The Grand Design of God

Ideas and Forms in English Literature

Edited by John Lawlor
Professor of English, University of Keele

The Grand Design of God

The literary form of the Christian view of history

C. A. Patrides

Reader in English and Related Literature
University of York

London
Routledge & Kegan Paul

Toronto
University of Toronto Press

First published 1972
by Routledge & Kegan Paul Ltd.
and in Canada and in the United States of America by
University of Toronto Press
Toronto and Buffalo

Printed in Great Britain by
The Camelot Press Ltd, London and Southampton

RKP ISBN 0 7100 7401 8
UTP ISBN 0 8020 1932 3
UTP Microfiche ISBN 0 8020 0272 2

for

John Dixon Hunt

κι αὐτὸ ἀκόμη τὸ σκαλὶ τὸ πρῶτο
πολὺ ἀπὸ τὸν κοινὸ τὸν κόσμο ἀπέχει

General Editor's Introduction

This series aims to explore two main aspects of literary tradition in English. First, the role of particular literary forms, with due emphasis on the distinctive sorts of application they receive at English hands; second, the nature and function of influential ideas, varying from large general conceptions evident over long periods to those concepts which are peculiar to a given age.

Each book attempts an account of the form or idea, and treats in detail particular authors and works rather than offering a general survey. The aim throughout is evaluative and critical rather than descriptive and merely historical.

J. L.

Contents

Illustrations

Between pages 54 and 55

Acknowledgements

The present study is a much amplified version of a monograph first published as *The Phoenix and the Ladder: The Rise and Decline of the Christian View of History* (University of California Press, 1964). The revision attempted in these pages affected every part of the original discussion, but most conspicuously the rationale underlying the patristic formulations, the place of the Mystery Plays in the mediaeval synthesis, the nature of the evidence provided by Renaissance authors not fully discussed earlier, the extension of the tradition in New England, and the variegated developments to our own day. I have also taken the opportunity to mention the use which artists made of the Christian view of history, and to amend the bibliographical notes.

My title is borrowed from a phrase by Jonathan Edwards (below, p. 119); but it could as readily have come from several other writers, including John Smith, the Cambridge Platonist (p. 70).

I am grateful to the University of California Press for permission to adapt my original monograph, and to the John Simon Guggenheim Memorial Foundation for the award of a Fellowship which enabled me to undertake the crucial preliminary research.

The expression of my indebtedness to individuals must begin with V. H. Galbraith, Regius Professor Emeritus of Modern History at Oxford, who read an early draft of these pages and graciously endorsed my wild surmises. I am no less grateful to Professor G. E. Aylmer of the University of York, who generously encouraged me with his authoritative judgement; Professor John Lawlor of the University of Keele, the General Editor of the present series, who improved these pages through a host of indispensable suggestions; Professor Philip Brockbank of the University of York, who helped me to amend the sections on Shakespeare and Blake; and Dr Marjorie Reeves of St Anne's

Acknowledgements

College, Oxford, who discussed with me the Joachimist movement
– now definitively articulated in her study *The Influence of Prophecy
in the Later Middle Ages: A Study in Joachimism* (1969). I am also
pleased to acknowledge the advice and encouragement extended
to me by The Very Revd M. C. D'Arcy, S.J., The Very Revd
R. L. P. Milburn, Professor Wallace K. Ferguson of the University
of Western Ontario, Professor Myron P. Gilmore of Harvard
University, Professor Elizabeth Salter of the University of York,
and Professor E. W. Strong of the University of California at
Berkeley. Finally, Professor D. D. C. Chambers of Trinity College,
Toronto, called my attention to the unique plate from Didacus
Valades's *Rhetorica christiana* (Plate 1).

The illustrations are reproduced by permission of the Trustees
of the British Museum (Plates 1, 2 and 3); The Prado, Madrid
(Plates 4 and 5); Alinari (Plates 6 and 7); and the Phaidon Press
(Plate 8). Mr J. B. Trapp, Librarian of the Warburg Institute,
greatly assisted me in finding the plates.

As learned journals tend not to review monographs, the original
edition was noticed only spasmodically. The exception was
Professor Roland M. Frye's review in *Shakespeare Studies*, II (1966),
357–8, which in the end proved instrumental in my decision to
attempt the present revision. But I was also encouraged by the
notice in Professor J. A. W. Bennett's inaugural lecture at Cambridge, 'The Medieval Humanist' (1965), which appeared to
confirm that the original monograph did serve a purpose.

Abbreviations

The following abbreviations are used in the notes:

AHR	*American Historical Review*
AJP	*American Journal of Philology*
AK	*Archiv für Kulturgeschichte*
AL	*American Literature*
ANCL	*Ante-Nicene Christian Library* (Buffalo, 1884 ff.)
AQ	*American Quarterly*
AR	*Archiv für Reformationsgeschichte*
ATR	*Anglican Theological Review*
BHR	*Bibliothèque d'humanisme et Renaissance*
BIHR	*Bulletin of the Institute of Historical Research*
BISI	*Bullettino dell' Istituto Storico Italiano per il Medio Evo e Archivio Muratoriano*
BJRL	*Bulletin of the John Rylands Library*
BR	*Bucknell Review*
BT	Bibliotheca scriptorum graecorum et romanorum teubneriana (Leipzig, 1849 ff.)
CH	*Church History*
CHR	*Catholic Historical Review*
CJ	*Cambridge Journal*
CP	*Classical Philology*
CQ	*Cambridge Quarterly*
CQR	*Church Quarterly Review*
CR	*Contemporary Review*
CSHB	*Corpus scriptorum historiae byzantinae* (Bonn, 1828 ff.)
E&S	*Essays and Studies* by members of the English Association
EETS	Early English Text Society: OS (Original Series, 1864 ff.), and ES (Extra Series, 1867 ff.)
EHR	*English Historical Review*
EHS	English Historical Society
ELH	*Journal of English Literary History*

ELN	*English Language Notes*
FDG	*Forschungen zur deutschen Geschichte*
GDG	*Neues Archiv der Gesellschaft für ältere deutsche Geschichtskunde*
GRBS	*Greek, Roman and Byzantine Studies*
GTR	*Greek Orthodox Theological Review*
H&T	*History and Theory*
HJ	*Historisches Jahrbuch*
HLQ	*Huntington Library Quarterly*
HR	*Hudson Review*
HTR	*Harvard Theological Review*
HZ	*Historische Zeitschrift*
JEGP	*Journal of English and Germanic Philology*
JHI	*Journal of the History of Ideas*
JMH	*Journal of Modern History*
JPP	*Journal of Philosophy, Psychology and Scientific Methods*
JR	*Journal of Religion*
JTS	*Journal of Theological Studies*
JWCI	*Journal of the Warburg and Courtauld Institutes*
KR	*Kenyon Review*
LCC	*Library of Christian Classics*, ed. John Baillie *et al.* (1953 ff.)
LCL	Loeb Classical Library (Cambridge, Mass., 1912 ff.)
MGH	*Monumenta Germaniae historiae* ('Auctores antiquissimi' unless otherwise stated) (Berlin, 1877 ff.)
MH	*Medievalia et humanistica*
MLQ	*Modern Language Quarterly*
MLR	*Modern Language Review*
MP	*Modern Philology*
MRS	*Mediaeval and Renaissance Studies*
NPNF	*Nicene and Post-Nicene Fathers* (Buffalo: 1st Series, 1886 ff.; 2nd Series, 1890 ff.)
NS	*New Scholasticism*
NTS	*New Testament Studies*
PBA	*Proceedings of the British Academy*
PG	*Patrologia, Series graeca*, ed. J.-P. Migne (Paris, 1857 ff.)
PL	*Patrologia, Series latina*, ed. J.-P. Migne (Paris, 1844 ff.)
PMLA	*Publications of the Modern Language Association*
PQ	*Philological Quarterly*
PR	*Philosophical Review*
RB	Rerum Britannicarum medii aevi scriptores ['Rolls Series'] (1858 ff.)

RES	*Review of English Studies*
RH	*Revue historique*
RHE	*Revue d'histoire ecclésiastique*
RHPR	*Revue d'histoire et de philosophie religieuses*
RIP	*The Rice Institute Pamphlet*
RSR	*Recherches de science religieuse*
RT	*Recherches de théologie ancienne et médiévale*
RUO	*Revue de l'Université d'Ottawa*
SAQ	*South Atlantic Quarterly*
SCBO	Scriptorum classicorum Bibliotheca Oxoniensis (Oxford, 1900 ff.)
SEL	*Studies in English Literature*
SHR	*Scottish Historical Review*
SJT	*Scottish Journal of Theology*
SP	*Studies in Philology*
SQ	*Shakespeare Quarterly*
SR	*Sewanee Review*
SRen	*Studies in the Renaissance*
SRev	*Slavonic Review*
SS	*Shakespeare Survey*
TL	*Theologische Literaturzeitung*
TLS	*Times Literary Supplement*
TS	*Theological Studies*
TSL	*Tennessee Studies in Literature*
TSLL	*Texas Studies in Literature and Language*
TZ	*Theologische Zeitschrift*
UCE	University of California Publications in English
UMSE	*University of Mississippi Studies in English*
UTQ	*University of Toronto Quarterly*
VC	*Vigilae christianae*
WW	*Wissenschaft und Weisheit*
YR	*Yale Review*
YRS	*Yale Romanic Studies*
ZK	*Zeitschrift für Kirchengeschichte*

In the notes places of publication are given only if other than London or New York. Biblical quotations are from the King James ('Authorised') Version of 1611; the poetry is typographically distinguished from the prose in accordance with *The Reader's Bible* (1951).

We looke upon God, in History, in matter of fact, upon things done, and set before our eyes; and so that Majesty, and that holy amazement, is more to us than ever it was to any other Religion.

JOHN DONNE

One

The Phoenix and the Ladder: Gentiles and Jews

οἵη περ φύλλων γενεή, τοίη δὲ καὶ ἀνδρῶν.
φύλλα τὰ μέν τ᾽ ἄνεμος χαμάδις χέει, ἄλλα δέ θ᾽ ὕλη
τηλεθόωσα φύει, ἔαρος δ᾽ ἐπιγίγνεται ὥρῃ
ὣς ἀνδρῶν γενεὴ ἡ μὲν φύει ἡ δ᾽ ἀπολήγει.

As is the generation of leaves, so is that of humanity. The wind scatters the leaves on the ground, but the live timber burgeons with leaves again in the season of spring returning. So one generation of men will grow while another dies.

The idea of recurrence underlying these lines from the *Iliad*[1] is one of the most splendid commonplaces of ancient Greek thought. Throughout the millennium after Homer, the Greeks generally viewed temporality as a cyclical movement. From Greece the idea passed to Rome, where it was summarily asserted by Seneca when he wrote that 'all things are connected in a sort of circle; they flee and they are pursued. Night is close at the heels of day, day at the heels of night; summer ends in autumn, winter rushes after autumn, and winter softens into spring; all nature in this way passes, only to return.'[2] This view is encountered almost everywhere we turn, whether it is to Polybius's affirmation of 'the cycle of political revolution' (πολιτειῶν ἀνακύκλωσις), or to Virgil's celebration of the circling centuries ('magnus ab integro saeclorum nascitur ordo'), or to Marcus Aurelius's conviction of the 'periodical renovation' of all things (περιοδικὴ παλιγγενεσία)[3] – nor is it necessary to insist on its explicitness in both Plato and Aristotle.

Yet this widespread persuasion that events occur in a series of cycles did not constitute, either for the Greeks or for the Romans, an interpretation of history, much less a 'philosophy' of history.

Such a possibility was not even entertained by them, not because they were unconcerned with history but because the very nature of the cycles deprived history of any ultimate meaning. Even Polybius, who regarded Rome's conquest of the world as history's apex, still viewed the Roman era as the crest of one of numberless waves endlessly crashing against the shores of the eternal world. This is not to say, of course, that the Greeks and the Romans deemed history useless; we are well aware of their reiterated conviction that history is a teacher of the first importance: a logical enough deduction when events are said to occur in an interminable series of flux and reflux. The claim of Diodorus Siculus in the first century B.C. that history is 'the guardian of the high achievements of illustrious men, the witness which testifies to the evil deeds of the wicked, and the benefactor of the entire human race' echoes both the earlier expectation of Thucydides that history is 'profitable' and the persuasion of Polybius that it is 'the soundest education and training', and anticipates the later commendation of Livy that

> What chiefly makes the study of history wholesome and profitable is this, that you behold the lessons of every kind of experience set forth as on a conspicuous monument; from these you may choose for yourself and for your own state what to imitate, for these mark for avoidance what is shameful in the conception and shameful in the result.[4]

But the historians of Greece and Rome also realised that the generally inevitable and predictable is not necessarily so in particular, a realisation which, when accepted with their belief that 'only what is unchanging can be known', contributed towards a decisive anti-historical tendency, particularly among the Greeks.[5] Hence the absence of any surprise in the Aristotelian thesis that history is inferior to poetry; hence indeed the justice in claiming that, on the whole, the Greeks and the Romans, while vitally concerned with history, were not interested in propagating a 'philosophy' of history, much less any precise and rigid philosophy grafted to metaphysics. Their concern was capitally with the past and the present, and with the future only in so far as the notion of recurrence afforded – within the limitations suggested – opportunities for didacticism.

The Graeco-Roman cycles have their counterpart in nearly all

2

other civilisations, even those as far apart from each other as Aztec and Hindu.[6] However, among Israel's immediate neighbours we find a distinct exception to the rule,[7] while in Israel itself and within the Judaeo-Christian tradition at large, history attains a position of unrivalled prominence and unique importance.[8]

According to the Book of Daniel, 'the Most High ruleth in the kingdom of men, and giveth it to whomsoever he will'.[9] If such a notion was nonsense to the Greeks, to the Jews it stemmed naturally from their conception of God. For the God of Israel is not an impersonal abstraction, dwelling beyond the confines of the universe and utterly uncommunicable. On the contrary, as the Bible repeatedly insists, he is a 'living God',[10] and, because living, concerned actively with the affairs of his creatures, always preoccupied with their fortunes, constantly interfering in the course of human events whether to chastise or to reward, to punish or to commend, to destroy or to save. The psalmist, surveying the past history of Israel, typically saw the hand of God in every event:[11]

> We have heard with our ears, O God,
> Our fathers have told us,
> What work thou didst in their days, in the times of old,
> How thou didst drive out the heathen with thy hand, and
> plantedst them;
> How thou didst afflict the people, and cast them out.
> For they got not the land in possession by their own sword.
> Neither did their own arm save them:
> But thy right hand, and thine arm, and the light of thy
> countenance.

The psalmist, contemplating the future and the multitude of dangers still encompassing Israel, goes on:

> Through thee will we push down our enemies:
> Through thy name will we tread them under that rise up
> against us.

Such an attitude is more a faith than a 'philosophy'; but if we wish to state it in more sophisticated terms, we might concur that history is 'a process determined by the creative act of God vertically from above', or that 'the temporal is inwardly sustained, saturated, pervaded by the untemporal'.[12] In either case we take cognisance of the unique Jewish view that history unfolds under

3

the vigilant eye of God, that it is acted out within a sacred framework. But God, far from being a mere observer of the human drama, is responsible directly for its progress, because, as has been said, history is 'the arena wherein his will expresses itself as action'.[13] The logical inference, which the Jews did not hesitate to draw, is that God manipulates every aspect of the created order according to his eternal plan for mankind. Jewish historians and the great prophets manifest strikingly this outlook by asserting that God, in dispensing judgement, normally elects certain nations as instruments of his justice. Thus the tribes of Israel were repeatedly 'delivered', 'sold' to the Philistines,[14] while Babylon later became 'a golden cup in the Lord's hand', Nebuchadrezzar was appointed the sword of God, and Cyrus the Great was crowned the anointed of the Supreme Judge.[15] God's own words, transmitted through Isaiah, are explicit enough:[16]

> O Assyrian, the rod of mine anger,
> And the staff in their hands is mine indignation.
> I will send him against an hypocritical nation,
> And against the people of my wrath will I give him a
> charge,
> To take the spoil, and to take the prey,
> And to tread them down like the mire of the streets.

Yet once Israel was punished, God diverted his wrath against his former instruments, punishing the 'high looks' of the Assyrians and reducing Babylon to a 'desolation among the nations'.[17] The theory was adequately summarised by an apologist of the sixteenth century: 'God so maketh wicked Instruments to serue to his glorie, that by them he executeth his eternall ordenaunce, and yet neuerthelesse he punisheth them for their euill imaginations and wicked works.'[18] This view of the Divine Purpose might seem uncomfortably close to Thomas Hardy's President of the Immortals, whose hobby was to sport with his creatures. To the Jews, however, God was anything but unjust; even when they staggered under the burden of divine wrath, they were still persuaded of his justice. Moreover, despite Hardy and similar eccentrics, the emphasis in the Old Testament falls not so much on the winters of God's anger as upon the eternal spring of his infinite mercies. Jewish writers chose invariably as their theme God's covenant with Israel. That covenant is an explanation –

'the shadow of the future thrown back on to the past'[19] – of God's constant efforts to safeguard Israel. And those efforts, the Old Testament maintains, are historically demonstrable; indeed, they *are* history.

We often think of the God of Israel as preoccupied exclusively with the affairs of the chosen race, yet the Old Testament presents him not merely as the ruler of a part of humanity but as 'the God of the whole earth'.[20] In the chapter following the account of creation in Genesis, we are given in outline the Jewish theory of how, out of the first man, arose the various nations of the world. The seemingly endless lists of names, so tedious to us, were of fundamental importance to the compilers themselves. As we pass from the generations of Adam to those of Noah and his three sons, and on through Abraham and Isaac and Jacob to Joseph, we realise that the roll-call of names is included to stress the essential unity of mankind, that under the one Lord of the universe there exists but a single family of nations, divided at various points in history, yet retaining still their unity under God. Though subsequent historians of Israel went on proclaiming their belief in God's particular interest in their nation, they continued to regard him as the Lord of all nations. None couched this belief more explicitly or more forcefully than the great prophets. The very first, Amos, clearly asserted that, before God, all nations are equally deserving of his punishments and his mercies – especially his mercies. Did not God bring Israel out of Egypt, delivering also the Philistines from Caphtor and the Syrians from Kir?[21] God, speaking to Isaiah, used far more striking words:[22]

> Blessed be Egypt my people,
> And Assyria the work of my hands,
> And Israel mine inheritance.

The Jews never hesitated to face up to the implications of their monotheistic creed. In the captivating metaphor of another age they believed God to be a circle whose centre is everywhere and his circumference nowhere.

Yet the most important difference between the Jewish and extra-Biblical views of history is the Old Testament conviction, often repeated, about the 'Day of the Lord'. Belief in the end of the world, involving universal judgement and the advent of 'new heavens and a new earth',[23] was a late development in Jewish

5

thought, its most notable proponents being the prophets – particularly Amos, Isaiah, and Zephaniah – and the author of the apocalypse in the Book of Daniel.[24] This belief, once widespread, completed the Jewish view of history, seen now to be linear, proceeding in a straight line from the six days of creation to the single Day of Judgement. During this progress from one end-point of history to the other, God manifests his purposes in and through everyday events, until at last all rivers of temporal history tumble into the vast ocean of eternity.

Only the author of Ecclesiastes among Hebrew writers took exception to this view. His prolonged meditation upon the nature of things had directed him not to the traditional straight line leading to the Day of the Lord, but to interminable cycles:[25]

> One generation passeth away, and another generation cometh: but the earth abideth for ever. The sun also ariseth, and the sun goeth down, and hasteth to his place where he arose. The wind goeth toward the south, and turneth about unto the north: it whirleth about continually, and the wind returneth yet again according to his circuits. All the rivers run into the sea; yet the sea is not full: unto the place whence the rivers come, thither they return again.

The original work, obviously the labour of a 'schismatic', was considerably revised by later writers and defended heroically as orthodox by a host of commentators. Even so, the extent to which the book departs from the predominating tenor of the Bible is inescapable. As Biblical scholars now agree, the Book of Ecclesiastes is the work of a sceptic,[26] an early representative of a movement we shall again encounter as we near the later Renaissance.

But the mainstream of ideas moved on, disregarding imperiously such backwaters as Ecclesiastes. It bore along in its flow a fundamental idea emerging slowly out of a group of prophecies concerning the advent of the Messiah.[27] The salvation thereby envisaged was not expected to take place outside but inside history, in conformity with God's normal method of 'working salvation in the midst of the earth'.[28] Hence Luke's elaborate care in recording that Jesus began his ministry 'in the fifteenth year of the reign of Tiberius Caesar, Pontius Pilate being governor of

Judea, and Herod being tetrarch of Galilee, and his brother Philip tetrarch of Iturea and of the region of Trachonitis, and Lysanias the tetrarch of Abilene, Annas and Caiaphas being the high priests'.[29]

Jesus the Christ of God constitutes for Christianity history's 'constant uniqueness'[30] because his advent marks the direct entrance of God into the historical process. Moreover, the God-man in executing the divine purpose lends significance to the entire range of human events, past as well as future. Jesus, it must be insisted, did not establish a new religion; indeed, as the New Testament constantly maintains, his birth was not the commencement but the climax of God's gradual revelation of himself to Israel. As the opening words of the Epistle to the Hebrews declare, 'God, who at sundry times and in divers manners spake in time past unto the fathers by the prophets, hath in these last days spoken to us by his Son, whom he hath appointed heir of all things.' The historical continuity claimed from Adam himself by Old Testament writers thus assumed even greater importance to the writers of the New. The very first chapter of Matthew's Gospel traces appropriately the ancestry of Jesus back to Abraham, beyond whom, of course, stood Adam. St Paul made explicit the extension by stating that as through Adam all men were condemned, so through Jesus all were saved.[31] Using the traditional terms employed by Renaissance expositors, we may state that there is a 'streight and perfect line from *Adam* vnto *Christ*', 'a golden vaine, a golden chaine, consisting of many linkes, from the first *Adam* to the *second*'.[32] In this respect, we recall how extensive the historical typology of the New Testament is, how enthusiastic its reception by the early apologists, and how elaborate its further consideration by subsequent generations.[33] That impressive concern with types had the threefold purpose of confirming that historical events are non-recurring and irreversible, that they imply a design according to which the created order advances onward, and that they are meaningful only in so far as they are seen to relate to the advent of the Messiah. John Gaule's statement in 1629 is adequate: 'As doe Lines in their Point and Period; Circumferences in their Center; Riuers in the Sea: So doe both the Law, and the Prophets meet in Christ Iesus'.[34]

But the New Testament does not relate the Christ Jesus merely

7

to the past history of Israel; it maintains also his relevance not only to the future history of Israel but to that of the whole universe. For the God-man is both historical and supra-historical, transcending the two end-points of history. On the one hand, he existed 'before the foundation of the world', and 'by him were all things created, that are in heaven, and that are in earth, visible and invisible';[35] **on** the other hand, the Last Judgement is also his personal task, although 'when all things shall be subdued unto him, then shall the Son also himself be subject unto him that put all things under him, that God may be all in all'.[36] Thus the significance of the Christ is more than local or national, it is cosmic, for he 'was, and is, and is to come', 'the same yesterday, and today, and for ever'.[37] The affirmation of the Old Testament that the God of Israel is also the God of the entire universe is thus further expanded in the New Testament. All barriers are now shattered: 'there is neither Greek nor Jew, circumcision nor uncircumcision, Barbarian, Scythian, bond nor free', 'no more strangers and foreigners, but fellow citizens with the saints, and of the household of God' – a cosmic brotherhood marching inevitably along the straight line leading to the end of the world.[38]

The Old Testament views history theocentrically, the New Testament Christocentrically. The chronology in present use by Jews and Christians is an eloquent testimony of their different attitudes towards history; for while both compute events from a fixed point, Judaism harks back to the creation of the world by God,[39] but Christianity slices history in two with the designations 'B.C.' and 'A.D.'. The Christ Jesus stands for Christianity at the very centre of universal history. Before his advent, all events are similarly linked to him in retrospection of his Nativity, which is a historical reality. In T. S. Eliot's words,[40]

> Then came, at a predetermined moment, a moment in
> time and of time,
> A moment not out of time, but in time, in what we call
> history: transecting, bisecting the world of time, a
> moment in time but not like a moment of time,
> A moment in time but time was made through that
> moment: for without the meaning there is no time,
> and that moment of time gave the meaning.

The meaningless cycles of flux and reflux in the Graeco-Roman attitude towards history are like the legendary phoenix, dying periodically in order to revive again, while to Christians history is like Jacob's Ladder, 'ascending by degrees magnificent' towards the Eternal City, the Christ's presence not only suffused everywhere in the ladder but, according to Renaissance commentators, the ladder itself.[41]

Notes

1 *Iliad*, vi, 146–9; trans. Richmond Lattimore (1951). The descent of the Homeric image to the lyric and dramatic poets of Greece is sketched by T. B. L. Webster, *An Introduction to Sophocles* (Oxford, 1936), pp. 31 ff.

2 *Ad Lucilium epistulae morales*, xxiv, 26; trans. R. M. Gummere, LCL (1917). For the parallel statement in Ovid, see *Metamorphoses*, xv, 177 ff.

3 Polybius, *Historia*, vi, ix, 10 (trans. W. R. Patton, LCL [1922–7]); Virgil, *Ecloga* iv, 5; and Marcus Aurelius, xi, 1 (trans. George Long, *Thoughts*, rev. ed. [1889]). Cf. W. H. Walsh, 'Plato and the Philosophy of History', *H&T*, ii (1962), 3–16.

4 Seriatim: Diodorus Siculus, i, ii, 2 (trans. C. H. Oldfather, LCL [1933 ff.]); Thucydides, i, 22; Polybius, *Historia*, i, 1; Livy, *Ab urbe condita*, Preface (trans. B. O. Foster *et al.*, LCL, [1919–51]). See further J. B. Bury, *The Ancient Greek Historians* (1909), ch. viii, 'Views of the Ancients concerning the Use of History', and George W. Robinson, *Outlines of Historical Study* (1927), pp. 296–301. For later views, see below, p. 91, note 5.

5 R. G. Collingwood, *The Idea of History* (Oxford, 1946), pp. 20–1. I am indebted to Collingwood's thesis throughout this paragraph.

6 Sir Charles Eliot, *Hinduism and Buddhism* (1921), vol. i, pp. i–lxv and 42–7; Arthur O. Lovejoy and George Boas, *Primitivism and Related Ideas in Antiquity* (Baltimore, 1935), esp. chs i, v and vi *passim*; Arnold Toynbee, *A Study of History* (1939), vol. iv, pp. iv, 23–33; Mircea Eliade, *The Myth of the Eternal Return*, trans. W. R. Trask (1954), esp. chs ii–iii, and *Images and Symbols*, trans. P. Mairet (1961), ch. iii; Rammanohar Lohia, *Wheel of History* (Hyderabad, 1955), esp. ch. ii; W. K. C. Guthrie, *In the Beginning* (1957), ch. iv; Kostas Papaioannou, 'Nature and History in the Greek Conception of the Cosmos', *Diogenes*, xxv (1959), 1–27; Alban G. Widgery, *Interpretations of History* (1961), chs ii–iii; and *Man and Time*, ed. Joseph Campbell, Papers from the Eranos Yearbooks, iii (1957), notably the essays by Henry Corbin, 'Cyclical Time in Mazdaism and Ismailism', and Mircea Eliade, 'Time and Eternity in Indian Thought'.

7 See Albert T. E. Olmstead, *Assyrian Historiography* (1916); Hans-Gustav Güterbeck, 'Die historische Tradition und ihre literarische Gestaltung bei Babyloniern und Hethitern bis 1200', *Zeitschrift für Assyriologie*, xlii (1934), 1–91, and xliv (1938), 45–149; Burr C. Brundage, 'The Birth of Clio: A

Résumé and Interpretation of Ancient Near Eastern Historiography', in *Teachers of History*, ed. H. S. Hughes (Ithaca, N.Y., 1954), pp. 199–230; and the three studies by E. A. Speiser, George C. Cameron, and C. Bradford Wells, on Mesopotamia, Persia, and the Hellenistic Orient (respectively), in *The Idea of History in the Ancient Near East*, ed. R. C. Dentan (New Haven, 1955), pp. 35–97, 133–67.

8 Expositions of the Christian view of history include: Nicolas Berdyaev, *The Meaning of History*, trans. G. Reavy (1936), chs v–vi; S. G. F. Brandon, *Time and Mankind* (1951), chs iv–v, viii; Rudolph Bultmann, *History and Eschatology* (Edinburgh, 1957), chs ii–iii; Herbert Butterfield, *Christianity and History* (1954); A. C. Charity, *Events and their Afterlife* (Cambridge, 1966); Anton-Herman Chroust, 'The Metaphysics of Time and History in Early Christian Thought', *NS*, xix (1945), 322–52; Charles N. Cochrane, *Christianity and Classical Culture* (Oxford, 1940), ch. xii; Oscar Cullmann, *Christ and Time*, trans. F. V. Filson (Philadelphia, 1950), and *Salvation in History*, trans. S. G. Sowers et al. (1967); Jean Daniélou, 'The Conception of History in the Christian Tradition', *JR*, xxx (1950), 171–9, and *The Lord of History*, trans. N. Abercrombie (1958); M. C. D'Arcy, *The Sense of History* (1959); Christopher Dawson, *The Dynamics of World History*, ed. J. J. Mulley (1957); Georges Florovsky, 'Eschatology in the Patristic Age', *GTR*, ii [i] (1956), 27–40; T. Francis Glasson, *His Appearing and His Kingdom* (1953), ch. xvii; Karl Löwith, *Meaning in History* (Chicago, 1949); W. Manson,'The Son of Man and History', *SJT*, v (1952), 113–22; John Marsh, *The Fulness of Time* (1952); E. L. Mascall, *Theology and History* (1962); R. L. P. Milburn, *Early Christian Interpretations of History* (1954); Reinhold Niebuhr, *Faith and History* (1949); North (below, note 24); L. G. Patterson, *God and History in Early Christian Thought* (1967); Otto Piper, *God in History* (1939); E. Gordon Rupp, *Principalities and Powers* (1952); Eric C. Rust, *The Christian Understanding of History* (1947); Roger L. Shinn, 'Augustinian and Cyclical Views of History', *ATR*, xxxi (1949), 133–41; James T. Shotwell, *The History of History* (1939), vol. i, part v; Nathan Söderblom, *The Living God* (1933), chs viii–ix; William Temple, *Christianity as an Interpretation of History* (1945); and vol. iii of the Report on the Conference at Oxford (1937) on Church, Community, and State, *The Kingdom of God in History* (1938). Further references in the original version of the present work, *The Phoenix and the Ladder: The Rise and Decline of the Christian View of History* (1964), pp. 73–5. On the New Testament, see esp. T. A. Burkill, 'St. Mark's Philosophy of History', *NTS*, iii (1957), 142–8; Hans Conzelmann, *The Theology of St Luke*, trans. G. Buswell (1960), parts iii–iv; Violet Wilkinson, *The Centre of History* (1967); Nils A. Dahl, 'The Johannine Church and History', in *Current Issues in New Testament Interpretation*, ed. W. Klassen and G. F. Snyder (1962), pp. 124–42; etc.

9 Daniel 4:17.

10 Deuteronomy 5:26, Joshua 3:10, 1 Samuel 17:26, 11 Kings 19:4, Hosea 1:10, Jeremiah 10:10, etc. – as well as in the New Testament (Matthew 16:16, 1 Thessalonians 1:9, 1 Timothy 6:17).

11 Psalms 44:1–23.

12 C. H. Dodd, *History and the Gospel* (1938), p. 181, and Josef Pieper, *The End of Time*, trans. M. Bullock (1954), p. 67, respectively.

13 J. S. Whale, *Christian Doctrine* (Cambridge, 1952), p. 56.

14 Judges, *passim*; the 'cyclical' theory of punishment and redemption is outlined in Judges 2:11–23.

15 Jeremiah 51:7, Ezekiel 30:24, Isaiah 45:1.

16 Isaiah 10:5–6. See further H. H. Rowley, *The Biblical Doctrine of Election* (1950), ch. v.

17 Isaiah 10:12, Jeremiah 50:23.

18 Pierre Viret, *The Worlde Possessed with Deuils*, trans. Thomas Stocker (1583), sig. E6ᵛ.

19 Alfred North Whitehead, *Adventures in Ideas* (Cambridge, 1933), p. 82.

20 Isaiah 54:5.

21 Amos 9:7.

22 Isaiah 19:25.

23 Isaiah 65:17.

24 Christopher R. North, *The Old Testament Interpretation of History* (1946), ch. vii.

25 Ecclesiastes 1:4–7.

26 See esp. Morris Jastrow, Jr, *A Gentle Cynic* (Philadelphia, 1919), and Johs. Pedersen, 'Scepticisme israélite', *RHPR*, x (1930), 317–70.

27 The two fullest accounts are by Joseph Klausner, *The Messianic Idea in Israel*, trans. W. F. Stinespring (1956), and Sigmund Mowinckel, *He that Cometh: The Messianic Hope in the Old Testament and in the Time of Jesus*, trans. G. W. Anderson (Oxford, 1959). Also pertinent are the numerous studies by Robert H. Charles.

28 Psalms 74:12.

29 Luke 3:1–2.

30 Gerald Heard, *Is God in History?* (1950), p. 222.

31 Romans 5:18. On Paul's attitude towards history (esp. in Romans 9–11), see C. H. Dodd, *The Epistle of Paul to the Romans* (n.d.), pp. 148–88; W. M. Ramsey, 'St Paul's Philosophy of History', *CR*, xcii (1907), 327–43; Robert M. Hawkins, 'The Rejection of Israel: An Analysis of Romans ix–xi', *ATR*, xxiii (1941), 329–35; E. F. Scott, *Paul's Epistle to the Romans* (1947), pp. 54–65; Oliver C. Quick, *Doctrines of the Creed* (1951), pp. 304–6; and H. J. Schoeps, *Paul: The Theology of the Apostle in the Light of Jewish Religious History*, trans. Harold Knight (1961), ch. vi.

32 Lodowick Lloyd, *The Consent of Time* (1590), 'To the Reader', and John Stoughton, *XI. Choice Sermons* (1640), vol. ii, p. 69, respectively.

33 See *PL*, ccxix, 243–7, 'Index figurarum: figurae quae Christum praesignant'; the discussions by Leonhard Goppelt, *Typos: Die typologische Deutung des Alten Testaments in Neuen* (Gütersloh, 1939); A. G. Hebert, *The Throne of David* (1941); M. D. Goulder, *Type and History in Acts* (1964); R. A. Markus, 'Presuppositions of the Typological Approach to Scripture', *CQR*, clviii (1957), 442–51; Helen Gardner, *The Limits of Criticism* (1956), ch. iii; G. W. H. Lampe and K. J. Woollcombe, *Essays on Typology* (1957); Jean Daniélou, *From Shadows to Reality: Studies in the Biblical Typology of the*

Fathers, trans. W. Hibberd (1960). The rich tradition involving Samson as a type of Christ is set forth by F. Michael Krouse, *Milton's Samson and the Christian Tradition* (Princeton, 1949). The relevance of typology to literature is variously demonstrated by Rosemary Woolf, below, p. 45, note 63; Rosemond Tuve, *A Reading of George Herbert* (Chicago, 1952); Northrop Frye, 'The Typology of *Paradise Regained*', *MP*, liii (1956), 227–38; William G. Madsen, 'Earth the Shadow of Heaven: Typological Symbolism in *Paradise Lost*', *PMLA*, lxxv (1960), 519–26; J. M. Evans, *'Paradise Lost' and the Genesis Tradition* (Oxford, 1968), pp. 99–104; etc.

34 *Practique Theories* (1629), p. 23.

35 1 Peter 1:20, Colossians 1:16.

36 1 Corinthians 15:28. See further Rudolph Bultmann, 'History and Eschatology in the New Testament', *NTS*, i (1954), 5–16; Werner G. Kümmel, *Promise and Fulfilment: The Eschatological Message of Jesus*, trans. D. M. Barton (1957); and H. M. Féret, *The Apocalypse of St John*, trans. E. Corathiel (1958), ch. iv, 'The View of History according to the Apocalypse'. On Paul's pronounced eschatological thinking, see the numerous studies cited by E. Earle Ellis, 'II Corinthians v.1–10 in Pauline Eschatology', *NTS*, vi (1960), 211–24.

37 Revelation 4:8, Hebrews 13:8.

38 Colossians 3:11, Ephesians 2:19.

39 Dated 3761 B.C. Mohammedans date events from *anno hegirae* 1, the year of Mohammed's flight from Mecca to Medina (A.D. 622). No other major religion refers events to a fixed point; as for other civilisations, I am aware only of one exception to this rule, the ancient Mayas.

40 *The Rock* (1934), p. 50. Cf. 'The Meditation of Simeon', in W. H. Auden's *For the Time Being* (1950), esp. pp. 108–9: 'By the event of this birth the true significance of all other events is defined . . . for of every other creature it can be said that it has extrinsic importance but of this Child it is the case that He is in no sense a symbol.'

41 See my article on 'Renaissance Interpretations of Jacob's Ladder', *TZ*, xviii (1962), 411–18. I use the phoenix as symbolic of the attitude to history outside the Judaeo-Christian tradition; but Christianity – with characteristic genius! – soon absorbed that symbol as well, and applied it to the Resurrection. See Joanne S. Kantrowitz, 'The Anglo-Saxon *Phoenix* and Tradition', *PQ*, xliii (1964), 1–13, as well as Rudolf Gottfried, 'Milton, Lactantius, Claudian, and Tasso', *SP*, xxx (1933), 497–503, but especially R. van den Broek, *The Myth of the Phoenix according to Classical and Early Christian Traditions* (Leyden, 1972).

Two

Patristic Structures

ἀρχὴν κόσμου βλέπει, καὶ τέλος
κόσμου, καὶ μεσότητα χρόνων
CYRIL OF JERUSALEM[1]

I

The churches established by St Paul were soon after his death subjected to a number of severe trials. Yet the prolonged and often brutal persecutions they suffered were far less perilous than the threat posed by an enemy who frequently arose from within their own ranks: Gnosticism.

Of the numerous ideas advanced by the Gnostics as later by the Arians, the most pernicious was their tendency to shift Christianity's centre of gravity from history to philosophy, from the historical Jesus to a system of abstractions.[2] But the apologists of the early Church, like the greater theologians who later opposed Arianism, steadfastly refused to surrender the 'scandal' at the core of their faith. As a result Christianity was prevented from receding into a mere philosophical curiosity, interesting in itself but less than relevant to the life of man.

The first apologists and early Fathers, fully persuaded by the validity of the Christian interpretation of history, condemned also the cyclical view of temporal events with impressive unanimity. Long before St Augustine's decisive attack in the early fifth century, St Justin Martyr (c. 100–c. 165) had looked askance upon the pagan affirmation 'that things will always remain as they are, and further, that you and I shall live again as we are living now, without having become either better or worse'.[3] Belief in the cyclical theory appeared to undermine not only the promise of mankind's improvement held out by the Christian

13

faith; it negated in particular the unique claim of Christianity which is 'the single and unrepeatable event of Jesus Christ'.[4]

Not every Christian was able to accommodate himself to this idea, least of all Origen (*c.* 185–*c.* 254). True, he lashed out against the Graeco-Roman 'cycles', and dutifully protested that to accept their sway is to accept also that 'Jesus will again come to visit this life and will do the same things that he has done, not just once but an infinite number of times according to the cycles'.[5] But it was one thing to denounce the cyclical view and another to evade its mazes. Unable to resist the appeal of the Graeco-Roman theory, Origen repeatedly fell prey to its influence as in his espousal of a future 'apocatastasis' or restoration of all things to their pristine innocence.[6] The offence he gave was further compounded by his arrant propensity for allegory. St Jerome was not the only theologian to be incensed: 'he so allegorises Paradise as to destroy historical truth, understanding angels instead of trees, heavenly virtues instead of rivers, and he overthrows all that is contained in the history of Paradise by his figurative interpretation'.[7] The historical sense was henceforth to be upheld by Christians resolutely, even militantly.

Another aspect of early Christian thought proved even more decisive, providing the corner-stone that was to be fundamental to all subsequent expositions of the Christian faith. This was the claim that Christianity existed before the beginning of the world – a claim already advanced by the writers of the New Testament, but now the subject of further exposition by such divers commentators as Justin Martyr and Tertullian, Athenagoras and Clement of Alexandria, Origen and Augustine.[8] The shape of things to come began to grow noticeable towards the end of the second century in a treatise by St Theophilus of Antioch to Autolycus, where we find a partly systematised recital of events since 'the beginning of the foundation of the world'.[9] Shortly thereafter the Χρονικὰ (*Chronica*) of St Hippolytus (*c.* 170–*c.* 236)[10] and the highly influential Χρονογραφίαι (*Chronographiae*) of 'the father of Christian chronography' Julius Africanus (*c.* 160–*c.* 240)[11] further conventionalised the tendency to hark back to the creation of the universe.

But the difference between Christian and pagan historians, it might be objected, is rather one of degree than of kind; for even if the Greeks and Romans rarely commenced with the creation since they normally held the world to be eternal, they reached into the distant past no less frequently than did Christian historians. It had been so ever since the first 'universal' history outside the Judaeo-Christian tradition was written by the Greek historian Ephorus in the fourth century B.C.[12] Thereafter universalising tendencies became visibly manifest in many others, among them Fabius Pictor, Cato, Polybius, Atticus, Cornelius Nepos, Diodorus Siculus, Trogus, Livy, Appian, and Dio Cassius. To these should be added Joseph ben Matthias, author of the Ἰουδαϊκὴ Ἀρχαιολογία (*Antiquitates Judaicae*)[13] – a work which Christians may have accepted widely as we shall see later, but one which properly forms part of Graeco-Roman historiography. Flavius Josephus would have wished it no other way.

These 'precedents' notwithstanding, Christian historians carved a path distinctly their own. But the distinction cannot be inferred from the works of Theophilus, Hippolytus, or even Julius Africanus, for these were but heralds to the great synthesis achieved by Eusebius of Caesarea (*c.* 260–*c.* 340).

Eusebius's celebrated *opus maius* on chronology[14] is divided into two parts: the Χρονογραφία (*Chronographia*), a narrative account of events since the Chaldeans; and the Χρονικοὶ Κανόνες (*Chronici Canones*) – also extant in the Latin version by St Jerome[15] – a tabular compilation of synchronised dates drawn from Assyrian, Hebrew, Egyptian, Greek, and Roman history. Assuredly Eusebius's monumental labours were not entirely original, for he relied extensively on the work of Julius Africanus.[16] Yet he did revise and improve decidedly upon Julius Africanus, notably upon his synchronised tables. He also placed his epoch-making account of the growth of the Church, the celebrated Ἐκκλησιαστικὴ Ἱστορία (*Historia ecclesiastica*),[17] within his comprehensive chronological framework. With the composition of the *Historia* we have at last the clearest divorce between Christian and Graeco-Roman historians. In an attempt to demonstrate that Christianity is not a recent religion, Eusebius lifted the curtain upon his *Historia* to a stirring vision of the events preceding even the creation of the world, beholding the Christ Jesus 'God by the side of the Father, the first and only offspring of God, before all creation and fabrication, both visible and invisible, the captain of the spiritual and immortal host of heaven'.[18] Thereafter, descending to the realm of history, we are led to witness God's gradual revelation of himself to the people of Israel, until the grand climax is reached in the Incarnation of the pre-existent Word. Here the first book ends. The rest of the work is similar in tenor, at every turn moving further away from the pagan historians with the recurrent affirmation that God marches through history in judgement or in mercy, and always in glory.

But Eusebius may not be regarded as the greatest exponent of the Christian view of history, for one fundamental idea, eschatology, is absent from his work. Other apologists had already insisted, and were to insist again, on the teleological aspect of history, notably the resurrection of the dead, for they appreciated that the unity of mankind can be maintained only through an affirmation not merely of a common origin but also of a common *telos* or end. But Eusebius, persuaded as he was that the triumph of Christianity under Constantine the Great – ὁ τῷ Θεῷ φίλος[19] – was the terminal point in God's promises to mankind, neglected the ultimate end and thereby limited drastically his vision of history. However, he still occupies an honoured place in Christian historiography for his labours in chronology, for his ecclesiastical history, but most for disseminating still further the tendency to view history from 'the depth of the irreversible Divine Resolve'.[20] Numerous imitations of his *Historia* testify to its just popularity,[21] although only the continuations by three Eastern historians of the earlier fifth century, Socrates, Sozomen, and Theodoret, are worthy of their great predecessor. In the West the enthusiasm for Eusebius was greater still. Even before the fourth century had expired, the *Historia* was freely translated into Latin by Rufinus of Aquileia, with a supplement bringing the Eusebian account up to A.D. 395.[22] Latin Christendom was by that time already graced by her two greatest fathers, St Augustine and St Jerome.

II

St Augustine (354–430) may rightly be called the father of the Christian 'philosophy' of history.[23] His major work on the subject, *De civitate Dei contra paganos*, begun in 413 and completed in 426, was written in the apologetic and polemic vein typical of most of his writings.[24] It was occasioned by Alaric's capture of Rome on 24 August 410, an event that generated pessimism among Christians and pagans alike. The inviolability of Rome, containing the hallowed tombs of Peter, Paul, and thousands of martyrs, had been synonymous with the stability of the Christian religion itself. To pagans, the fall of the Mistress of the World could only mean violent disapproval by their gods of Christianity's triumphant rise. To friends and foes alike, therefore, Augustine resolved to address his great *apologia*. He concerned himself chiefly with two among numerous arguments: first, that the world had known far greater disasters in the past than the invasion of Rome; and second, that the importance attached to Rome was totally erroneous. What is a mere city in the progress of history from creation to the Last Judgement? Rome, indeed, is but a second Babylon, of the earth, and mortal. All that matters is the Eternal City in the Kingdom of God, of the heavens, and immortal. In the course of his arguments, Augustine dilated upon his sharp division between the two 'cities', the *civitas Dei* and the *civitas terrena*:[25]

> Two loves have given origin to these two cities, self-love in contempt of God unto the earthly, love of God in contempt of one's self to the heavenly. The first seeks the glory of men, and the latter desires God only as the testimony of the conscience, the greatest glory. That glories in itself, and this in God. That exalts itself in self-glory: this says to God: 'My glory and the lifter up of my head'. That boasts of the ambitious conquerors led by the lust of sovereignty: in this all serve each other in charity, both the rulers in counselling and the subjects in obeying. That loves worldly virtue in the potentates: this says unto God: 'I will love thee, O Lord, my strength'.

The greater part of *De civitate Dei* is devoted to an exposition of, and commentary on, the progress of the world under the shadow of these two cities or states, now inclined towards the one and now towards the other. Augustine, like Eusebius, began his account with the supra-historical era before the creation of the universe; but unlike his great predecessor, he went ahead to affirm the end of the world and the consummation of all things in God. Inestimably influential, Augustine, by capping the history of temporal events with the Last Judgement, gave more weight than ever before to the linear nature of history, beginning with Adam, with its 'central datum' in Jesus, and with its 'uni-dimensional movement in time' leading to the end.[26]

In his sweeping view of history acted out *sub specie aeternitatis,* Augustine was at one with some of his predecessors in measuring the progress of the world by the Six Ages corresponding to the six days of creation. The First Age extends from Adam to Noah, the Second thence to Abraham, the Third to David, the Fourth to the Babylonian captivity, and the Fifth to the Incarnation; the Sixth Age is presently unfolding, to be terminated at the Second Coming, with the beginning of the Seventh Age in which we are to rest eternally as God rested on the seventh day of creation.[27] Such a scheme clearly precludes the Graeco-Roman cycles; yet the thorough Augustine lost no opportunity to castigate the notion of the 'continual rotation of ages past and present'.[28] Triumphantly seizing on the psalmist's words that 'the wicked walk in a circle', he affirmed their application to the adherents of the cyclical view of history: 'not because their life (as they think) is to run circularly, but because their false doctrine runs round in a circular maze.'[29]

Augustine's discussion of the rise and development of the two 'cities' stands at the outset of Book XI of *De civitate Dei.* Earlier, in the first ten books, he was concerned to defend the one true God against the multiplicity of false gods, and to demonstrate the superiority of Christianity over paganism. At the same time he elaborated further the providential view of history which the prophet Isaiah had long since consolidated, whereby God 'giveth kingdoms to good and to bad: not rashly, nor casually, but as the time is appointed, which is well known to him, though hidden from us'.[30] Yet Augustine's contributions did not end here, for he also formulated, if not the traditional, certainly the most widespread Christian view of time and eternity.[31]

St Augustine is the greatest theologian among the Latin Fathers. His contemporary St Jerome (*c.* 342–420) is beyond doubt the greatest scholar.[32] Considering their contributions to the Christian view of history alone, we can readily see why their successors numbered them both among the four supreme *doctores ecclesiae.* Between them they shaped the course invariably followed by all historians until the Renaissance. All accepted Augustine's philosophy and Jerome's chronology. Jerome's *Chronicon*[33] is, indeed, but a translation of the chronicle of Eusebius, made while Jerome was in Constantinople for studies under St Gregory of Nazianzus and other Eastern theologians; yet it was Jerome's prestige as the translator of the Vulgate that guaranteed general acceptance of Eusebius in the West. In any event Jerome did more than translate the original into Latin; he carried forward the chronicle to his own day. Jerome's additions to Eusebius's basic structure soon invited further extensions by others, among them Bishop Hydatius of Chaves, followed by Marcellinus Comes, Victor of Tunnuna, and Joannes of Gerona.[34]

Early in the fifth century Augustine in a letter commended to Jerome 'a religious young man, a brother in the Catholic fold, in age a son, in dignity a fellow priest, alert of mind, ready of speech, burning with eagerness, longing to be a useful vessel in the house of the Lord'.[35] The recipient of this high praise, Paulus Orosius (*c.* 380–*c.* 420), did not fail to measure up to Augustine's faith in his abilities. He was assigned the important task of elaborating the argument of *De civitate Dei* that the sacking of Rome, far from being the greatest calamity in world history, was only one of numerous similar catastrophes instigated by the Supreme Judge. The result of Orosius's labours, the *Historia adversus paganos*,[36] so far surpassed Augustine's expectations, and had such an immense influence on later writers, that we might justly speak of the Christian philosophy of history as being Orosian rather than Augustinian.[37] For his dates, Orosius made free use of Eusebius's *Chronicon*, by now the standard authority on chronology; for his argument, he summarised the thought of his predecessors, though relying always on Augustine. Yet Orosius was not a slavish imitator. There is something very moving in his majestic survey of universal history from the creation to A.D. 417, tracing the rise and fall of the four great civilisations of the past, Babylon, Macedon, Carthage, and Rome, discerning in their fortunes the hand of a divinity shaping their ends, now supporting the righteous, and now smashing the proud and the wicked. So earnestly did Orosius try to impose upon history an orderly pattern that we are tempted to forgive his liberal manipulation of dates, as when he claims that since Babylon was conquered by the Medes 1,164 years from her foundation, so Rome was invaded by Goths 'after an equal number of years'.[38] Ultimately, however, years and even centuries are of no consequence; what matters is that 'one God has directed the course of history'.[39] Before the fifth century ended, Orosius's lucid exposition of the Christian view of history was officially approved by the Bishop of Rome;

thereafter he enjoyed a popularity often unrivalled even by Augustine himself. Dante's verdict that Orosius was 'avvocato dei tempi cristiani'[40] stands as the common view of the entire period until the end of the seventeenth century.

III

If the style of Orosius leaves much to be desired, that of Sulpicius Severus (*c.* 363–*c.* 425) rises to the occasion of his epic subject. His *Historia sacra*,[41] completed some fifteen years before Orosius's history was even begun, is another product of the same tradition in that it is a demonstration of the providential rule of history from the creation to A.D. 400. Notwithstanding its undoubted literary merit, it proved less than popular throughout the millennium following its composition. The injustice was more than redressed during the Renaissance, Scaliger leading the chorus of praise with his tribute to Sulpicius as 'ecclesiasticorum purissimus scriptor'.[42] By virtue of his style, indeed, Sulpicius outlived not only Orosius but even the Christian view of history. Gibbon, who dismissed Orosius as the author of 'pious nonsense', hailed Sulpicius as 'a correct and original writer'.[43]

The legacy bequeathed to the future by Eusebius and Jerome on the one hand, and by Augustine and Orosius on the other, was confirmed by two works written before the end of the fifth century. One was the *Chronicum integrum*[44] of St Prosper of Aquitaine (*c.* 390–*c.* 463), a world chronicle in annalistic form outlining the principal events from Adam to A.D. 455; the other was *De gubernatione Dei*[45] of Salvian of Marseilles (*c.* 400–*c.* 480), a narrative survey of history since the creation, single-mindedly attempting to establish that God is present throughout history as 'a most anxious watcher, a most tender ruler, and a most just judge'.[46] In other words, we have the stage set, the principal plays already written, and different actors giving essentially similar performances. And so it was to be for more than a thousand years.

But significant innovations continued apace. Christian writers up to the first half of the sixth century employed various systems of chronology. One common practice was to date events in relation to the reigns of Roman emperors, and another to use the year of the world's creation as the standard point of reference. Neither method was satisfactory, however, since the first involved the commemoration of Christianity's enemies, while the second created serious problems in so far as the differences of opinion were often enormous. The honour of initiating the traditional scheme fell to Dionysius Exiguus, a Scythian monk living in Rome, who ventured his proposal in 525. Dionysius and his contemporaries were not themselves aware of the significance of his contribution; indeed, although his invention was used on a limited scale shortly after its inception and became widely diffused in Spain during the last half of the seventh century, it was not adopted by any noteworthy authority until its appearance in Bede's *Historia ecclesiastica*. The scheme finally came into use at the Vatican from 963 onwards.[47]

The sixth century is also significant because of the contributions of Cassiodorus (*c.* 485–*c.* 580) and St Gregory of Tours (*c.* 540–594). The least of Cassiodorus's achievements was the compilation of a table of events from Adam to A.D. 519.[48] Far more important was his role in the preparation of the *Historia tripartita* which he and his associates compiled from the ecclesiastical histories of Socrates, Sozomen, and Theodoret, all recently translated from the Greek by Epiphanius.[49] As the necessary supplement to Rufinus's version of the *Historia ecclesiastica* of Eusebius, the composite work of Cassiodorus enjoyed immediate popularity and remained one of the standard texts until the Renaissance.

No less important was the work of the far greater historian of the sixth century, Gregory of Tours, whose account of the birth of Merovingian culture in the *Historia francorum*[50] begins from the creation. Gregory's summary of universal history in Book I is now dismissed as dull and useless. The dullness must be admitted, but not the uselessness; for the book places the entire account under the shadow of eternity, thereby forging yet another major link in the chain of tradition stretching all the way to the Renaissance.

The chain was further strengthened at the turn of the sixth century into the seventh by St Isidore of Seville (*c.* 560–636). His *Chronica maiora* is a compilation of yet another table of events from the creation to A.D. 615,[51] while his *Etymologiae* or *Origines* is the first authoritative encyclopaedia of nearly catholic scope which includes a condensed version of a world chronicle in annalistic form.[52] This last version utilises the division of universal history into Six Ages, already propounded by Augustine and others, but now incorporated for the first time into a formal chronology. But since ideas never remain static, this concept also underwent transformation at the hands of the Venerable Bede (*c.* 673–735).

The major work of St Bede, the *Historia ecclesiastica gentis anglorum*,[53] demonstrates fully the traditional approach to history which unfolds, as did its prototype, the work of Eusebius, under the eye of Providence. In two other works also, *De temporibus* and *De temporum ratione*,[54] Bede made use of the traditional idea of the Six Ages; but unlike Isidore, who terminated his account with the Sixth Age, Bede concluded on an eschatological note of 'sublime devotion' by advancing not only to a description of the Last Judgement but even to the Seventh and Eighth Ages that are to follow the last events of temporal history.[55] Earlier exposition of these *eschata* in *De civitate Dei* may obscure Bede's originality, yet it is there, in degree if not in kind, for Bede's conception first authoritatively introduced into chronology the Christian view of history. But neither Augustine nor Bede could have foreseen that eschatology, espoused by both in their attempts to demonstrate the linear nature of history, was until the fifteenth century to remain a capital interest of Christian historiography.[56]

Notes

1 *Catechesis*, xvi, 16 (*PG*, xxxiii, 941): 'to see the origin of the world, and the end of the world, and the intervening time'.

2 Adam F. Findlay, *Byways in Early Christian Literature* (Edinburgh, 1923), pp. 143 ff.

3 *Dialogus cum Tryphone*, i, 5; trans. A. Lukyn Williams (1930).

4 Jaroslav Pelikan, *The Shape of Death* (1962), p. 49; see also pp. 19 f., 48 f., 89 f.

5 *Contra Celsum*, iv, 67–8; v, 20–1; etc. The quoted passage is cited from J. Pelikan (as in note 4), p. 90.

6 See my article 'The Salvation of Satan', *JHI*, xxviii (1967), 467–78.

7 'To Pammachius against John of Jerusalem', vii; trans. in *NPNF*, 2nd Series, vi, 428. On Origen see further J. Pelikan (as before, note 4), ch. iv, and R. P. C. Hanson, *Allegory and Event: A Study of the Sources and Significance of Origen's Interpretation of Scripture* (1959), esp. ch. x.

8 Consult Johannes Beumer, 'Die altchristliche Idee einer präexistierenden Kirche und ihre theologische Auswertung', *WW*, ix (1942), 13–22.

9 *Ad Autolycum libri tres*, iii, 24–8, in *PG*, vi, 1023–1168; trans. J. A. Giles, *The Writings of the Early Christians* (1857), pp. 119–92. Theophilus also refers (ii, 30) to another work he had written 'concerning history', but this has

been lost. See further Otto Bardenhewer, *Geschichte der altkirchlichen Literatur* (Freiburg, 1913), vol. i, p. 310, and Robert M. Grant, 'Theophilus of Antioch to Autolycus', *HTR*, xl (1947), 227–56.

10 The work is now extant in two Latin versions. See the edition of the *Liber generationis ab Adam*, in *Chronicon Paschale, CSHB*, ix (ii), 96–111; Theodor Mommsen, 'Über den Chronographen vom J.354', *Abhandlungen der königlich Sächsischen Gesellschaft der Wissenschaften* (Leipzig, 1850), vol. ii, 549–668. Hippolytus's chronicle is discussed by Christopher Wordsworth, *St. Hippolytus and the Church of Rome*, 2nd ed. (1880), pp. 218–19, and J. B. Lightfoot, *The Apostolic Fathers* (1890), vol. ii (i), 399.

11 The work survives in fragments preserved in a number of Eastern chronicles. See the edition by M. J. Routh, *Reliquiae Sacrae* (Oxford, 1846), vol. ii, pp. 238–309; trans. in *ANCL*, vi, 125–40; and the discussion by Heinrich Gelzer, *Sextus Julius Africanus und die Byzantinische Chronographie* (Leipzig, 1880), vol. i, pp. 52 ff.; and further: James W. Johnson, 'Chronological Writing: its Concepts and Developments', *H&T*, ii (1962), 124–45.

12 Ephorus's history survives in fragments, collected in *Fragmenta Historicorum Graecorum*, ed. Carl and Theodore Müller (Paris, 1841), vol. i, pp. 234–77; see further Godfrey L. Barber, *The Historian Ephorus* (Cambridge, 1935), esp. ch. ii.

13 Ed. and trans. by H. St John Thackeray and Ralph Marcus, LCL (1930 ff.), 9 vols in progress; see further H. St John Thackeray, *Josephus: The Man and the Historian* (1929), ch. iii, and F. J. Foakes-Jackson, *Josephus and the Jews* (1930), chs xiv–xv.

14 The complete text survives in a seventh-century Armenian version. The Armenian text, with a Latin translation and the extant Greek fragments, has been edited by J. B. Aucher, *Eusebii Pamphili Chronicon Bipartitum* (Venice, 1818), 2 vols. Another Latin version, again including the Greek fragments, is the *Evsebi Chronicorum libri dvo*, ed. Alfred Schoene, 2nd ed. (Berlin, 1962), 2 vols.

15 *Evsebii Pamphili Chronici Canones*, ed. John K. Fotheringham (1923); discussed by Alfred Schoene, *Die Weltchronik des Eusebius in ihrer Bearbeitung durch Hieronymus* (Berlin, 1900); C. H. Turner, 'The Early Episcopal Lists: I. Eusebius of Caesarea and his *Chronicle*', *JTS*, i (1900), 184 ff.; James T. Shotwell, 'Christianity and History: III. Chronology and Church History', *JPP*, xvii (1920), 141–50; J. Stevenson, *Studies in Eusebius* (Cambridge, 1929), pp. 35 ff.; F. J. Foakes-Jackson, *Eusebius Pamphili* (Cambridge, 1933), pp. 142 ff.; and D. S. Wallace-Hadrill, *Eusebius of Caesarea* (1960), ch. viii.

16 Eusebius's debt to Julius Africanus is argued by Gelzer (above, note 11), vol. ii, pp. 23–107.

17 The text, trans. Kirsopp Lake and J. E. L. Oulton, is in LCL (1926–32), 2 vols. One of the finest accounts of Eusebius is by Milburn (above, p. 10, note 8), ch. iv; but see also Roy J. Deferrari, 'Eusebius', in *Church Historians*, ed. Peter Guilday (1926), pp. 3–29; Norman H. Baynes, 'Eusebius and the Christian Empire', in his *Byzantine Studies* (1955), ch. ix; and of the studies cited above (note 15), esp. Wallace-Hadrill, ch. ix, 'The Purpose of God and Human History'. For further references see the latter (pp. 209–14) as well as Johannes Quasten, *Patrology* (Utrecht, 1960), vol. iii, pp. 309–45.

18 Ibid., I, ii, 3.
19 Ibid., x, ix, 2.
20 Anton-Herman Chroust, 'The Relation of Religion to History in Early Christian Thought', *The Thomist*, xviii (1955), 62.
21 See Berthold Altaner, *Patrology*, trans. H. C. Graef (Freiburg, 1960), pp. 272 ff.
22 Ed. Eduard Schwartz and Theodor Mommsen, *Die griechischen christlichen Schriftsteller der ersten drei Jahrhunderte, II: Eusebius Werke* (Leipzig, 1902–9), 3 vols. See J. E. L. Oulton, 'Rufinus's Translation of the Church History of Eusebius', *JTS*, xxx (1928–9), 150–74; Henrich Hoppe, 'Rufin als Ueber-setzer', in *Studi dedicati alla memoria di Paolo Ubaldi*, ed. Agostino Gemelli (Milan, 1937), pp. 133–50; Francis X. Murphy, *Rufinus of Aquileia* (Washington, D.C., 1945), pp. 158–75; Sister M. Monica Wagner, *Rufinus the Translator* (Washington, D.C., 1945); and Maurice Villain, 'Rufin d'Aquilée et l'Histoire Ecclésiastique', *RSR*, xxxiii (1946), 164–210.
23 On Augustine, and particularly his 'philosophy' of history, see the studies by Giuseppe Amari, *Il Concetto di Storia in Sant' Agostino* (Rome, 1950); Norman H. Baynes, *The Political Ideas of St. Augustine's 'De Civitate Dei'* (1936); Edgar H. Brookes, *The City of God and the Politics of Crisis* (1960); John H. S. Burleigh, *The City of God: A Study of St. Augustine's Philosophy* (1949); Jules Chaix-Ruy, *Saint Augustin: temps et histoire* (Paris, 1956), esp. part ii; Cochrane (above, p. 10, note 8); Christopher Dawson, 'St. Augustine and his Age: The City of God', in his *The Dynamics of World History* (1957), pp. 294–325; Roy J. Deferrari and M. Jerome Keeler, 'St. Augustine's *City of God*: Its Plan and Development', *AJP*, l (1929), 109–37; Alois Dempf, *Sacrum Imperium* (Munich and Berlin, 1929), part ii, ch. iii; John N. Figgis, *The Political Aspects of St. Augustine's 'City of God'* (1921), esp. ch. ii; Cataldo Gallo, *La filosofia della storia nel 'De civitate Dei'* (Bari, n.d.); P. Gerosa, 'S. Agostino e l'Imperialismo Romano', in *Miscellanea agostiniana* (Rome, 1931), vol. ii, pp. 977–1040; William A. Green, *Augustine on the Teaching of History*, University of California Publications in Classical Philology, xii, 18 (1944); F. J. C. Hearnshaw and A. J. Carlyle, 'St. Augustine and the City of God', in *The Social and Political Ideas of Some Great Mediaeval Thinkers*, ed. Hearnshaw (1923), pp. 34–52; G. L. Keyes, *Christian Faith and the Interpretation of History: A Study of St Augustine's Philosophy of History* (Lincoln, 1966), with further references; Ernst Lewalter, 'Eschatologie und Weltgeschichte in der Gedankenwelt Augustins', *ZK*, liii (1934), 1–51; Karl Löwith, *Meaning in History* (Chicago, 1949), ch. iv; R. A. Markus, *Saeculum: History and Society in the Theology of St. Augustine* (Cambridge, 1970), with further references; Milburn (above, p. 10, note 8), pp. 74–88; Theodor E. Mommsen, 'St. Augustine and the Christian Idea of Progress: The Background of *The City of God*', in his *Mediaeval and Renaissance Studies* (Ithaca, N.Y., 1959), ch. xii; Joseph Rickaby, *St. Augustine's 'City of God': A View of its Contents* (1925); Giuseppe Ruotolo, *La filosofia della storia e la Città di Dio*, 2nd ed. (Rome, 1950); Ferdinand Schevill, *Six Historians* (Chicago, 1956), pp. 33–60; Heinrich Scholz, *Glaube und Unglaube in der Weltgeschichte: Ein Kommentar zu Augustins De Civitate Dei* (Leipzig, 1911); Georg Seyrich, *Die Geschichtsphilosophie*

Augustins (Chemnitz, 1891); Roger L. Shinn, *Christianity and the Problem of History* (1953), ch. ii; James T. Shotwell, *The History of History* (1939), vol. i, ch. xxviii; Georges Simard, 'Philosophie et théologie de l'histoire d'après *La Cité de Dieu*', *RUO*, vii (1937), 441–8; Johannes Thyssen, *Geschichte der Geschichtsphilosophie*, 2nd ed. (Bonn, 1954), pp. 10–16; Ernst Troeltsch, *Augustin, die christliche Antike und das Mittelalter im Anschluss an die Schrift 'De Civitate Dei'* (Munich and Berlin, 1915); Marthinus Versfeld, *A Guide to 'The City of God'* (1958), chs vii–viii; Alois Wachtel, *Beiträge zur Geschichtstheologie des Aurelius Augustinus* (Benn, 1960).

24 Ed. J. E. C. Welldon (1924), 2 vols; trans. John Healey (1610), revised by R. V. G. Tasker (1942), 2 vols. The LCL ed., in 7 vols, is currently in progress.

25 *De civitate Dei*, xiv, 28; the quoted Scriptural verses are Psalms 3:3 and 18:1, respectively. The actual division between the two 'cities' was also proposed earlier by Tertullian and Tyconius (Dawson [above, note 23], pp. 298 ff., 308 ff.).

26 Ernst Hoffmann, 'Platonism in Augustine's Philosophy of History', in *Philosophy and History*, ed. Raymond Klibansky and H. J. Paton (Oxford, 1936), p. 174.

27 This highly influential concept is set forth capitally in *De civitate Dei*, xxii, 30, and *De Genesi contra Manichaeos*, i, 23. Numerous references to its use both before and after Augustine are cited by Charles W. Jones, ed., *Bedae Opera de Temporibus* (Cambridge, Mass., 1943), p. 345, and W. A. Green (above, note 23), pp. 322 ff. For discussions, see Hugo Hertzberg, 'Über die Chroniken des Isidorus von Sevilla', *FDG*, xv (1875), esp. pp. 327 ff., 349 ff.; Franz Hipler, *Die christliche Geschichts-Auffasung* (Cologne, 1884), chs i–ii *passim*; Dempf (above, note 23), pp. 117 ff.; Jones (below, note 47), pp. 23 ff.; Levison (below, note 53), pp. 115 ff.; cf. Jean Daniélou, 'La typologie de la semaine au IVe siècle', *RSR*, xxxv (1948), 382–411, and Auguste Laneau, *L'Histoire du salut chez les Pères de l'Église: La doctrine des âges du monde* (Paris, 1964).

28 See *De civitate Dei*, esp. xii, 13–14, 17–20.

29 Ibid., xii, 13; the same metaphor is used in xii, 17. The Biblical reference is Psalms 12:8[9], but in the Vulgate: 'in circuitu impii ambulant'; the King James Version reads: 'The wicked walk on every side'.

30 Ibid., iv, 33.

31 See Herman Hausheer, 'St. Augustine's Conception of Time', *PR*, xlvi (1937), 503–12; John F. Callahan, *Four Views of Time in Ancient Philosophy* (Cambridge, Mass., 1948); Robert E. Cushman, 'Greek and Christian Views of Time', *JR*, xxxiii (1953), 254–65; J. L. Russell, 'Time in Christian Thought', in *The Voices of Time*, ed. J. T. Fraser (1966), pp. 59–76.

32 The best short account of Jerome in English is by Edward K. Rand, *Founders of the Middle Ages* (Cambridge, Mass., 1928), ch. iv.

33 See above, note 15. The work is discussed by Francis X. Murphy, 'St. Jerome as an Historian', in *A Monument to St. Jerome* (1952), pp. 113–41.

34 Hydatius Lemicensis, Marcellinus Comes, Victor Tunnunensis, Joannes Biclarensis, *et al.*, ed. Theodor Mommsen, *MGH*, xi (*Chronica Minora*, ii) (1894).

35 Letter clxvi, 2; trans. Wilfrid Parsons, *Saint Augustine: Letters* (1955), vol. iv, p. 7.
36 *Historiarum adversum paganos libri vii*, ed. Carl Zangemeister, BT (1889); trans. Irving W. Raymond (1936).
37 Theodor E. Mommsen, 'Orosius and Augustine', in his *Mediaeval and Renaissance Studies* (Ithaca, N.Y., 1959), ch. xiv. See further Pierre de Labriolle, *History and Literature of Christianity from Tertullian to Boethius*, trans. Herbert Wilson (1924), pp. 434 ff.; William M. T. Gimble, 'Orosius', in *Church Historians*, ed. Peter Guilday (1926), pp. 30–70; Eleanor S. Duckett, *Latin Writers of the Fifth Century* (1930), pp. 158 ff.; M. L. W. Laistner, 'Some Reflections on Latin Historical Writing in the Fifth Century', *CP*, xxxv (1940), 241–58.
38 Op. cit., ii, 3.
39 Ibid.
40 *Paradiso*, x, 119.
41 *PL*, xx, 95–460; trans. in *NPNF*, 2nd Series, xi, 71–122. On Sulpicius, see Terrot R. Glover, *Life and Letters in the Fourth Century* (Cambridge, 1901), ch. xii; and of the studies cited above (note 37), Labriolle, pp. 380 ff., and Duckett, pp. 51 ff.
42 *Apud* Edward Leigh, *Fœlix Consortium* (1663), p. 324.
43 *The Decline and Fall of the Roman Empire*, ed. J. B. Bury (1897), vol. iii, pp. 266n. and 153n., respectively.
44 *PL*, li, 535–608.
45 Salvianus Massiliensis, *MGH*, i, 1–108; trans. Eva M. Sanford (1930). See the study by Michele Pellegrino, *Salviano di Marsiglia* (Rome, 1940), with further references.
46 Ibid., ii, 1.
47 Franz Rühl, *Chronologie des Mittelalters und der Neuzeit* (Berlin, 1897); Bruno Krusch, 'Studien zur christlich–mittelalterlichen Chronologie', *Abhandlungen der Preussischen Akademie der Wissenschaften*, Philosophisch–historische Klasse (1937), no. 8, 59–87; and esp. Reginald L. Poole: *Mediaeval Reckonings of Time* (1918), pp. 39–40; 'The Earliest Use of the Easter Cycle of Dionysius', *EHR*, xxxiii (1918), 57–62, 210–13 (reprinted in his *Studies in Chronology and History*, ed. A. L. Poole [Oxford, 1934], ch. ii); and *Chronicles and Annals* (Oxford, 1926), pp. 16–26. Poole's fundamental studies have been amended by Charles W. Jones, 'The Victorian and Dionysiac Paschal Tables in the West', *Speculum*, ix (1934), esp. 413 ff., and *Saints' Lives and Chronicles in Early England* (Ithaca, N.Y., 1947), ch. iii and Appendix. See further George Ogg, 'Hippolytus and the Introduction of the Christian Era', *VC*, xvi (1962), 2–18.
48 *Chronica*, *MGH*, xi (1894), 120–61.
49 *PL*, lxix, 879–1214; discussed by M. L. W. Laistner, 'The Value and Influence of Cassiodorus' Ecclesiastical History', *HTR*, xli (1948), 51–67. For more general accounts, see G. C. Minasi, *M. A. Cassiodoro* (Milan, 1895); Richard W. Church, 'Cassiodorus', in his *Miscellaneous Essays* (1888), pp. 155–204; A. van der Vyver, 'Cassiodore et son œuvre', *Speculum*, vi (1931), 244–92; and E. S. Duckett, *The Gateway to the Middle Ages* (1938), ch. ii. For a survey of the historiographical methods of Socrates

et al., see Glanville Downey, 'The Perspective of the Early Church Historians', *GRBS*, vi (1965), 57–70.

50 Andreas du Chesne, ed., *Historiæ Francorum Scriptores coætanei* (Paris, 1636), vol. i, pp. 251–459; more readily accessible in *PL*, lxxi, 161–572; trans. O. M. Dalton (Oxford, 1927).

51 Ed. Theodor Mommsen, *MGH*, xi (1894), 391–494.

52 Ed. W. M. Lindsay, SCBO (1911), 2 vols; the chronicle is in v, xxxix ('De descriptione temporvm'). See Hugo Hertzberg, *Die Historien und Chroniken des Isidorus von Sevilla* (Göttingen, 1894), esp. pp. 43 ff.; Maximilianus Manitius, *Geschichte der lateinischen Literatur des Mittelalters* (Munich, 1911–31), vol. i, pp. 52–70; Ernest Brehaut, *An Encyclopedist of the Dark Ages*, Columbia University Studies in History, Economics and Public Law, xlviii (1912), 1–274; and Paul Séjourné, *Le dernier Père de l'Église* (Paris, 1929). For the various editions consult Robert B. Brown, *The Printed Works of Isidore of Seville* (Lexington, 1949).

53 Ed. Charles Plummer (Oxford, 1896), 2 vols: ed. and trans. Bertram Colgrave and R. A. B. Mynors (Oxford, 1969); discussed by Jones, *Saints' Lives* (above, note 47), ch. v. The standard accounts of Bede's historiography are by Wilhelm Levison, 'Bede as Historian', in *Bede: His Life, Times, and Writings*, ed. A. H. Thompson (Oxford, 1935), ch. v; Charles W. Jones, 'Bede as Early Mediaeval Historian', *MH*, iv (1946), 26–36; and Robert W. Hanning, *The Vision of History in Early Britain* (1966), ch. iii. See also the comprehensive study by Peter H. Blair, *The World of Bede* (1970).

54 Ed. C. W. Jones (Cambridge, Mass., 1943).

55 The seven concluding chapters of *De temporibus* (xvi–xxii) comprise a brief chronicle from Adam to the date of composition (A.D. 703). *De temporum ratione* has as its chapter lxvi ('Chronicon sive de sex huius saeculi aetatibus') an extensive chronicle of the same Six Ages extending to the date of composition (A.D. 725); mediaeval scribes often copied this chapter as a separate work. Thereafter, chapters lxvii to lxx consider the *eschata* of the Sixth Age; and chapter lxxi is concerned with the Seventh Age (the dead saints in their current state) and an Eighth Age (eternity after the end of the world). See *MGH*, xiii (*Chronica Minora*, iii) (1898), 247–327.

56 The progress toward a millennial kingdom which so fired the imagination of chiliasts was to have an even longer history. Consult: Norman Cohn, who in *The Pursuit of the Millennium*, rev. ed. (1970), describes the influence of eschatology on revolutionary movements from the late eleventh to the seventeenth century; and Ernest L. Tuveson, who in *Millennium and Utopia* (Berkeley, 1949), discusses the secularisation of Christian expectations. On later developments, see below, pp. 121–2.

Three

Mediaeval Formulations:
West and East

The day is commen of catyfnes,
   all those to care that are vncleyn,
The day of batell and bitternes,
   ffull long abiden has it beyn.
The Towneley Plays: 'The Judgement'[1]

I

The standard expositions of the Christian view of history enjoyed widespread popularity throughout the Middle Ages.[2] According to Einhard, Charlemagne was partial to *De civitate Dei*,[3] and the imperial preference appears to have been shared throughout the Middle Ages. The *apologia* of Paulus Orosius was easily the second most popular work, with Jerome's version of the chronicle of Eusebius, the *Historia ecclesiastica* of Eusebius, the *Historia tripartita* of Cassiodorus, the encyclopaedia of Isidore, and the chronological and historical works of Bede coming after. To these must be added the *Antiquitates Judaicae* of Josephus, widely respected not only as the universal history that it is, but also as a non-Christian source furnishing 'proof' concerning the divinity of Jesus.[4]

The historians of the Middle Ages, like their predecessors in Israel, were both particular and universal. They were universal because they attempted to be all-encompassing, thereby upholding the total jurisdiction of Providence throughout the created order. They were particular because each believed his nation to be God's ultimate concern. Of the strictly 'ecumenical' works written during the Middle Ages, the most popular universal history was the *Chronica* of Sigebert of Gembloux (*c.* 1030–1112), seemingly concerned only with the period from A.D. 381 to 1111, yet continuing further the chronicle of Eusebius, Jerome, and Prosper of Aquitaine.[5] Similarly, works concerned with 'origins' far outweigh those that are not. Some modest historians such as Hugo of Fleury in the eleventh century[6] were content to hark back only as far as Abraham, while others – among them Regino of Prüm in the tenth century, Hugo of Flavigny in the twelfth, and Sicard of Cremona in the thirteenth[7] – preferred the Nativity as their starting-point. The majority, however, elected to commence their labours with an account of the creation. Though it is not possible to enumerate all the universal chroniclers, a representative list exclusive of anonymous works[8] is called for, if only in order to demonstrate the variety of the writers' nationalities, callings, and stations in life. In the ninth century, soon after Bede's death, we already find universal chroniclers at work, two of the most noteworthy being Freculph of Lisieux and St Ado of Vienne.[9] By 1100, it has been estimated, Western Europe possessed nearly sixty universal chronicles.[10] As the dam finally burst, originality struggled for a time to survive but was drowned; by the eleventh century its epitaph was to be read in the world chronicles of Hermann of Reichenau, Marianus Scotus, and Lambert of Hersfeld, all of which propound the scheme of the Six Ages.[11] The most noteworthy of twelfth-century chronicles were Honorius of Autun's *Summa totius de omnipoda historia*, a world history which he also rehearsed, in abridged form and divided into the traditional Six Ages, in Book III of his encyclopaedic *Imago mundi*; Peter Comestor's *Historia scholastica*, a refreshing variation in that it is a universal chronicle in the form of commentaries on individual books of the Bible; the ecclesiastical history of the Anglo-Norman Orderic Vitalis; Gottfried of Viterbo's *Pantheon*, predominantly in verse; the *Kaiserchronik*, the oldest metrical world history in the vernacular; and Ekkehard of Aura's *Chronicon universale*.[12] In the next century, the thirteenth, we find Robert of Auxerre's *Chronologia* and Lucas of Tuy's *Chronicon mundi*, both of which elaborate the concept of the Six Ages.[13] Universal histories continued to be written throughout the thirteenth century, mostly in Latin, but occasionally in the vernacular – in French, Brunetto Latini's brief section in his encyclopaedic *Trésor*;[14] in Spanish, the well-known *Primera crónica general* of King Alfonso X surnamed El Sabio;[15] and in German, the *Sächsische Weltchronik* usually attributed to Eike of

Repgow,[16] and the metrical world chronicles of Jansen Enikel and Rudolf of Ems.[17]

Otto of Freising, Joachim of Fiore, and Vincent of Beauvais represent in the vast area of mediaeval historiography the most characteristic inclinations. The first, the Bishop of Freising (1114?–58), was unquestionably the most highly placed, for in addition to his ecclesiastical position he was the son of the Margrave of Austria, and uncle to Emperor Frederick Barbarossa. Yet his major work, the *Chronica sive historia de duabus civitatibus*,[18] is anything but worldly; it is on the contrary the most eloquent statement eschatologically of the Christian view of history, often enough proclaimed before, but emerging now to the forefront because of contemporary pessimism over this world, which stirred conviction that the Last Judgement was at hand.[19] If in his prologue Otto acknowledges his indebtedness to 'those illustrious lights of the Church, Augustine and Orosius', the similarities between them are more apparent than real. Unlike Augustine and Orosius, Otto was neither apologetic nor polemic; he also inclined the scales away from the Incarnation towards the Second Advent. In outline his work is traditional enough. The two opening books review the history of the world from the creation of the first Adam to the birth of the second, with a running commentary interpreting the rise and fall of civilisations as evidence of God's constant presence in history; the next five books carry the narrative, still providentially oriented, from the Nativity to Otto's own time; and the last book sets forth the *eschata* of history, including the Last Judgement, the final conflagration, and the cessation of time in the Eternal Present. Throughout, however, the stress is on the *miseria rerum mutabilium*, constantly accompanied by reminders that Otto and his contemporaries stood witness to 'the closing days' of history, that their times were 'threatening the approaching end of the world in consequence of the enormity of its sinfulness, and indicating that the kingdom of Christ is soon to come'.[20] Such is Otto's pessimism that, through his excessive emphasis on life's vicissitudes, he comes perilously close at times to an affirmation of the cyclical view of history; yet ultimately he did not lose sight of its linear nature, even though his stress was not on the alpha but on the omega.

However profound and forceful Otto of Freising may have been, he was never so influential as the almost legendary Joachim of Fiore (*c.* 1132–1202), the father of a movement that spread expeditiously from Italy to Northern Europe and persisted, in one form or another, even to our own day. Joachim's principal works are three: the *Liber concordiae novi ac veteris testamenti*, the *Expositio in apocalypsim*, and the *Psalterium decem cordatum*.[21] If these were orderly and disciplined, the same cannot be said of the works later attributed to Joachim, notably the *Evangelium aeternum*, an 'anthology' compiled with generous additions by his followers and so successfully suppressed that not a single copy is extant. The spurious works, and reputedly the 'eternal gospel' in particular, constitute the most striking mediaeval amalgam of ingenious flights of fancy, prophecies run wild, and incredible attempts to establish multiple correspondences throughout the levels of the universe. From this chaos emerges at least one idea, on occasion espoused by Joachim himself and fundamental to the Joachimist 'philosophy' of history: the concept of the three eras of Nature, Law, and Grace. Earlier, when Augustine and others expounded a similar scheme, the era of Nature referred to the pre-Mosaic period, that of Law to the Mosaic, and the era of Grace to the period since the Incarnation.[22] But now all three were drastically reapportioned. The first era, under the jurisdiction of the Father, was readjusted in order to comprehend the entire period from Adam to the Christ; the second, regarded as the province of the Son, was said to have commenced with the Incarnation and to be nearing its terminal point; while the third, assigned to the province of the Holy Spirit, was proclaimed as the last era, its duration unknown, its nature temporal, its rulers celibate, and marked by the revelation of a new and final dispensation, the so-called 'evangelium aeternum'. Joachim himself interpreted the third era less as a distinct 'age' and more as the last period of mankind's development prior to the Second Advent. But lesser intellects so misconstrued his views as to lapse into tritheism and, because of the fuller revelation involved under the new dispensation, threatened to remove Jesus from the centre of history. Joachim's own pronounced tendencies toward tritheism profoundly disturbed the ecclesiastical authorities, but it was not possible to censure a person with his ample reputation for sanctity. The compilers of the *Evangelium aeternum*, however, were condemned without hesitation. Yet despite the anathema decreed by the Council of Arles in 1263, the misunderstanding of Joachim's views persisted;

31

and in the centuries following the Joachimist apocalypse of the third dispensation often verged on, and frequently merged with, such visions of a brighter temporal future as that advanced by the millenarians – witness even the 'Third Reich' which significantly was expected to last a thousand years.[23] Up to and including the Renaissance, at any rate, the appeal of Joachim's apocalyptic notions remained so powerful that a century after his death, and the uncertain ecclesiastical attitude notwithstanding, he was elevated by Dante to Heaven. In the poet's words,[24]

> lucemi da lato
> il Calabrese abate Gioacchino,
> di spirito profetico dotato.

The third towering figure of mediaeval historiography is Vincent of Beauvais (*c.* 1190–1264), the author of the most ambitious project undertaken in Christendom either before or since. His astonishing goal was a compendium of all available knowledge in his time. The wonder is that although Vincent fails to impress us with his critical acumen, he still succeeded in preserving within the confines of a single work the chief preoccupations of the period up to the Renaissance. His *Speculum maius* is not merely long; it is colossal. Of its three parts,[25] the one that interests us here, the *Speculum historiale,* itself comprises nearly four thousand chapters and has been estimated to contain one and a quarter million words. Inevitably, the *Speculum historiale* is a synthesis of traditional views. Beginning with an account of the creation, it progresses to the middle of the thirteenth century; but the *telos* is also kept firmly in view through an epilogue that describes in detail the last events of temporal history.[26] And with this, appropriately enough, Vincent's work concludes.

If I have given the impression that during the Middle Ages original thinking had come to a standstill, we must remember that the mediaeval historians wrote under outrageously adverse conditions; that they wrote at all is a recognisably significant achievement: for they did not possess the satisfactory chronology that is the backbone of history, nor did they have the opportunities for research we have grown accustomed to accept. Moreover such was the force of tradition – 'the gathered force of immemorial tradition'[27] – that minds bent before it naturally. Mediaeval education itself reflected this servitude to tradition, for instead of attaching any importance to the study of temporal events, it excluded history from its liberal arts altogether. Thus the composition of histories, beyond the compilation of merely derivative annals, marked by discriminating selection of facts, sound evaluation of the events recounted, and a style commensurate to the argument,[28] remains a considerable achievement. We must allow for the plethora of world chronicles which even the champion of the renaissance of the twelfth century confessed to.[29] Even so, there sprang up during the Middle Ages most competent historians, like Adam of Bremen in the eleventh century, Villehardouin and Matthew Paris in the thirteenth, Froissart and Marsilius of Padua in the fourteenth; and at the peak of the period, the twelfth century, we have Eadmer and Orderic Vitalis, Peter Comestor and William of Tyre, Otto of Freising and William of Malmesbury. This same century was moreover the age of John of Salisbury and Abélard, no less than the age of St Bernard of Clairvaux and the 'Master of the Sentences', of Averroës and Maimonides, of translations from the Arabic and of advances in science and jurisprudence, of the *Poema de mio Cid* and the *Chanson de Roland*, of the high Romanesque and the early Gothic, of the school of Chartres and its platonising Chancellors, and of the emerging institutions of higher learning at Bologna and Paris and Oxford. Lastly it stands out as the age of heresy.

These developments notwithstanding, the spokesmen for the Middle Ages categorically refused to tamper with the traditional emphasis on the historical nature of the Christian faith. True, the approach to the Bible was often by way of the notorious 'four senses';[30] but the historical sense was never actually surrendered, least of all by great minds of the order of St Thomas Aquinas. Its primacy is firmly upheld even in the well-known formulation by Rabanus Maurus: 'in nostræ ergo animæ domo *historia* fundamentum ponit, *allegoria* parietes erigit, *anagogia* tectum supponit, *tropologia* vero tam interius per affectum quam exterius per effectum boni operis, variis ornatibus depingit'.[31] Ironically it is to the excessive fondness for the literal sense that we must in part attribute the mediaeval predilection for apocalyptic visions. However strenuously St Thomas may have resisted the common stress on the Book of Revelation, millennial expectations were largely sustained by a literalistic interpretation of its prophecies. As if to compound the irony, the belief in progress implicit in all such expectations gradually discarded its Biblical origins and advanced into the Age of Enlightenment in all its glorious naïvety.[32]

II

But it is time to glance, however briefly, at the situation in Eastern Christendom. The great schism of 1054 was the climax of a process of alienation which extended over several centuries and was as much exacerbated by differences in language and mental outlook as by conflicting claims involving both State and Church. The widespread acceptance by the West of Augustinianism was not calculated to reduce the tension, especially as Eastern theologians thought it excessively dogmatic and unduly morbid.[33] The philosophy of history expounded in *De civitate Dei* was consequently unknown in the East. Even so, there is no appreciable difference between the Eastern and Western attitudes to history. If the Christians of the East were unaware of St Augustine, they were bound to reach similar conclusions so long as they did not deviate from the road marked out by Julius Africanus and Eusebius.

And they did not. In a rare display of unity, the pattern we have been tracing in the West was repeated in the East. During the twelve centuries from the death of Julius Africanus to the fall of Constantinople in 1453, the providential theory of history was a commonplace among Eastern historians, while universal histories were composed with an indefatigable enthusiasm fully analogous to that in the West.[34] But the teleological aspect of history was neglected as much by Byzantine historians as it had been by Eusebius. Eschatology intruded upon Eastern historiography only during the Empire's declining years, when the sunset of Constantinople was increasingly interpreted as heralding the sunrise of the Second Advent.[35]

The Eastern tradition may be said to have come properly into its own when Philippos Sidetes, a contemporary of Paulus Orosius, composed his encyclopaedic Χριστιανικὴ Ἱστορία (*Historia Christiana*)[36] which aspired to relate all events from the creation to A.D. 430. Worthy of imitation as this precedent was, other Eastern historians similarly resolved to commence their accounts with the creation – but with the understandable difference that they regarded their own Empire as the culminating point of universal history, in line with their intensely nationalistic conviction that Constantinople had become 'the heart of the universe' (ἡ τῆς οἰκουμένης καρδία).[37]

Of the numerous world chronicles written in the East, the following are no less noteworthy than they were popular: in the sixth century, the Ἱστορία of Hesychios Milesios and the Χρονογραφία of Joannes Malalas; in the seventh century, the anonymous Πασχάλιον; in the ninth, the Χρονογραφία of Georgios Synkellos – thereafter continued by Theophanes Homologetes – and the Χρονικὸν Σύντομον of Georgios Monachos or Hamartolos; in the tenth century, the Χρονογραφία uncertainly attributed to the famous hagiographer Symeon Metaphrastes; in the eleventh, the Σύνοψις Ἱστοριῶν of Georgios Cedrenos; and in the twelfth, the Ἐπιτομὴ Ἱστοριῶν of Ioannes Zonaras, the Βίβλος Χρονικὴ of Michael Glykas, and the metrical Σύνοψις Χρονικὴ of Constantinos Manasses.[38] The pattern, repeated throughout Eastern Europe,[39] was particularly noticeable in Russia, where under the all-pervasive influence of the Eastern Orthodox Church the tradition was extended in numerous imitations of the Byzantine chronicles, notably the universal histories of Malalas and Monachos.[40] Russian chroniclers differed from their Byzantine counterparts in one significant respect. In what had already become a meaningful extension of Hebrew historiography as well as a common manifestation of nationalistic aspirations, they viewed the course of world history as focusing ultimately, by the grace of God, on Russia.[41]

Yet our brief survey of Byzantine historical writing requires drastic qualification, since Eastern Christendom possessed not only a host of mere world chroniclers but a number of great historians who wrote on a far higher intellectual level than did any historian in the West.[42] Foremost among them was Michael Psellus (c. 1019–c. 1078), who not only redeemed the Greek language from the evil times into which it had fallen, but was also responsible for a revival of classical learning and himself contributed a historical work of capital importance, the Χρονογραφία (*Chronographia*).[43] The work covers the period from the death of Joannes I Tzimisces in 976 to the reign of Michael VII Ducas (1071–78); yet Psellus, unlike the chroniclers, neither relied upon any preceding compilation, nor resorted to any indiscriminate accumulation of details. Involved as he was with the personalities of his time, he composed an imaginative and highly readable history which is distinguished by an uncommonly excellent style, overpowering learning, psychological insight, and a noble attempt at impartiality in accordance with the highest ideal of all Byzantine historians, the presentation of 'truth'.[44] But he did not fail to adopt some of the most time-honoured aspects of Christian historiography. He adhered to the traditional view of history as directed by Providence; and while he did not commence his account with the creation, he was less than prepared to reject such an approach. As he himself states, his work is a continuation of Leo Diaconus's well-wrought Ἱστορία (*Historia*),[45] which in turn dates all events from the foundation of the universe.

III

Developments in Britain were in the meantime keeping pace with those on the Continent and deriving from the foundations laid by Bede. We must, on the other hand, note the passion of Anglo-Saxon writers for *De civitate Dei*,[46] and note also four early native works that prefigure conspicuously the capital preoccupations of British historians throughout the Middle Ages. One is the *De excidio et conquestu Britanniae* of St Gildas (516?–70), which sees history progressing *sub specie aeternitatis*; another is the chaotic *Historia Britonum* associated with the name of Nennius (*fl.* 796), which begins with the creation and adopts, among other schemes, the division of universal history into the traditional Six Ages; the third is the translation of Orosius's *Historia* by King Alfred (848?–99), which confirms the widespread acceptance of the providential view of history; while the fourth is the group of texts constituting the *Anglo-Saxon Chronicle*, according to which events occur precisely 'as God had foreseen' them, the overthrow of enemies is the gift of 'the Lord of Victories', and disasters are the just punishment inflicted by the offended and incensed God ('such things happen because of the people's sins').[47] While some of the works written in Britain during the Middle Ages were inevitably lost, the majority survive albeit mostly in manuscript form.[48] From world chronicles that are typical and all-inclusive, we may single out from the twelfth century Florence of Worcester's encyclopaedic *Chronicon ex chronicis* and the anonymous *Chronicum Scotorum*;[49] from the thirteenth, John of Oxnead's *Chronica*;[50] from the fourteenth, Thomas of Malmesbury's *Eulogium*, Richard of Cirencester's *Speculum historiale*, and Ranulf Higden's incredibly popular *Polychronicon*;[51] and from the early fifteenth century, Andrew of Wyntoun's metrical world chronicle of Scotland as well as its English counterpart by John Capgrave, who glances tenderly back to Adam ('Adam was mad on a Friday, withoute modir, withoute fader').[52] All these writers commenced their accounts with the creation, but others, who did not, began either with Noah[53] or with the times of Brut, as we shall see.

Neither the mediaeval period in Europe nor the Middle Ages in Britain lend themselves to ready generalisations. In the twelfth century, for example, we come across that phenomenon, William of Malmesbury, whose *Gesta regum anglorum*[54] begins not with the creation but with the year of our Lord 449. It is a work of rare impartiality, wide learning, and exceptional style, while paying all proper attention to characterisation and description. As its author self-consciously observes in his preface, he wrote it to extract from posterity 'if not a reputation for eloquence, at least credit for diligence'. Then the early thirteenth century saw established at St Albans a 'school of history' which began with Roger of Wendover shortly after 1215, continued with his successor Matthew Paris, and terminated with Thomas Walsingham well into the fifteenth century. Until recently the most serious problem confronting students of this period was the relationship between three of its earliest works: the *Flores historiarum* of Roger of Wendover, the *Chronica maiora* of Matthew Paris, and the *Flores historiarum* of 'Matthew of Westminster'. It is now believed that Wendover's work, extending from the creation to 1235, derives in its earliest part from other chronicles and strikes originality only after 1201.[55] The *Chronica maiora*, beginning with the creation and terminating in or about 1259, is a revision of Wendover's work, but after 1235 continues in singularly original vein.[56] The third, again starting from the creation, is largely borrowed from Matthew Paris and was erroneously attributed to the non-existent 'Matthew of Westminster' upon its publication in 1567.[57] Of all English historians of the Middle Ages – our own great respect for William of Malmesbury notwithstanding[58] – Matthew Paris (*c.* 1199–1259) traditionally earns the highest praise. No less discriminating an authority than Milton described Paris as 'the best of our Historians'.[59] We are told Paris was fond of saying that 'laziness is the enemy of the soul'. The massive work he left behind is ample testimony of fidelity to his acceptance of this principle. Nevertheless it is assuredly not his prolific tendencies that have exalted him to the rank he occupies, nor his originality of thinking and research into original sources, both of which he avoided like temptations to sin. But he was endowed with a personality as strong as that of his Byzantine counterpart, Michael Psellus. Both are picturesque and vivacious writers, both held decidedly personal views, both commend and denounce with equal vehemence, both colour their works with their personalities and decorate them with captivating anecdotes and lively descriptions. The praise bestowed by posterity upon Paris and Psellus was not misplaced.

The Christian view of history influenced mediaeval literature greatly. The fourteenth-century poem *Cursor mundi*[60] can hardly be overlooked since it is the most ambitious lyrical endeavour to envisage history as a sequence of Six Ages terminating in a Seventh through and beyond the Last Judgement. The authors of the *Cursor mundi* may have hoped to achieve in poetry what Vincent of Beauvais had already attempted in prose: for the poem is interminably long, extending to nearly thirty thousand lines.

But there is also mediaeval drama. The Passion Plays were indeed often preceded by a dramatic representation of the Fall of Man, and followed by a Judgement;[61] but it is not until the formation during the fourteenth century of the great cycles of the Mystery Plays that we obtain the most sustained literary interpretation of historical events as cosmic in scope, and advancing along a linear path *sub specie aeternitatis*. The four cycles traditionally apportioned to York, Chester, Wakefield, and 'Coventry'[62] are essentially different manifestations of one and the same play, 'the plaie called Corpus Christi'. Unique in its comprehensive vision of history, the play would frequently begin in eternity with God in self-contemplation ('gracyus and grete, god withoutyn begynnyng'); progress thereafter to the Fall of Lucifer, or else the creation of the world and man's first disobedience; advance thence through a series of typologically-significant episodes drawn from the Old Testament, to the advent of the Christ;[63] and terminate with a stirring account of Doomsday, the 'chosen childir' ascending to Heaven, the 'cursed kaitiffs' confined for ever to Hell. 'The plaie called Corpus Christi' is therefore not simply a universal history in that it endeavours 'the mimesis of total human time'; it is fundamentally a Christocentric interpretation of historical events in that it posits the omnipresence of the Christ whether typologically, historically, or in anticipation of his Second Advent. Finally, while its selection of seven basic episodes for dramatisation looks back upon the traditional division of history into Seven Ages, its espousal of the providential theory of history looks ahead to the Elizabethan chronicle drama.[64]

IV

If we were to pause here, nearly a thousand years after St Augustine, to seek the finest exposition of the Christian view of history, we would discover it neither in Britain nor in Byzantium, nor among such impressive chroniclers of Latin Christendom as Otto of Freising and Vincent of Beauvais. It is to be discovered in a poet – not indeed any of the versifiers responsible for the *Cursor mundi* or the Mystery Plays, but a poet whose style is answerable to his great argument. Dante does not win this distinction either for extending the traditional view of history in *De monarchia*,[65] or for echoing Augustine and Orosius,[66] but because in his *Commedia* he surveys history from the divine standpoint. His is an eloquent testimony that all temporal events, however haphazard they may seem and however tragic they may be, are vital links in the golden chain of history stretching from the creation to the Last Judgement. This truth struck him like a flash of lightning when, from the vantage-point of the Eternal Present, he beheld the 'universal form' of all things.[67]

> legato con amore in un volume,
> ciò che per l'universo si squaderna;
>
> sustanzia ed accidenti, e lor costume,
> quasi conflati insieme per tal modo,
> che ciò ch'io dico è un semplice lume.

Notes

1 *The Towneley Plays*, ed. George England, EETS: ES (1897), p. 379.
2 On mediaeval historiography see the *Early Chroniclers of Europe* by Ugo Balzani on Italy, Gustave Mossen on France, James Gairdner on England

(1883), 3 vols; the fundamental survey by Maximilianus Manitius, *Geschichte der lateinischen Literatur des Mittelalters* (Munich, 1911–31), 3 vols; T. F. Tout, 'The Study of Mediæval Chronicles', *BJRL*, vi (1921–2), 414–38 (reprinted in his *Collected Papers* [Manchester, 1934], vol. iii, pp. 1–25); Silvio Vismara, *Il concetto della storia nel pensiere scolastico* (Milan, 1924); C. H. Haskins (below, note 29), ch. viii; Floyd S. Lear, 'The Mediaeval Attitude toward History', *RIP*, xx (1923), 156–77; Harry E. Barnes, *A History of Historical Writing* (Norman, Okla., 1937), ch. iii; Herbert Grundmann, 'Die Grundzüge der mittelalterlichen Geschichtsanschauungen', *AK*, xxiv (1934), 326–36; Ludovico D. Macnab, *El concepto escolastico de la historia* (Buenos Aires, 1940); Etienne Gilson, *The Spirit of Mediæval Philosophy*, trans. A. H. C. Downes (1940), ch. xix; Ricardo Orta Nadal, 'La conception cristiana de la historia on la Edad Media', in *Anales de Historia Antigua y Mediæval* (Buenos Aires, 1950), pp. 85–101; Johannes Thyssen, *Geschichte der Geschichtsphilosophie*, 2nd ed. (Bonn, 1954), pp. 16 ff.; *et al.* On the historical works that were particularly popular during the Middle Ages, see James S. Beddie, 'Libraries in the Twelfth Century: their Catalogues and Contents', in *Haskins Anniversary Essays* (Boston, 1929), pp. 1–23. The nearly total ignorance of the historians of Greece and Rome is admirably documented by Eva M. Sanford, 'The Study of Ancient History in the Middle Ages', *JHI*, v (1944), 21–43.

3 *Vita Karoli Imperatoris*, xxiv, 2.

4 The celebrated *testimonium Flavianum* is in *Antiquitates Judaicae*, xviii, iii, 3. On this controversial statement, see below, p. 119, note 4.

5 Sigebertus Gemblacensis, *PL*, clx, 57–546.

6 Hugo Floriacensis, *Chronicon*, ed. Bernhard Rottendorff (Westphalia, 1638).

7 Regino Prumiensis, *Chronicon*, *PL*, cxxxii, 15–150; Hugo Flaviniacensis, *Chronicon*, *PL*, cliv, 21–404; Sicardus Cremonensis, *Chronicon*, *PL*, ccxiii, 441–540.

8 For which see August Potthast, *Bibliotheca Historica Medii Aevi*, 2nd ed. (Berlin, 1896), pp. 223–318 *passim*.

9 Freculphus Lexoviensis, *Chronicon*, *PL*, cvi, 917–1258; Ado Viennensis, *Chronicon*, *PL*, cxxiii, 23–138.

10 Louis L. Myers, 'Universal History in the Twelfth Century', *HLQ*, v (1942), 162. Cf. below, note 29.

11 Hermannus Contractus, *Chronicon*, in *Chronica*, ed. Joannes Sichardus (Basle, 1579), folios 185ᵛ–223; Marianus Scotus, *Chronicon*, in *Rervm Germanicarvm Scriptores*, ed. Joannes Pistorius (Regensburg, 1726), vol. i, pp. 448–656; Lambertus Hersfeldensis, *Chronicon*, in *Historicum opus*, ed. Simon Schardius (Basle, 1574), vol. i, pp. 694–815.

12 Honorius Augustodunensis, *PL*, clxxii, 115–86 (the *Imago*) and 187–96 (the *Summa*, but only the section for A.D. 726–1133); Petrus Comestor, *PL*, cxcviii, 1055–1722; Ordericus Vitalis, *Ecclesiastical History*, ed. and trans. Marjorie Chibnall (Oxford, 1969); Godefridus Viterbiensis, *Pantheon, sive vniuersitatis libri, qui chronici appelantur*, *XX* (Basle, 1559); *Die Kaiserchronik*, *MGH* ('Scriptorvm qvi vernacvla lingva vsi svnt'), i (1892); Ekkehardus Uraugiensis, *PL*, cliv, 498–1058.

13 Robertus Altissiodorensis, *Chronologia seriem temporvm* (Utrecht, 1608); Lucas Tudensis ('El Tudense'), *Chronicon* in *Hispaniæ illvstrata sev vrbivm rervmque hispanicarvm*, ed. Andreas Schottus (Frankfurt, 1608), vol. iv, pp. 1–116. The latter is merely an amplified version of the formulation by Isidore.

14 *Li Livres dou Trésor*, ed. Francis J. Carmody, University of California Publications in Modern Philology, xxii (1948), pp. 32–81; discussed by F. J. Carmody in 'Latin Sources of Brunetto Latini's World History', *Speculum*, xi (1936), 359–70.

15 Ed. Ramón Menéndez Pidal (Madrid, 1906), vol. 1.

16 *MGH* ('Scriptorvm qvi vernacvla lingva vsi svnt'), ii (1877), 65–384.

17 Jansen Enikel, *Weltchronik*, ibid., iii (1900), 1–596; Rudolf vom Ems, *Weltchronik*, ed. Gustav Ehrismann (Berlin, 1915).

18 Ed. Adolf Hofmeister (Hanover and Leipzig, 1912); trans. Charles C. Mierow (1928). See the estimates by Justus Hashagen, *Otto von Freising als Geschichtsphilosoph und Kirchenpolitiker* (Dresden, 1900); Joseph Schmidlin, *Die Geschichtsphilosophie und Kirchenpolitische Weltanschauung* (Freiburg, 1906); Adolf Hofmeister, 'Studien über Otto von Freising', *GDG*, xxxvii (1912), 99–161, 633–768; Felix Fellner, 'The *Two Cities* of Otto of Freising and its Influence on the Catholic Philosophy of History', *CHR*, xx (1934–5), 154–74 (reprinted in *The Catholic Philosophy of History*, ed. Peter Guilday [1936], pp. 45–82); Paolo Brezzi, 'Ottone di Frisinga', *BISI*, liv (1939), 129–328, with an extensive bibliography; Werner Kaegi, *Grundformen der Geschichtschreibung seit dem Mittelalter* (Utrecht, 1947), ch. i.

19 G. G. Coulton, *From St. Francis to Dante*, 2nd ed. (1907), pp. 55 ff.

20 *Chronica*, ii, 13, and vii, 9, respectively. See further the comprehensive survey by Vasiliev (below, note 35).

21 The standard account of Joachimism is by Marjorie Reeves, *The Influence of Prophecy in the Later Middle Ages* (Oxford, 1969), which also cites several of her other studies (p. 546). Further accounts, especially by Continental scholars, are named by Eugène Anitchkof, *Joachim de Flore et les milieux courtois* (Rome, 1931), pp. ix–xxiii; Herbert Grundmann, *Neue Forschungen über Joachim von Fiore* (Marburg, 1950); and Francesco Russo, *Bibliographia gioachimita* (Florence, 1954). Studies of Joachimist influences on literature include Morton W. Bloomfield's *'Piers Plowman' as a Fourteenth-Century Apocalypse* (New Brunswick, N.J., 1961).

22 For the rise and development of this idea, see my article cited below, p. 63, note 32.

23 The idea has had an incredibly tortuous history. On its antecedents see especially Ruth Kestenberg-Gladstein, 'The "Third Reich"', *JWCI*, xviii (1955), 245–95.

24 *Paradiso*, xii, 139–41: 'there shineth at my side the Calabrian abbott Joachim, dowed with prophetic spirit' (trans. Philip H. Wicksteed). On Joachim's influence on Dante, see Leone Tondelli, *Il Libro delle Figure dell' abate Gioachino da Fiore* (Turin, 1939), vol. i, pp. 185–334, and the studies cited by Bloomfield (above, note 21), pp. 310 f.

25 The *Speculum naturale*, the *Speculum doctrinale*, and the *Speculum historiale*; a fourth part, the *Speculum morale*, was compiled by another writer. Pertinent details on the entire work are provided by B. L. Ullman, 'A Project for a

New Edition of Vincent of Beauvais', *Speculum*, viii (1953), 312–26. The edition I consulted was: *Bibliotheca mvndi. sev specvli maioris Vincentii . . . Bellovacensis . . . Tomvs quartvs, qvi specvlvm historiale inscribitvr: in qvo vniuersa totius orbis, omniumque populorum ab orbe condito vsque ad auctoris tempus historia continetur, pulcherrimum actionum ciuilium & ecclesiasticarum theatrvm* (Douai, 1624).

26 'Epilogvs specvli historialis: continens tractatvm de ultimis temporis', ibid., pp. 1323–32.

27 V. H. Galbraith, *Roger Wendover and Matthew Paris* (Glasgow, 1944), p. 12.

28 Cf. Gervase of Canterbury's distinction between histories and annals, in *Historical Works*, ed. William Stubbs, RB (1879), vol. i, pp. 87–8; as expounded by V. H. Galbraith, *Historical Research in Medieval England* (1951), p. 2.

29 Charles H. Haskins, *The Renaissance of the Twelfth Century* (Cambridge, Mass., 1927), p. 237: 'The universal chronicle is a conspicuous feature of historical writing in the twelfth century.'

30 Harry Caplan, 'The Four Senses of Scriptural Interpretation and the Mediaeval Theory of Preaching', *Speculum*, iv (1929), 282–90. For two mediaeval articulations of this scheme, see the translations available in *Studies in Rhetoric . . . in Honor of J. A. Winans* (1925), pp. 61–90, and in *LCC*, ix, 291–2.

31 *Allegoriæ in Sacram Scripturam*, Preface (*PL*, cxii, 849): 'in the house of our soul, history lays the foundation, allegory erects the walls, anagogy puts on the roof, while tropology provides ornament, within through the disposition, without through the effect, of the good work' (trans. H. O. Taylor, *The Mediaeval Mind*, 4th ed. [1925], vol. ii, p. 74). On St Thomas as exponent of the primacy of the literal sense, consult Robert M. Grant, *A Short History of the Interpretation of the Bible* (1965), pp. 97 ff.

32 See the suggestive survey by Ernest L. Tuveson, 'Ideas of Progress', *History of Ideas News Letter*, iii (1957), 2–6, and his seminal study *Millennium and Utopia* (Berkeley, 1949). Cf. above, p. 27, note 56.

33 Despite their limited knowledge of Augustine's actual writings (Berthold Altaner, 'Augustinus in der griechischen Kirche bis auf Photius', *HJ*, lxxi [1951], 37–76).

34 On Byzantine historiography, see Karl Krumbacher, *Geschichte der byzantinischen Litteratur*, 2nd ed. (Munich, 1897), pp. 319–408; Ferdinand Hirsch, *Byzantinische Studien* (Leipzig, 1876), esp. chs i, vi; Giovanni Montelatici, *Storia della letteratura bizantina* (Milan, 1916), esp. pp. 149 ff., 233 ff.; Constantinos I. Amantos, Ἱστορία τοῦ Βυζαντινοῦ Κράτους (Athens, 1947), vol. ii, pp. 374 ff.; F. H. Marshall, 'Byzantine Literature', in *Byzantium*, ed. N. H. Baynes and H. St L. B. Moss (Oxford, 1948), pp. 234 ff.; Louis Bréhier, *Le monde byzantine* (Paris, 1950), vol. iii, pp. 346 ff.; G. Georgiades Arnakis, 'The Eastern Imperial Tradition', in *The Development of Historiography*, ed. M. A. Fitzsimmons et al. (Harrisburg, Pa., 1954), ch. vi; cf. Francis Dvornik, *Early Christian and Byzantine Political Philosophy* (Washington, D.C., 1966), 2 vols. Further references are cited in the comprehensive bibliography by A. A. Vasiliev, *History of the Byzantine Empire* (Madison, 1958), vol. ii, pp. 735–99; and more generally in *The Cambridge Medieval*

History, IV: The Byzantine Empire, ed. J. M. Hussey (Cambridge, 1966–7), 2 parts.

35 See A. A. Vasiliev, 'Medieval Ideas of the End of the World: West and East', *Byzantion*, xvi (1942–3), 462–502.

36 For references to the few extant fragments of this work and to pertinent studies, see Otto Bardenhewer, *Geschichte der altkirchlichen Literatur* (Freiburg, 1924), vol. iv, pp. 135–7.

37 Theodoros Prodromos, *Epist. II, PG*, cxxxiii, 1246.

38 Hesychios, ed. Carl Müller, *Fragmenta Historicorum Græcorum* (Paris, 1851), vol. iv, pp. 145–77; Malalas, ed. Ludwig Dindorf, *CSHB*, viii; *Chronicon Paschale, PG*, xcii, 67–1160; Synkellos, ed. Carl Wilhelm Dindorf, *CSHB*, vii; Homologetes, ed. Johann Classen, *CSHB*, xxvi; Monachos, *PG*, cx; Metaphrastes (?), *PG*, cix, 663–822; Cedrenos, *PG*, cxxi and cxxii, 9–368; Zonaras, ed. Ludwig Dindorf, BT (1868–71), 4 vols; Glykas, *PG*, clviii, 1–624; Manasses, *PG*, cxxvii, 219–472. Further afield, another world history originally written in Greek was the seventh-century *Chronicle* of John the Coptic bishop of Nikiu; it also begins with Adam and Eve. The work was translated into Arabic and thence into Ethiopic (the latter, ed. H. Zotenberg [Paris, 1883], trans. R. H. Charles [1916]).

39 For the situation in Bulgaria, for example, see Francis Dvornik, *The Slavs: their Early History and Civilization* (Boston, 1956), pp. 181 ff.; on Croatia: Michael B. Petrovich, 'Dalmatian Historiography in the Age of Humanism', *MH*, xii (1958), 84–103; on Hungary: Josef Trostler, 'Die Anfänge der ungarischen Geschichtsprosa', in *Denkschrift für Jakob Bleyer* (Berlin and Leipzig, 1934), pp. 116–31, and Bálint Hóman, 'La première période de l'historiographie hongroise', *Revue des études hongroises et finno-ougriennes*, iii (1925), 125–64; etc.

40 A. N. Puipin, *Istoriya russkoi literaturii*, 4th ed. (St Petersburg, 1811), vol. i, pp. 271 ff.; N. K. Gudzy, *History of Early Russian Literature*, trans. S. W. Jones (1949), pp. 51 ff. Cf. Nevill Forbes, 'The Composition of the Earlier Russian Chronicles', *SRev*, i (1922), 73–85 – an essay unfortunately marred by the author's unnecessary censure of the 'narrow outlook' of the Russian chroniclers because they believed history to be 'conducted from on high'.

41 Thus the *Primary Chronicle*, in an attempt to trace the origin of the Russians, begins with the division of the earth among Shem, Ham, and Japheth; see *The Russian Primary Chronicle*, trans. Samuel H. Cross, Harvard Studies and Notes in Philology and Literature, xii (1930), p. 136.

42 Charles Diehl, *Byzantium: Greatness and Decline*, trans. Naomi Walford (New Brunswick, N.J., 1957), p. 241; J. M. Hussey, *Church and Learning in the Byzantine Empire* (1937), p. 109; Steven Runciman, *Byzantine Civilization* (1933, repr. 1958), p. 196.

43 Ed. Constantine Sathas (1899); trans. E. R. A. Sewter (1953). For a general account of Psellus, see Amantos (above, note 34), vol. ii, pp. 247–51. The best English study of his philosophy is by Hussey (previous note), ch. iv; his merits as a historian are discussed by J. B. Bury, 'Roman Emperors from Basil II to Isaac Komnênos', *EHR*, iv (1889), 41–64, 251–85 (reprinted in his *Selected Essays*, ed. Harold Temperley [Cambridge, 1930], pp. 126–214); and J. M. Hussey, 'Michael Psellus, the Byzantine Historian',

Speculum, x (1935), 81–90. The literary aspect of Psellus's work has been exhaustively studied by Émile Renauld, *Étude de la langue et du style de Michel Psellos* (Paris, 1920), with bibliography, pp. ix–xxix.

44 The Byzantine ideal of historiography is competently summarised by Georgina Buckler, *Anna Comnena* (Oxford, 1929), pp. 225–9.

45 Ed. Carl Benedict Hase, *CSHB,* ii, 1–178.

46 J. D. A. Ogilvy, *Books Known to Anglo-Latin Writers from Aldhelm to Alcuin* (Cambridge, Mass., 1936), p. 14.

47 Gildas: ed. Joseph Stevenson, EHS (1838), trans. J. A. Giles, *Six Old English Chronicles* (1878), pp. 295–380; 'Nennius': ed. Joseph Stevenson, EHS (1838), trans. A. W. Wade-Evans (1938); *King Alfred's Anglo-Saxon Version of the Compendious History of the World by Orosius,* ed. Joseph Bosworth (1859), and (together with the original Latin) ed. Henry Sweet, EETS: OS, lxxix (1883); *The Anglo-Saxon Chronicle:* trans. S. I. Tucker (1953), ed. Dorothy Whitelock *et al.* (1961) – my quotations are extracts from the entries under A.D. 973, 1067, and 1087: in Whitelock's ed., pp. 77, 147, and 162. Further references in Whitelock's bibliography, pp. xxv–xxix. On Gildas and 'Nennius' see esp. Robert W. Hanning, *The Vision of History in Early Britain* (1966), chs ii, iv.

48 R. M. Wilson, *The Lost Literature of Medieval England* (1952), ch. ii; Thomas D. Hardy, *Descriptive Catalogue of Materials relating to the History of Great Britain and Ireland,* RB (1862–71), 3 vols.

49 *Chronicum Scotorum,* ed. and trans. William M. Hennessy, RB (1866). The edition of Florence of Worcester by Benjamin Thorpe, EHS (1848–9), 2 vols, contains only the text from A.D. 450 to 1117, with a continuation to 1295; the same ground is covered in the translation of Thomas Forester (1854). I have consulted the complete version: *Chronicon ex chronicis, ab initio mundi vsque ad Annum Domini. 1118. deductum* (1592).

50 Ed. Sir Henry Ellis, RB (1858).

51 Malmesbury (probable author): ed. Frank S. Haydon, RB (1858–63), 3 vols; Cirencester: ed. John E. B. Mayer, RB (1863–9), 2 vols, trans. J. A. Giles, *Six Old English Chronicles* (1878), pp. 419–71; Higden: ed. Churchill Babington and Joseph R. Lumby, RB (1865–6), 9 vols, with the translations of John of Trevisa (1387) and an anonymous fifteenth-century writer. These and similar chronicles, inevitably continued by others, were supplemented by translations of earlier works, such as Trevisa's(?) abbreviated version of Methodius's universal history (ed. Aaron J. Perry, EETS: OS, clxvii [1925], 94–112).

52 Wyntoun, *The Orygynale Cronykil of Scotland,* ed. David Laing, in *Historians o, Scotland* (Edinburgh, 1872–9), vols ii, iii, ix; Capgrave, *The Chronicle of England,* ed. Francis C. Fingeston, RB (1858).

53 For example, *The Story of England by Robert of Brunne,* ed. Frederick J. Furnivall, RB (1887), 2 vols.

54 Ed. Sir Henry Savile, *Rervm Anglicarvm scriptores post Bedam* (1596), folios 1–98ᵛ; more readily accessible in the edition of William Stubbs, RB (1887–9), 2 vols; trans. J. A. Giles (1866). On Malmesbury and his contemporaries, see R. R. Darlington, *Anglo-Norman Historians* (1947), and V. H. Galbraith, *Historical Research in Medieval England* (1951), pp. 15–28; there is

also a competent survey by Heinz Richter, *Englische Geschichtschreiber des 12. Jahrhunderte* (Berlin, 1938), pp. 54–125.

55 Ed. Henry O. Coxe, EHS (1841–2), 4 vols (covering the period A.D. 447 to 1235); ed. Henry G. Hewlett, RB (1886–9), 3 vols (A.D. 1154–1235); trans. J. A. Giles (1849), 2 vols (A.D. 447–1257).

56 Ed. Henry R. Luard, RB (1872–83), 7 vols. Since the thirteenth century revised portions of the *Chronica maiora* have also been issued as the *Historia Anglorum*; the best modern edition is by Sir Frederick Madden, RB (1866–9), 3 vols; trans. J. A. Giles (1852–4), 3 vols.

57 The error was made by Archbishop Matthew Parker, editor of Matthew Paris's *Historia Anglorum* (*Historia maior*, 1571) as well as of the complete text of 'Matthew of Westminster' (*Flores historiarum*, 1567). The latter is now available in the edition by Henry R. Luard, RB (1890), 3 vols; trans. Charles D. Yonge (1853), 2 vols.

58 David Knowles, while acknowledging the traditional respect for Matthew Paris, observes that 'as a critical historian' he is at present thought to be inferior to Malmesbury (*Saints and Scholars* [Cambridge, 1962], p. 110).

59 *The Tenure of Kings and Magistrates* (1649), in *Works*, gen. ed. F. A. Patterson (1932), vol. v, p. 25. For my account of Paris, I am indebted to the brilliant lecture by V. H. Galbraith, *Roger Wendover and Matthew Paris* (Glasgow, 1944); but I have also benefited from Richard Vaughan, *Matthew Paris* (Cambridge, 1958), esp. ch. viii. See further David Knowles, *The Religious Orders in England* (Cambridge, 1948), vol. i, ch. xxv, and the introduction by V. H. Galbraith, ed., *The St. Albans Chronicle 1406–1420* (Oxford, 1937), pp. ix–lxxv.

60 Its four versions are edited by Richard Morris, EETS: OS (1874–93), 3 vols. In a sense, Lydgate's *Siege of Thebes* can also be regarded as reflecting attitudes characteristic of the Christian view of history; cf. Robert W. Ayers, 'Medieval History, Moral Purpose, and the Structure of Lydgate's *Siege of Thebes*', *PMLA*, lxxiii (1958), 463–74.

61 Hence A. P. Rossiter's suggestion that the Passion Plays contributed to the formation of the Mystery Plays (*English Drama from Early Times to the Elizabethans* [1950], pp. 50–1).

62 *York Plays*, ed. Lucy Toulmin Smith (Oxford, 1885), from which I quote here; *The Chester Plays*, ed. H. Deimling and J. Matthews, EETS: ES (1893–6); *The Towneley Plays*, ed. G. England and A. W. Pollard, EETS: ES (1897); and *Ludus Coventriae*, ed. K. S. Block, EETS: ES (1922). Perhaps the finest adaptation of selections into modern English is John Bowen's *The Fall and Redemption of Man* (1968). But this version, perhaps significantly, avoids the Last Judgement altogether.

63 Cf. Rosemary Woolf, 'The Effect of Typology on the English Medieval Plays of Abraham and Isaac', *Speculum*, xxxii (1957), 805–25; and Kolve (next note), *passim*. But the typological approach to mediaeval drama has its limitations; for a warning against over-enthusiastic readings, see Arnold Williams, 'Typology and the Cycle Plays: Some Criteria', *Speculum*, xliii (1968), 677–84.

64 My account was greatly influenced by the studies of Elfie MacKinnon, 'Notes on the Dramatic Structure of the York Cycle', *SP*, xxviii (1931),

433–49; E. Catherine Dunn, 'The Medieval "Cycle" as History Play: An Approach to the Wakefield Plays', *SRen*, vii (1960), 76–89; Arnold Williams, *The Drama of Medieval England* (East Lansing, 1961), ch. vi, 'From Eden to Doomsday'; and particularly V. A. Kolve, *The Play called Corpus Christi* (Stanford, 1966), esp. chs iii–v. See also David J. Leigh, 'The Doomsday Mystery Play: An Eschatological Morality', *MP*, lxvii (1970), 211–23.

65 On Dante's interpretation of history see Romano Guardini, 'Dante', in *Grosse Geschichtsdenker*, ed. Rudolf Stadelmann (Tübingen and Stuttgart, 1949), pp. 77–94; A. P. d'Entrèves, *Dante as a Political Thinker* (Oxford, 1952); U. Limentari, ed., *The Mind of Dante* (Cambridge, 1965), ch. v; but especially Charles T. Davis, *Dante and the Idea of Rome* (Oxford, 1957).

66 On the influence of Augustine, see Edward Moore, *Studies in Dante*, 1st Series (Oxford, 1896), pp. 291–4; Edmund G. Gardner, *Dante and the Mystics* (1912), ch. ii; and Edward K. Rand, *Founders of the Middle Ages* (Cambridge, Mass., 1928), ch. viii. The Orosian influence has been studied by Edoardo Zama, 'Orosio e Dante', *La Cultura*, n.s., ii [1] (1892), 429–35; Paget Toynbee, 'Dante's Obligations to Orosius', *Romania*, xxiv (1895); and Edward Moore, op. cit., 279–82.

67 *Paradiso*, xxxiii, 86–90: 'bound by love in one volume, the scattered leaves of all the universe; substance and accidents and their relationships, as though together fused, after such fashion that what I tell of is one simple flame' (trans. P. H. Wicksteed). See further Charles S. Singleton, *Dante Studies II: Journey to Beatrice* (Cambridge, Mass., 1958), pp. 86 ff., and Gerald G. Walsh, 'Dante's Philosophy of History', *CHR*, xx (1934–5), 117–34 (reprinted in *The Catholic Philosophy of History*, ed. Peter Guilday [1936], pp. 113–46), as well as A. C. Charity's wide-ranging *Events and Their Afterlife: The Dialectics of Christian Typology in the Bible and Dante* (Cambridge, 1966).

Four

The Renaissance in Europe:
Tradition and Innovation

In this light of eternity alone, is the Work of God seen aright, in the entire piece, in the whole design, from the beginning to the end.

PETER STERRY[1]

I

The achievement of Gutenberg (or whoever was responsible for the invention of movable metal type) offered Renaissance historians the delightful opportunity to prepare world histories that were to be at once more widely read and – if it were possible – even longer than their predecessors. One such massive work was Hartmann Schedel's *Nürnberger Chronik* (1493), which is distinguished less by its formidable size than by the handsome woodcuts of Michael Wolgemut and Wilhelm Pleydenwurf (Plate 3). The *Nürnberger Chronik* follows the traditional pattern, commencing with the creation and dividing history into Six Ages. There follows a description of the Last Judgement with appropriately terrifying illustrations ingeniously introduced by six folio pages left totally blank.[2] This very blankness constitutes an obvious invitation to readers to take an inventory of their lives before the horrid end. The chronicle ends with a detailed account of the Seventh Age when, as Spenser was to say in the last extant stanza of *The Faerie Queene*,

> no more *Change* shall be,
> But stedfast rest of all things firmely stayd
> Vpon the pillours of Eternity.

The Renaissance ushered in a series of new ideas which were to pave the way for the ultimate secularisation of history. Before turning our attention to those ideas, however, let us consider the attitude of Protestant reformers. Generally speaking, Protestants adhered to the traditional interpretation of history, for despite their professed lack of interest in the accretions of tradition, their debt to St Augustine for numerous aspects of their thought almost necessarily dictated their acceptance of his philosophy of history as well. Protestant historians have no surprises for us. Luther's widely influential annals, the *Supputatio annorum mundi* (1541),[3] typify their efforts, for they commence, predictably, with the creation. The *Chronica* of Sebastian Franck (1531), deriving largely from the *Nürnberger Chronik*, likewise comprehends world history from the creation to the rise of Protestantism.[4]

Luther also set the stage for the common Protestant insistence on the primacy of the historical sense. He dismissed allegories contemptuously as 'inania somnia', empty dreams,[5] in full agreement with that later apologist who equally feared lest 'all the Articles of our Faith that respect the History of *Christ* might be most frivolously and whifflingly allegorized into a mere Romance or Fable'.[6] This essentially patristic argument was further extended by Luther in his vision of history as a series of events manipulated by God in such a way that all aspects of the created order appear to be so many divine masks. 'He himself works through us', wrote Luther, 'and we are only his masks behind which he conceals himself and works all in all.' His acceptance of the Augustinian theory of history was total, even if its articulation was decidedly his own: 'God has collected a fine, splendid, and strong deck of cards representing mighty, great men, such as emperors, kings, princes, etc.; and he defeats the one with the other.'[7] Isaiah's interpretation of Assyria and Babylonia as instruments of divine justice was updated by Luther to include that formidable threat to sixteenth-century Europe, 'the bloody and cruell Turke', widely regarded as 'the scourge of the East and the Terror of the West'.[8] Luther's conviction that the Turks were agents of God's justice[9] generated any number of enthusiastic endorsements, among them a detailed treatise by Theodor Buchmann or Bibliander, first published in 1542. 'It is not the cruelty and tyrănye of the Turkes that fyghteth agaynste vs', warned Bibliander, 'but the wrath of god from aboue is sore kyndeled and waxeth cruell vpon vs by a cruell people'. Suleiman the Magnificent, continued Bibliander,[10] is onely the whyppe with the whych the holy and ryghteous Lorde dothe beate and scourge vs for owre vicious lyuynge. He is the rasoure wyth the whych he hath determyned to pare vs to the quycke. He is the sworde wherewith all the transgressors of Gods lawes be slayne. He is the fell and vengeable instrument wherwith we must ether be amended or els be vtterly destroyed.

Protestant historians, without sharing the occasional pessimism of their mediaeval forerunners, believed fanatically that the end of the world was very near. They were also sincerely persuaded that they were themselves accredited to warn mankind of the imminent Judgement. This attitude links all reformers within the Judaeo-Christian tradition, weaving into the pattern the Hebrew prophets, Jesus and the early Christians, the puritans both of the Middle Ages and of the Renaissance, the societies of saints in England as well as in New England, and finally the evangelists of our own era. Most histories written by early Protestants, coloured by this viewpoint, were thus marked strongly by eschatological tendencies which showed usually in their efforts to interpret world history on the basis of the Book of Daniel, especially according to its vision of the Four Monarchies.[11] The extremely popular *Chronica* of Johann Carion (1531), edited and subsequently enlarged by Melanchthon,[12] and the more explicit *De quatuor summis imperiis* of Johann Philippson surnamed Sleidanus (1556), constitute two of the most important works written in this mould. Both begin with the creation of the world, and both recount the fortunes of four monarchies: Babylon, Persia, Greece, and Rome. Of them Rome was dealt with in greater detail because of the persistent German view that the Christian empire stemmed from the Roman to form sixteenth-century Europe, now approaching its end in fulfilment of Daniel's prophecy. This end was not necessarily expedited by the Turkish scourge, however. As Sleidanus remarked, again appealing to the Book of Daniel:[13]

A few yeres past yᵉ Turkes passed yᵉ straight of Thracia, and proyed and spoyled al ouer Europa: and at this present [i.e. 1556] haue so enlarged them selues that theyr dominion bordereth vpon Germanye. Where-through she is in great daunger as well as Italy, for the nearenes. Howbeit if we marke Daniel more narowly, it is to be hoped that their strength & power is come euer to the vttermost steppe. For Daniel attributeth vnto them but only thre hornes[14] . . . the which they now obtain, first of al in possessing the dominion of Asia, afterwards of Grecia & of Egypt.

Even more crucial to the Protestant interpretation of history was the acceptance of the Book of Revelation as prophetic of actual events.[15] This approach fathered a body of theological literature whose vast dimensions cannot possibly be suggested here. But one author may be mentioned as representative of Protestant tendencies: the great French poet Agrippa d'Aubigné (1552–1630). Not the least of d'Aubigné's labours was the composition of fifteen 'songs' celebrating the creation of the world. But his major work is the apocalyptically-oriented *Les Tragiques*, first published in 1616 though composed over the preceding forty years. Its seven books draw heavily both on the imagery and the thematic patterns of the Book of Revelation as the vision unfolds through contemporary events to the final apocalypse in 'Le Jugement'. The conflict is between the newly-chosen race of Protestants and the agents of darkness represented by Roman Catholicism. The outcome is of course predetermined, for d'Aubigné never doubts either God's absolute control of world history or his extreme partiality to Protestants. But the path of the elect is through the flames of martyrdom:[16]

> le feu violent
> Ne brusloit pas encor son cœur en la bruslant;
> Il court pas ses costés; en fin, leger, il vole
> Porter dedans le ciel et l'ame et la parole.

II

Fundamental expositions of the Christian view of history abounded during the Renaissance. *De civitate Dei* was one of the first works to be printed and, in France, one of the first to be translated into the vernacular.[17] Orosius's *apologia* proved just as popular,[18] and by the beginning of the seventeenth century the works of nearly all mediaeval historians, foremost among them Vincent of Beauvais, had appeared in print.[19] The humanists were directly concerned in all this activity: Scaliger reconstructed Eusebius's chronicle and its continuations,[20] Erasmus introduced the 1522 edition of *De civitate Dei*, and Vives compiled the well-known commentary on the same work. Two other works, produced during the golden age of Italian humanist historiography, demonstrate convincingly the continuity of tradition; both are histories of the universe from the creation. The first was the *Chronica* of Archbishop Pierozi of Florence, better known as St Antoninus (1389–1459);[21] the second was the *Enneades* of the famed humanist Marcantonio Coccio surnamed Sabellicus (*c.* 1436–1506).[22] But other massive universal histories continued to be written until well into the seventeenth century, all commencing with the creation, and variously originating from every corner of Europe: France,[23] Italy,[24] the Netherlands,[25] Denmark,[26] Portugal,[27] Spain,[28] Hungary,[29] Germany.[30] It is by no means an exaggeration to claim that the province of these works was the universe. Here for example is the title-page of the fifth edition of Christoph Helwig's compilation, first published in 1616:[31]

> Theatrvm historicvm et chronologicvm, æqualibvs denariorvm, quinquagenariorvm & centenariorum intervallis; cum assignatione imperiorvm, regnorvm, dynastiarvm regvm, aliorvmqve virorvm, celebrivm, prophetarvm, theologorum, iureconsultorum, medicorum, philosophorum, oratorum, historicorum, poëtarum, hæreticorum, rabbinorum, conciliorum, synodorum, academiarum, &c. itémque usitatarum epocharum, ita digestum, ut vniuersa temporvm et historiarvm series à primo mundi exordio ad annum M.DC.L. quasi in speculo videri possit.

Such histories of the universe are related to numerous other works of the period, not only the innumerable chronologies[32] but even the comprehensive bibliographies which also began 'ab initio mundi'.[33] But affinities are even more extensive. In Portugal, for example, when António Galvão, the 'Apostle of the Moluccas', wrote a history of the passage to India, he began his survey with the discoveries since the Flood;[34] in Switzerland, Bullinger's demonstration of the antiquity of Christianity began with the creation;[35] while in France, Gabriel Naudé in his historical study of the occult sciences reverted to Adam.[36] The same universalising tendencies are apparent in the numerous histories of the Church, and even in martyrologies generally and the Anabaptist theory of martyrdom in particular.[37] Two works, catholic in scope and staggering in length, offer good examples. The violently partisan *Ecclesiastica historia*, in thirteen folio volumes (1559-74), which was a co-operative labour supervised by the Lutheran theologian Matthias Flacius surnamed Illyricus, traces the development of the Church to the year 1400, century by century (hence the other title of the work, *Centuriae Magdeburgenses*).[38] The *Annales ecclesiastici* of Caesar Cardinal Baronius, in twelve folio volumes (1588-1607), is a year-by-year account completed to 1198 before its author's death, and continued by other great scholars like Henri de Spondee and Odorico Rinaldi.[39]

Although we consider such works in isolation, the Renaissance thinkers did not. We may dwell for a moment on the scheme visualised in the plate reproduced here (Plate 1), the elaborate hierarchical system of analogies and correspondences which was thought to extend vertically – as an English writer phrased it – 'from the Mushrome to the Angels'.[40] The world histories lent vital support to this scheme: for as the Scale of Nature upheld a vertical unity in the universe, so the world histories affirmed a horizontal unity throughout the created order, from its inception at the act of creation to its termination upon the Last Judgement. The prime aim of both cosmic scheme and world histories was to proclaim the order pervading all existence. They fused into a conception of the universe so magnificent that, even if not quite responsible to demonstrable reality, it was at least grandiose enough to offer a poet of the future the necessary background for a major epic.

III

Printing helped widely to disseminate world chronicles (cf. p. 47) but also provided opportunities to argue the linear nature of historical events in visual terms. Henry Isaacson's tabular compilation of world history, the *Saturni ephemerides sive tabula historico-chronologica* (1633), includes the two pages partially reproduced here (Plate 2): the first page, which is restricted to a single entry on Adam and Eve, and a later page, which generously lists events of the years A.D. 1601-5. The solitary entry on page 1 may seem absurdly pedantic, but it argues the origin of the world's history in Adam and its linear progress thereafter to the seventeenth century. The implications of Isaacson's tables are also proclaimed on the elaborate title-page, especially in that the title itself is flanked by two massive columns respectively borne by representations of the creation and the Last Judgement. Richard Crashaw provided the commentary in verse:[41]

> their base
> Shewes the two termes and limits of *Time*'s race:
> That, the *Creation* is; the *Judgement*, this;
> That, the World's *Morning*, this her *Midnight* is.

Isaacson's tables were one type of visual argument; illustrations were another. The common mediaeval practice of illustrating manuscripts of the Bible[42] was extended after the discovery of printing to include the use of plates embedded within editions of the Bible. The approach was soon adjusted to encompass world histories, witness the impressive illustrations in the *Nürnberger Chronik* noted earlier. Its one plate reproduced here (Plate 3) demonstrates the frequent conflation of several episodes within one composition ('continuous narration'), in this instance the Fall and the Expulsion.

Visual expositions of the Christian view of history were even more memorably undertaken by several great artists. Here we encounter yet another imposing tradition, for the artists of the Renaissance had been preceded by the artists of the Middle Ages. Mediaeval representations were commonly sequential arrangements of the principal events from the creation to the Last Judgement; they were most often executed in stained glass or painted panels, and not infrequently in sculpture. Examples in stained glass are legion; some are major works of art in their own right, like the Great East Window (1405–8) of the York Minster – the work of John Thornton of Coventry – whose central panels depict twenty-seven episodes from the Old Testament starting with the creation, followed by eighty-one illustrations of the Johannine Apocalypse. The continuity of tradition is even more interestingly displayed at Exeter Cathedral. The elaborately-carved pulpitum or quire screen erected in the early fourteenth century is crowned by a series of thirteen panels painted in the seventeenth century[43] and so arranged as to advance from the creation and the Expulsion, through several episodes drawn from the Old Testament, to the ascent of the Christ into Heaven and the descent of the Holy Spirit into history. The Lady Chapel, moreover, extends the tradition into the twentieth century in terms of Eve and Mary: the stained glass of its east window contains a series of seven lancets whose representations progress from the Fall of Eve, through the Nativity, to the final glorification of Mary.

The events in Eden were greatly favoured by artists of the Renaissance as of the Middle Ages.[44] Their representation during the early fifteenth century in both the *Très riches heures du duc de Berry* and the Bedford Book of Hours – alike 'continuous narrations' – have innumerable precedents in mediaeval art even as they anticipate later interests.[45] Even more relevant to our purposes, however, is another major work of the early fifteenth century the Ghent altarpiece (*c.* 1420–32) executed by Hubert(?) and Jan van Eyck.[46] The upper tier of this polyptych is dominated by God the Father, flanked by several panels which terminate in representations of Adam on the left, and Eve on the right. In the lower tier, immediately beneath God the Father, is the Adoration of the Lamb. The wings of the polyptych, when closed, merge into a representation of the Annunciation.

The Ghent altarpiece depends for its unity on a complex series of typological equations which align the Fall and the Redemption within a cosmic scheme controlled by God.[47] Its argument is far more lucidly set out in the so-called Cambrai altarpiece, *The Triptych of the Redemption,* associated with the workshop of Rogier van der Weyden (Plate 4).[48] The Crucifixion as the central event of history is here placed centrally. The panel on the left represents the Expulsion, with the Fall in the background; both events are acted *sub specie aeternitatis,* and lead from the disobedience of Adam and Eve to the obedience of Jesus and Mary. The panel on the right completes the vision of history by anticipating the Redeemer's Second Advent.

The 'unique and truly divine' Hieronymus Bosch likewise provided two interpretations of the Christian view of history, first in *The Hay-Wain* (1485–90?),[49] and later in *The Garden of Earthly Delights* (1500–5?).[50] Both are triptychs; and while their phantasmagoric details will necessarily continue to defy full comprehension, their argument is clearly to be understood. *The Garden of*

1   The Scale of Nature. From Didacus Valades, *Rhetorica
christiana* (1579)

2 Continuity in history: left, the first page of world history; and below, the section for A.D. 1601–5. From Henry Isaacson, *Saturni ephemerides* (1633)

3 The sequence of the events in Eden: the Fall (right) and the
Expulsion (left). From Hartmann Schedel, *Nuremberg Chronicle*
(1493)

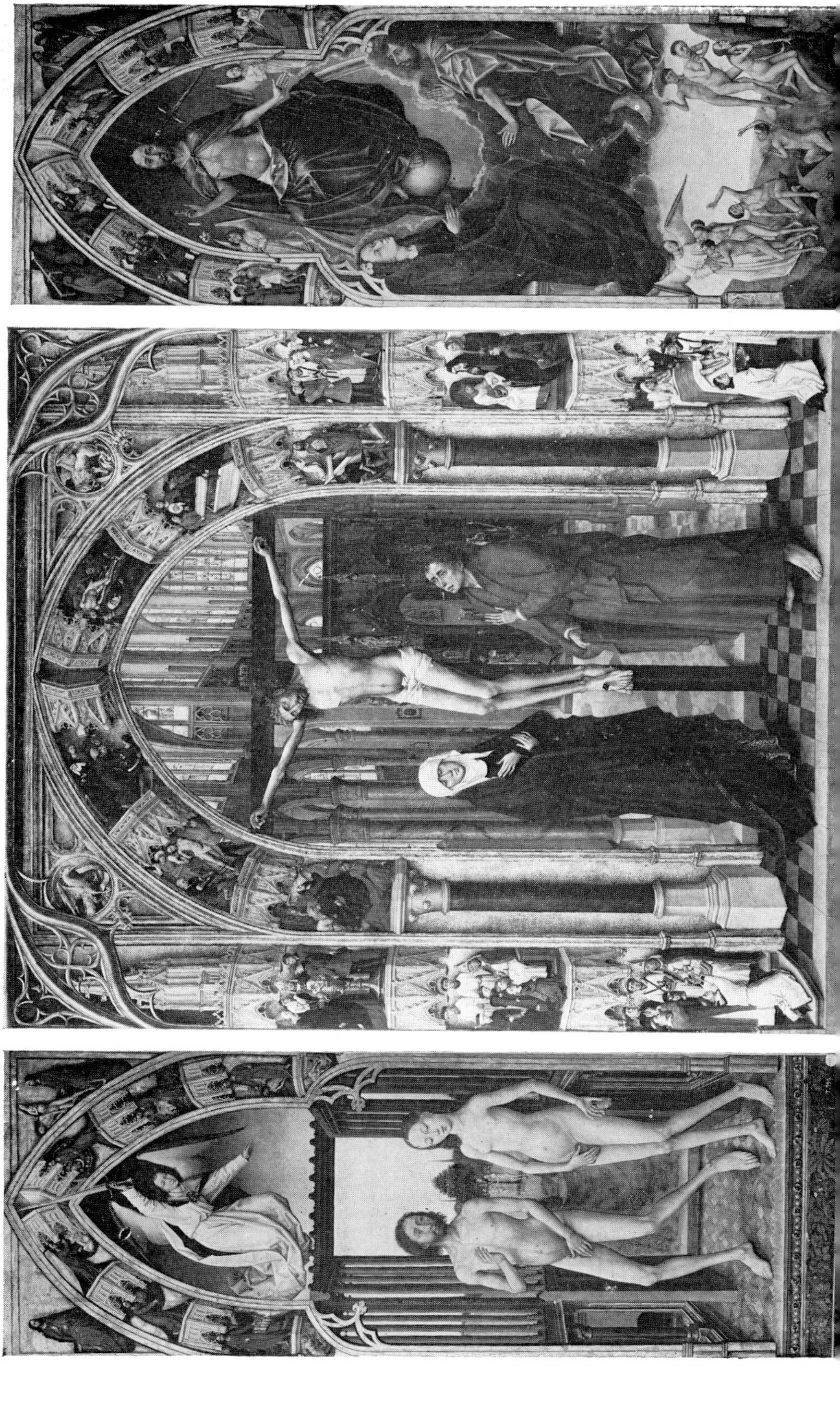

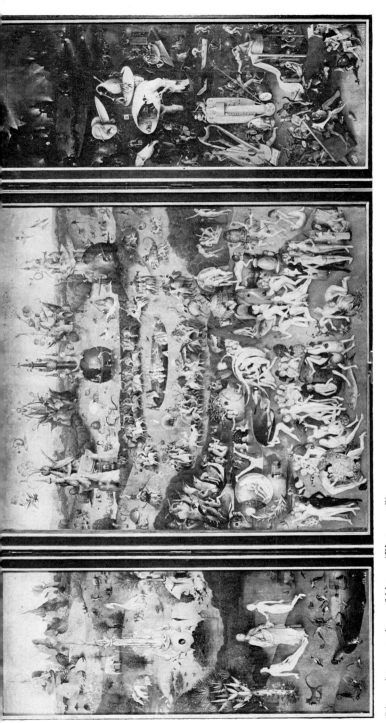

Linear interpretations of history (Plates 4–8)

4 (opposite page) School of Rogier van der Weyden, *The Triptych of the Redemption* (second half of the fifteenth century): the Expulsion, the Crucifixion, and the Last Judgement. Prado, Madrid

5 (above) Hieronymus Bosch, *The Garden of Earthly Delights* (c. 1500–5?): the Garden of Eden, the fallen world, and eternal torments. Prado, Madrid

6   The sequence from the Creation . . .
Ghiberti, *The Gates of Paradise* (1436–52): the first of ten panels.
East door, Baptistery, Florence

7 . . . to the Last Judgement
Mosaics in the cupola of the Baptistery, Florence (thirteenth
century)

8   Michelangelo's sequence from the Creation to the Last Judgement.
The Sistine Chapel: the ceiling frescoes (1508–12)
and the fresco over the altar (1536–41)

Earthly Delights as a spectacular display of Bosch's fecund imagination is more impressive than the earlier triptych. Its wings, when closed, join to reveal the sphere of the newly-created world suspended in chaos; above it are inscribed the words 'ipse dixit et facta sunt, ipse mandavit et creata sunt'.[51] The open triptych (Plate 5) begins with a panel which represents the prelapsarian state in 'continuous narration'. But the actual Fall is anticipated by the preying animals and unnatural forms in the foreground, the demeanour of Adam as he beholds Eve for the first time, the owl ominously watching from the centre, and the flight of birds moving in the distance like so many flies. These harbingers of disaster lead us to the central panel's macabre vision of the fallen world, now utterly overwhelmed by orgiastic sensuality. The last panel represents the inheritance of sin. It is a hallucinatory vision of the dolorous realm, where nature is annihilated, displaced by perverse shapes and monstrous forms set against a background of spectral flames.

The serialised sequence of world events was also adapted in another medium by Lorenzo Ghiberti. *The Gates of Paradise*, on the East Door of the Florence Baptistery (1436–52),[52] was never more justly praised than by Ghiberti himself. 'Executed with the greatest study and perseverance', he wrote, 'of all my work it is the most remarkable I have done and it was finished with skill, correct proportions, and understanding.'[53] The first of its ten bronze panels (Plate 6) is a 'continuous narration' of four scenes set in the Garden of Eden; the other nine panels advance through a series of episodes drawn from the Old Testament, to terminate in the reigns of David and Solomon. The series may be said to relate to another work by Ghiberti, the bronze panels he had executed earlier for the North Door of the Baptistery,[54] which focus on events drawn from the New Testament. But the vision of history is not completed until we enter the Baptistery to behold the sequence of thirteenth-century Byzantine mosaics in the cupola, executed by several Venetian and Florentine artists who may have included Cimabue. The mosaics carry the narrative from the first events in the Garden of Eden to the final episode of world history, the Last Judgement, here dominated by the imposing figure of the Pantocrator (Plate 7).[55]

Ghiberti's bronze panels and the mosaics of the Florence Baptistery are by no means the only expositions of the traditional view in media other than panel painting. Mediaeval sculptors had already used the façades of several cathedrals to advantage, and Renaissance sculptors provided – however spasmodically – their own versions.[56] In graphic art, moreover, Dürer executed *The Small Passion* (1509–11), a series of woodcuts advancing serially from the Fall and the Expulsion, through several plates depicting the Passion, to the Last Judgement.[57] But the most brilliant visual interpretation of the Christian view of history was, in the end, achieved in frescoes.

One major achievement in fresco-painting is the so-called 'Bible of Raphael' (1517–19) in the loggia of the palace of Nicholas III in the Vatican. Designed though not executed by Raphael, it is a series arranged in groups of four frescoes set in each of the loggia's thirteen arches.[58] The first arch contains four scenes from the creation of the world, and the second, four episodes from the story of Adam and Eve; there follows a survey of the principal events in the Old Testament, terminating in the Nativity, the Epiphany, the Baptism, and the Last Supper. As an interpretation of universal history, therefore, the 'Bible of Raphael' is not complete, and hardly compares with Michelangelo's frescoes then in progress (1508 ff.) in the Sistine Chapel (Plate 8).

Michelangelo did not tamper with the frescoes already *in situ* on the lower walls, representing scenes from the lives of Moses and the Christ. He drew them within his comprehensive design by providing the history of the world before Moses, and a grandiose vision of the Last Judgement. The ceiling frescoes were executed first (1508–12).[59] Centrally he located nine scenes, arranged in groups of three episodes: first, God hovering over chaos during the act of creation, the genesis of the heavens, and the blessing of the newly-emergent universe; second, the creation of Adam followed by that of Eve, and the Fall together with the Expulsion; and finally three scenes from the story of Noah. Peripherally he placed figures and episodes which one way or another relate to the advent of the Christ. But the vision was not completed until, nearly three decades later, Michelangelo painted over the altar his great fresco of the Last Judgement (1536–41).[60] History's crowning event is dominated by the Supreme Judge, with the Virgin on his right. Apostles and Patriarchs press forward to gaze on him expectantly, while below, the angels trumpet the living and the dead to judgement. On one side the elect ascend to eternal life; on the other, writhing bodies are catapulted through vast spaces to eternal perdition. The sense of orderly progress pervading the confined area of the ceiling frescoes surrenders here to a limitless universe at the moment of its final transformation. It was the highest orb to which the imagination of man has ever soared.

IV

During the Italian Renaissance the Christian view of history found still another champion in Giovanni Villani (*c.* 1275–1348). His *Croniche fiorentine,* of universal scope, begins with the period immediately after the Flood; and because it is providentially oriented, it views Totila, for example, as *flagellum Dei,* the destroyer of Florence by divine decree.[61] Villani was in this traditional enough. His novelty is that he concentrated on the fortunes of a single city. Two centuries divide Villani's *Croniche fiorentine* and Machiavelli's *Historie fiorentine,* yet within this period the broad framework of universal histories broke and other aspects of the Christian view of history were damaged irreparably. Machiavelli did not demolish finally the traditional concepts because no man could single-handed have accomplished that. Nevertheless he affords the extreme example of deviation from traditional methods of historiography.[62] One such deviation was readily noted by Thomas Fuller: 'I know *Machiavel* was wont to say; That *he who undertakes to write a History, must be of no Religion*: if so, *he* himselfe was the best qualified of any in *his Age* to be a *good Historian*.'[63] Fuller meant, of course, to insult; yet to the brave new wits of the time his statement was, ironically, a compliment.

Deviations from tradition occurred very slowly, and if we may liken their aggregate to a play, then it was a long play featuring a variety of actors, foremost among them Leonardo Bruni surnamed Aretino (1370–1444), whose *Historiae florentini populi* represents current efforts to exclude all fables and legends and to rely only on authenticated fact;[64] Erasmus (1466?–1536), whose *Novum instrumentum* practises what he and other humanists so often preached, by paying attention to primary sources;[65] Francesco Guicciardini (1483–1540), whose *Storia d'Italia* is the most strictly political history of the era, so half-heartedly oriented to the idea of providential control as to draw criticism;[66] and Jean Bodin

(1530–96), whose *Methodus ad facilem historiarum cognitionem* is in part a violent attack on the concept of the Four Monarchies.[67] These spokesmen for the new historiography resuscitated all the historians of Greece and Rome[68] as models worthy of imitation for their comparative veracity no less than for their stylistic excellence. Fidelity to truth led to the dismissal of sacrosanct authorities like Isidore of Seville, now unceremoniously described by Valla as the 'most arrogant of the unlearned: one who, since he knows nothing, teaches everything'.[69] The ever-increasing attention to style, on the other hand, resulted in the abandonment of the annalistic chronicle in favour of narratives, and in the emergence of Livy as the most pervasive influence on Renaissance historians writing in Latin,[70] with Tacitus trailing not far behind. Developments in Portugal were typical of those in Western Europe at large; for notwithstanding the universally-minded Galvão mentioned earlier (p. 51), most of the other chroniclers of Portugal's maritime exploits were far more inclined towards the classical historians, João de Barros clearly manifesting the influence of Livy, and Diogo do Couto that of Tacitus.

The secularisation of history became so widespread that it was undertaken even by exponents of other disciplines like the science of international law which Alberico Gentili and Hugo Grotius developed at this time.[71] International law, by uniting the human race under the auspices of an authority other than Providence, ultimately advanced its own view of history, whose secular character was acknowledged, cautiously, by Grotius, who observed that the existence of God was inessential to the validity of his theory.[72] Others proposed new theories of history or revived old ones like the cyclical view which figures in Bodin's numerological mazes in the *Methodus* and in Louis Le Roy's eloquent statement of mutability in his popular treatise *De la vicissitude ou varieté des choses en l'univers*.[73] Such developments signal the abandonment of the providential view of history.[74] Indeed, the scope of histories became ever more limited as the focus of attention gradually shifted from the supernatural to the natural, from the universe to nation, principality, city, and, as hagiographies were displaced by secular biographies, to individual members of the *civitas terrena*. The refusal to revert to the creation or to utilise the traditional framework is also evident in visual art, notably the two cycles of paintings by Piero di Cosimo (1461–1521), which set forth the evolution of man without recourse to the Christian myth of man's creation, Fall and Redemption.[75]

During the Renaissance the division of history into Six Ages, together with the concept of the Four Monarchies, was accepted by 'ye moste parte of approued Authours'.[76] But the hallmark of the new historiographical temper is to be found in novel schemes of periodisation. Their extensive variations[77] are not nearly so important as is the concerted effort itself to formulate and to adopt non-traditional schemes. One such scheme was proposed impressively early, had clear-cut implications, and exercised a decisive influence upon later historians. Petrarch, its author, located history's most crucial point in the decline of the Roman Empire, thus neatly disavowing the Christian claim that the Incarnation stands as history's central event. Later humanists, varying Petrarch, concluded that the sum of their activities amounted not to any 'renaissance' chronologically separate from preceding eras but to a revival of the Graeco-Roman civilisation which had succumbed with the decline of Rome. The period of Greece and Rome thus became 'classical', the age ushered in by the humanists became 'modern', while the intervening centuries were termed – not always with consistency – 'Middle Ages'. All three designations were standardised by the end of the seventeenth century and represented a scheme of periodisation in diametric opposition to the Christian division of history into 'B.C.' and 'A.D.'.[78]

Notes

1 *A Discourse of the Freedom of the Will* (1675), p. 166.
2 *Registrum huius operis libri cronicarum* (Nuremberg, 1493), folios 259–61ᵛ. The work is described fully by T. F. Dibdin, *Bibliotheca Spenceriana* (1814), vol. iii, pp. 255–80, and discussed by Paul Joachimsen, *Geschichtsauffassung und Geschichtschreibung in Deutschland unter dem Einfluss des Humanismus* (Leipzig, 1910), pp. 87 ff., and Rudolph Bernoulli, 'Das Weltallbild in Hartmann Schedels Weltchronik', in *Buch und Bucheinband* [Essays presented to Hans Loubier] (Leipzig, 1923), pp. 48–58.
3 Trans. into German by Johann Aurifaber as *Chronica* (Wittenberg, 1551). The work is discussed by Hans Henning-Pflanz, *Geschichte und Eschatologie bei Martin Luther* (Stuttgart, 1939), esp. pp. 34–44; but see further Hans Lilje, *Luthers Geschichtsanschauung* (Zurich, 1932); Anders Nygren, 'Luthers Lehre von den zwei Reichen', *TL*, lxxiv (1949), 1–8; and John M. Headley,

Luther's View of Church History (New Haven, 1963). On Protestant historiography, see Franz X. von Wegele, Geschichte der deutschen Historiographie (Munich, 1885), pp. 178 ff.; Emil Menke-Glückert, Die Geschichtschreibung der Reformation und Gegenreformation (Leipzig, 1912); Eduart Feuter, Geschichte der neueren Historiographie, 3rd ed. (Munich, 1936), pp. 186 ff.; Harry E. Barnes, A History of Historical Writing (Norman, Okla., 1937), ch. vi; and Wallace K. Ferguson, The Renaissance in Historical Thought (Boston, 1948), pp. 46 ff. See further Joachimsen (previous note), ch. iv, 'Humanistische Weltchroniken'.

4 Chronica, Z̓eÿt-büch und geschycht-bibel von anbegyn biss inn diss genenwertig MDXXXJ̓ jar (Strasbourg, 1531). On Franck, see Rufus M. Jones, Spiritual Reformers in the 16th and 17th Centuries (1914), ch. iv.

5 Werke (Weimar, 1911), vol. xlii, p. 173; further discussed by A. Skevington Wood, Luther's Principles of Biblical Interpretation (1960), pp. 24 ff. See also Robert M. Grant, A Short History of the Interpretation of the Bible (1965), pp. 97 ff., and James S. Preus, From Shadow to Promise: Old Testament Interpretation from Augustine to the Young Luther (Cambridge, Mass., 1969).

6 Henry More, 'A Brief Discourse of the True Grounds of the Certainty of Faith', in his Divine Dialogues (1668), ii, 482. The stage for the attitude of English Protestants had been set much earlier by Tyndale. In discussing the four approaches to the Bible, Tyndale protested that the literal sense was reduced to 'nothinge at all'. 'Thou shalt vnderstōde therfore', said Tyndale, 'that yᵉ scripture hath but one sence wᶜ is the litterall sence. And the litterall sence is yᵉ rote & grounde of all & the ancre that neuer faileth' (The Obedience of a Christian Man, rev. ed. [Marlborow in the land of Hesse, 1535], folios 129–37, 'The iiii. senses of yᵉ scripture').

7 Quoted, and further discussed, by Heinrich Bornkamm, Luther's World of Thought, trans. M. H. Bertram (St Louis, 1958), pp. 195–217, 'God and History'.

8 René de Lucinge, The Beginning, Continuance, and Decay of Estates, trans. John Finet (1606), sig. bᵛ. See my article ' "The Bloody and Cruell Turke": The Background of a Renaissance Commonplace', SRen, x (1963), 126–35. On the reflection of this particular prejudice in Renaissance literature, consult Franklin L. Baumer, 'England, the Turk, and the Common Corps of Christendom', AHR, l (1944), 26–48, and esp. Samuel C. Chew, The Crescent and the Rose (1937), ch. iii, ' "The Present Terror of the World" '.

9 See G. Simon, 'Luther's Attitude toward Islam', Moslem World, xxi (1931), 257–62; H. Buchanan, 'Luther and the Turks 1519–1529', AR, xlvii (1956), 145–60; Roger L. Shinn, Christianity and the Problem of History (1953), pp. 80 f.; Chew (previous note), pp. 101 f.; and Dorothy M. Vaughan, Europe and the Turk (Liverpool, 1954), pp. 135 ff. Consult also the broader study by Robert Schwoebel, The Shadow of the Crescent: The Renaissance Image of the Turk 1453–1517 (Nieuwkoop, 1967).

10 A Godly consultation . . . By what meanes the cruell power of the Turkes both may and ought for to be repelled of the Christen people (1542), fo. 6v. The original treatise was published in Latin earlier in the same year.

11 Daniel 7:2 ff. The best account of this idea is by H. H. Rowley, Darius the Mede and the Four World Empires in the Book of Daniel (Cardiff, 1935). But see

further Joseph W. Swain, 'The Theory of the Four Monarchies: Opposition History under the Roman Empire', *CP*, xxxv (1940), 1–21. Cf. the notion of the Six Ages, above, p. 25, note 27.

12 Carion, *Chronica durch Magistrū*, ed. Melanchthon (Wittenberg, 1532); Melanchthon, *Chronicon absolvtissimvm ab orbe condito vsque ad Christum deductum, in quo non Carionis solùm opus continetur* (Basle, 1560); and *Chronicorvm ab orbe condito pars secvnda* (Basle, 1560). Consult Menke-Glückert (above, note 3), ch. iii. Carion's work, repeatedly printed in the original German and in a Latin version, was also translated into Dutch, French, and English (below, p. 92, note 18); there were in addition numerous abridgements. The work was continued not only by Melanchthon but by the widely-respected Caspar Peucer.

13 *De quatuor summis imperiis* (Strasbourg, 1556); trans. Stephen Wythers, *A Briefe Chronicle of the Foure Principall Empyres* (1563), fo. 104.

14 The reference is to Daniel's vision (8:3–8) of the two-horned goat and the one-horned he-ram. Notwithstanding this interpretation, Sleidanus was aware that in fact 'the Ramme with two hornes signifieth the kings of the Medes & Persians, but the Goate the Greke empyre' (as in previous note, fo. 102ᵛ).

15 The acceptance was sanctioned by Luther; see Ernest L. Tuveson, *Millennium and Utopia* (Berkeley, 1949), pp. 24 ff., and further: Michael Fixler, *Milton and the Kingdoms of God* (1964). Protestants also utilised Joachimist 'prophecies'; see Marjorie Reeves, *The Influence of Prophecy in the Later Middle Ages* (Oxford, 1969), pp. 107 ff. During the seventeenth century the most extreme form of apocalyptic thought was developed by the militants who looked eagerly to the advent of a Fifth Monarchy, i.e. in succession to the world's four secular monarchies prophesied by Daniel (above, p. 49). See the account by P. G. Rogers, *The Fifth Monarchy Men* (1966).

16 *Oeuvres completes de Theodore Agrippa d'Aubigné*, ed. E. Réaume and F. de Caussade (Paris, 1873–92), 6 vols; *La Creation* is in vol. iii, pp. 350–444; *Les Tragiques* in vol. iv. My account summarises Richard Regosin's 'D'Aubigné's *Les Tragiques*: A Protestant Apocalypse', *PMLA*, lxxxi (1966), 363–8, which emphasises the influence of Heinrich Bullinger's *Cent sermons sur l'Apocalypse* (1558), a work no less popular in England where it was first translated in 1561.

17 By Raoul de Presles (1486); in the sixteenth century, *De civitate Dei* was translated anew by Jacques Tigeou and Gentian Hervet. By 1490 the Latin text was already in print at Basle, Strasbourg, Venice, Rome, Naples, etc.

18 Among the editors of the Latin text: Joannes Caesarius, Margarinus de la Bigne, Aeneas Vulpes, Andreas Schottus. Translations were undertaken into French by Claude de Seyssel; into Italian, by Giovanni Guerini; into German, anonymously.

19 Vincent's *Speculum historiale* was translated *in toto* into French, German, and Spanish (see Ullman, above, p. 41, note 25). Numerous other mediaeval chronicles were also issued in the massive collections of Schardius, Savile, *et al.* (cited above, pp. 40 ff., notes 11, 54, etc.). The work of the historians of Greece and Byzantium, as well as of Rome and mediaeval Europe, is surveyed in the encyclopaedic volumes of the German scholar Gerhard

Johannes Vossius, *De historicis græcis* and *De historicis latinis*, rev. edns (Leyden, 1651).

20 *Thesavrvs temporvm* (Leyden, 1606), including the continuations by Jerome, Prosper, *et al.* (above, p. 25, notes 34 and 44).

21 *Opus excellentissimū historiarū seu cronicarū* (Leyden, 1512), 3 vols; discussed by James B. Walker, *The 'Chronicles' of Saint Antoninus* (Washington, D.C., 1933), esp. ch. v.

22 *Enneades Marci Antonij Sabellici ab orbe condito ad inclinationem Romane Imperij* (Venice, 1498).

23 Charles de Bouelles, *Aetatvm mundi septem supputatio* (Paris, 1520); Matthieu Beroalde, *Chronicvm, scriptvræ sacræ autoritate constitvtvm* (Geneva, 1575), with one portion (book v) in annalistic form; Philippe Briet, *Annales mundi, sive Chronicon universale*, 'ultima Editione' (Augsburg and Dillingen, 1696); Jean de Bussières, *Flosculi historici delibati . . . sive historia universalis*, 5th ed. (Oxford, 1663); Gilbert Génébrard, *Chronographiæ libri quatuor* (Leyden, 1609); Philippe Labbé, *Chronologia historica* (Paris, 1670), 5 vols; Antoine Le Grand, *Historia sacra a mundi exordio* (1685); Denis Pétau, *Rationarivm temporvm*, 'editio ultima' (Paris, 1652); Jacques Salian, *Annales ecclesiastici veteris testamēti* (Cologne, 1620–4), 6 vols. A typical anonymous French work: *Cronica cronicarum . . . cōtenans deux parties . . . la premiere cōmēcāt a la creation du Monde* (Paris, 1521), with illustrations in colour.

24 Girolamo Bardi, *Chronologia vniversale* (Venice, 1581), 4 vols; Donato Bossio, *Chronica bossiana . . . ab orbis initio* (Milan, 1492); Giovanni Nicolò Doglioni, *Compendio historico vniversale* (Venice, 1594); Agostino Ferentilli, *Discorso vniversale* (Venice, 1574); J. P. Foresti [Philip of Bergamo], *Supplementum chronicarum* (Venice, 1492); Giovanni Lucido, *Tabvlæ annales temporvm*, in *Chronicon . . . ab orbe condito* (Venice, 1575), part ii; Giuseppe Rosaccio, *Le sei età del mondo* (Venice, 1598); Orazio Scoglius, *Chronologia ab orbe condito*, prefixed to *A Primordio ecclesiæ historiarum* (Rome, 1622); Agostino Tornielli, *Annales sacri & profani, ab orbe condito* (Frankfurt, 1611), later abridged by Henri de Sponde (Paris, 1647); Orazio Torsellino, *Epitomæ historiarum libri XX*, 2nd ed. (Leyden, 1621). These works stand quite apart from the popularisations of histories which became increasingly more common in sixteenth-century Italy; see Paul F. Grendler, 'Francesco Sansovino and Italian Popular History', *SRen*, xvi (1969), 139–80.

25 Ubbe Emmen, *Canon chronicvs*, appended to *Opvs chronologicvm novvm* (Groningen, 1619); Hendrik Guthberleth, *Chronologia*, 2nd ed. (Amsterdam, 1656); Gerhard Kremer (Mercator), *Chronologia . . . ab initio mundi* (Cologne, 1569); Pieter van Opmeer, *Chronographia . . . a mvndi exordio* (Cologne, 1625), 2 vols; Christiaan Schotanus, *Continuationis historiæ sacræ Sulpicii Severi libri tres* (Franeker, 1656), and *Bibliotheca historiæ sacræ veteris testamenti . . . per modum commentarii in historiam sacram Sulpici Severi* (Franeker, 1661–2), 2 vols.

26 Jens Bircherod, *Lumen historiæ sacræ veteris testamenti*, 'opus posthumus . . . ab ipsius filiis editum' (Copenhagen, 1687).

27 Manuel de Faria y Sousa, *Evropa portuguesa* (Lisbon, 1675), 2 vols.

28 Jerónimo de Chaves, *Chronographia ò reportorio de los tiempos* (Seville, 1561); Alonso Maldonado, *Chronica vniuersal* (Madrid, 1624); Juan de Pineda, *Los treynta libros de la monarchia ecclesiastica, o historia universal* (Barcelona, 1620),

5 vols; Francisco Vicente de Tornamira, *Chronographia, y repertorio delos tiempos* (Pamplona, 1585); Alonso de Acevedo, *Creación del mundo* (1615; in *Biblioteca de autores españoles* [Madrid, 1854], vol. ii, pp. 245–87).

29 István Székely, *Chronica ez vilagnac yeles dolgairol* (Cracow, 1599).

30 Johann Heinrich Alsted, *Thesaurus chronologiæ*, 4th ed. (Heibron, 1650); Gabriel Bucelin, *Nuclei historiæ universalis* (Augsburg, 1658); Abraham Bucholzer, *Index chronologicvs* (Görlitz, 1599); Heinrich Bünting, *Chronologia catholica* . . . *ab initio mvndi* (Magdeburg, 1608); David Chytraeus, *Series temporvm mvndi*, in *Chronologia* . . . *ab initio mundi* (Rostock, 1573), pp. 215 ff.; Johann Clüver, *Historiarvm epitome* (Leyden, 1645); Matthäus Dresser, *Isagoge historica* (Leipzig, 1598–9), vols i–ii; Johann Thomas Freig, *Historiæ synopsis* (Basle, 1580), and *Mosaicvs* (Basle, 1583); Johann Funck, *Chronologia* . . . *ab initio mvndi* (Wittenberg, 1601); Achilles Gasser, *Historiarvm et chronicorum mundi epitome* (Antwerp, 1533); Johann Ludwig Gottfried, *Historische chronica* . . . *von Anfang der Welt* (Frankfurt, 1657); Albert Otto Horn, *Idea polyhistoriæ* (Heidelberg, 1660); Georg Horn, two versions: *Historia ecclesiastica et politica* (Leyden and Rotterdam, 1665), and *Arca Noæ. sive historia imperiorum et regnorum à condito orbe* (Leyden and Rotterdam, 1660): another work, entitled *Arca Mosis sive historia mundi* (1669), is actually a 'natural' history; Seth Kallwitz (Calvisius), *Chronologia* (Leipzig, 1605); Johann Micraelius, *Tabellæ historicæ* (Stettin, 1652); Elias Reusner, *Isagoges historicæ libri dvo* (Jena, 1600); Friederich Spanheim, *Introductio ad historiam et antiquitates sacras* (Leyden, 1657), later expanded into *Introductio ad chronologiam* (Leyden, 1683). Two typical anonymous German works: *Chronica* . . . *vonn aller Wellt herkommen* (Frankfurt, 1535), illustrated; and *Cronica oder Zeit Register* . . . *von Anfang der Welt* (Augsburg, 1601?), a metrical version.

31 Ed. Joannes Balthasar, 5th ed. (Oxford, 1651); an English version appeared in 1687.

32 See my article 'Renaissance Estimates of the Year of Creation', *HLQ*, xxvi (1963), 315–22, and the broader survey by Francis C. Haber, *The Age of the World: Moses to Darwin* (Baltimore, 1959).

33 Archer Taylor, *Renaissance Guides to Books* (Berkeley, 1945), ch. iii; this excellent study concentrates on Conrad Gesner's *Bibliotheca universalis* (1545).

34 *Tratado* . . . *dos diuersos & desuayarados caminhos, por onde nos tempos passados a pimenta & especearia veyo da India ás nossas partes*, ed. Francisco de Sousa Tavares (Lisbon, 1563). For a survey of the Portuguese historians of the sixteenth century, including Galvão, see Aubrey F. G. Bell, *Portuguese Literature* (Oxford, 1922), ch. iii (5), and Boies Penrose, *Travel and Discovery in the Renaissance* (Cambridge, Mass., 1952; repr. 1962), ch. xvii, with bibliography.

35 *Der alt gloub. Das der Christen gloub von anfang der waelt gewart habe* (Zurich, 1539); discussed by John E. Parish, 'Pre-Miltonic Representations of Adam as a Christian', *RIP*, xl (1953), 1–24. Something similar was attempted in France by Simon de Voyon, *Catalogue des Docteurs de l'Eglise*, trans. into English by William Fiston (1560?) and John Golburne (1598).

36 *Apologie povr tovs les grands personnages qui ont esté faussement soupçonnez de Magie*

(Paris, 1625); discussed by James V. Rice, *Gabriel Naudé*, Johns Hopkins Studies in Romance Literatures and Languages, xxxv (1939), pp. 47–72. Something similar was attempted in England by Thomas Vaughan in *Magia adamica* (1650).

37 The Anabaptists, persuaded that the congregation of martyrs constitutes the true Church, supported their view with studies of history usually commencing with the persecution of 'primitive' Christians (cf. Tieleman Jans van Braght, *Het bloedigh tooneel* [Dordrecht, 1669]), but sometimes harking back to the creation of the world (cf. the Hutterite *Geschichtbuech*, ed. A. J. F. Zieglschmid, *Die älteste Chronik der Huttersichen Brüder* [Ithaca, N.Y., 1943]). See the accounts by Ethelbert Stauffer, 'Märtyrertheologie und Täuferbewegung', *ZK*, lii (1933), 545–98, trans. Robert Friedmann, 'The Anabaptist Theology of Martyrdom', *Mennonite Quarterly Review*, xix (1945), 179–214; and Franklin H. Littell, *The Anabaptist View of the Church* (Philadelphia, 1952), pp. 99 ff., 108 ff.

38 See Wilhelm Preger, *Matthias Flacius Illyricus und seine Zeit* (Erlangen, 1859–1961), vol. ii, ch. viii; and P. Polman, 'Flacius Illyricus, historien de l'Église', *RHE*, xxvii (1931), 27–73.

39 On the labours of the other great champion of sixteenth-century Catholicism, Cardinal Bellarmine, see E. A. Ryan, *The Historical Scholarship of Saint Bellarmine* (Louvain, 1936).

40 Samuel Ward, *The Life of Faith*, 3rd ed. (1622), p. 2. The classic study of the concept is by Arthur O. Lovejoy, *The Great Chain of Being* (Cambridge, Mass., 1936). I discuss its survival into the seventeenth century in *Milton and the Christian Tradition* (Oxford, 1966), ch. iii; see also the survey I provided in 'Hierarchy and Order', forthcoming in the *Dictionary of the History of Ideas*.

41 Crashaw's lines are reprinted in his *Poems*, ed. L. C. Martin, 2nd ed. (Oxford, 1957), p. 191. The engraved title-page was by William Marshall, the recipient of Milton's unflattering verses.

42 Notably narrative picture Bibles; cf. François Bucher, *The Pamplona Bibles* (New Haven, 1971), 2 vols.

43 Most likely during the reign of Charles I. I am grateful to the Librarian of Exeter Cathedral for providing me with V. Hope's notes on the pulpitum, and an article by Sir Cyril Fox on the Lady Chapel's east window (designed by D. Marion Grant).

44 See the discussions (with reproductions) by Sir Kenneth Clark, *The Nude: A Study in Ideal Art* (1956), and J. B. Trapp, 'The Iconography of the Fall of Man', in *Approaches to 'Paradise Lost'*, ed. C. A. Patrides (1968), pp. 223–65.

45 These include the masterpieces of Masaccio (*c.* 1425), Hugo van der Goes (*c.* 1470), Dürer (the engraving of 1504 and the twin panels of 1507), Raphael (the fresco in the Stanza della Segnatura, 1509–11), Albrecht Altdorfer (*c.* 1525), Bronzino(?) (mid sixteenth century), Tintoretto (*c.* 1550), Titian (*c.* 1570), Rubens (with Jan Breughel, *c.* 1620), and the incredible interpretation by Rembrandt (1638). Lucas Cranach the Elder was particularly prolific; his most ambitious painting of the events in Eden (1532), in 'continuous narration', is now in Vienna's Kunsthistorisches Museum.

46 Discussed by Erwin Panofsky, *Early Netherlandish Painting* (Cambridge, Mass., 1966), vol. i, ch. vii; and Max J. Friedländer, *Early Netherlandish Painting* (Leyden, 1967), vol. i, pp. 24 ff.; reproduced ibid., plates 1–16, and in the same author's *From Van Eyck to Breughel*, ed. F. Grossmann, trans. M. Kay, 3rd ed. (1969), plates 1–7.

47 The Fall and the Redemption are no less important in the equally typologically-oriented triptych by Mabuse, and in Mantegna's *Madonna della Vittoria*. Both are mentioned, and the latter is reproduced, by J. B. Trapp (above, note 44), p. 226 and plate 1.

48 Discussed by Paul Lafond, *Roger van der Weyden* (Brussels, 1912), pp. 58 ff.; Jules Destrée, *Roger de la Pasture van der Weyden* (Paris and Brussels, 1930), vol. i, pp. 140 ff.; and Friedländer, *From Van Eyck to Breughel*, pp. 23 f. Reproduced in Destrée, plates 77–9, and Friedländer, *Early Netherlandish Painting* (Leyden, 1967), vol. ii, plates 66–7. For a similar work, cf. Master Bertram's Grabower Altar of the later fourteenth century: its numerous panels begin with a sequence representing the creation of the world. See the reproductions in Hans Platte, *Meister Bertram in der Hamburger Kunsthalle* (Hamburg, c. 1960), plates 1–25, and the further references in Jens Christian Jensen, 'Meister Bertram: Quellen und Untersuchungen', *Zeitschrift des Vereins für hamburgische Geschichte*, xliv (1958), 141–203.

49 Discussed by Charles de Tolnay, *Hieronymus Bosch* (1966), pp. 355–6. Reproduced ibid., plates 116–33; also in Ludwig von Baldass, *Hieronymus Bosch* (1960), plates 13, 23–35; and more readily accessible in Mario Bussagli, *Bosch* (1967), plates 12–23.

50 Discussed by Tolnay, pp. 360–3, and Wolfgang Hirsch, *The Garden of Delights* (1954); see also E. H. Gombrich, in *JWCI*, xxxii (1969), 162–70. Reproduced in Tolnay, plates 202–47; Hirsch, who provides sixteen plates in colour; Baldass, plates 58–74, which include the best reproductions of the closed wings; and more readily accessible in Bussagli, plates 60–79.

51 The Vulgate's version of Psalm 148:5 ('he commanded, and they were created').

52 Discussed briefly by Charles Avery, *Florentine Renaissance Sculpture* (1970), pp. 49–53, and more fully by Richard Krautheimer, *Lorenzo Ghiberti* (Princeton, 1956), pp. 157–225. Reproduced in profuse detail by Krautheimer, plates 81–138.

53 *Commentaries*; in *A Documentary History of Art*, ed. Elizabeth G. Holt, 2nd rev. ed. (1957), vol. i, p. 63.

54 Reproduced in Krautheimer (above, note 52), plates 18–68.

55 Discussion with reproductions in Antony de Witt, *I Mosaici del Battistero di Firenze* (Florence, 1954–9), 5 vols. The mosaic of the Last Judgement in the cupola of the Florence Baptistery corresponds to the later fresco by Vasari and Zuccari in the interior of Brunelleschi's dome in the Duomo.

56 For example the marble reliefs flanking the West Door of the Cathedral of San Petronio in Bologna, carved (c. 1420–38) by Jacopo della Quercia. The most celebrated predecessor of Ghiberti's *Gates of Paradise* is Lorenzo Maitani's serialised version of universal history in the Orvietto Duomo. Renaissance works include the early sixteenth-century monument of Pope Paul II, by Mino da Fiesole and Giovanni Dalmata; its surviving fragments

and engravings indicate that the work progressed in a series of low reliefs from the creation and the Fall, through the Resurrection, to the Last Judgement. See John Pope-Hennessy, *Italian Renaissance Sculpture* (1958), p. 335, fig. 116, and plate 110.

57 Discussed by Erwin Panofsky, *Albrecht Dürer*, 3rd ed. (Princeton, 1948), vol. i, pp. 139–45; the sequence of the plates is listed ibid., vol. ii, Catalogue Numbers 236–72; reproduced in Karl-Adolf Knappe, *Dürer* (1965), plates 254–90. Panofsky also places Dürer's great altarpiece *The Adoration of the Trinity* (1507–11) within the context of the Augustinian vision of history in terms of the two 'cities' (op. cit., vol. i, pp. 125–31).

58 Serially reproduced in *All the Frescoes of Raphael*, ed. Ettore Camesasca, trans. Paul Colacicchi (n.d.), part ii, plates 128–53, and esp. Rumer Godden, *The Raphael Bible* (1970); partially reproduced in Luitpold Dussler, *Raphael: A Critical Catalogue* (1971), plates 145–52.

59 Discussed by Heinrich Wölfflin, *Classic Art*, trans. Peter and Linda Murray, 2nd ed. (1953), pp. 50–67; Rolf Schott, *Michelangelo*, trans. Constance McNab (1963), pp. 53–110; and Charles de Tolnay, *Michelangelo, II: The Sistine Ceiling* (Princeton, 1949). Reproduced in profuse detail in *Michelangelo*, ed. Ludwig Goldscheider, 4th ed. (1962), plates 49–144; in Tolnay; and in the magnificent volume *La Capella Sistina in Vaticano*, ed. Roberto Salvini (Milan, 1965), vol. ii, plates 1–4.

60 Discussed by Schott, pp. 173–92, and Charles de Tolnay, *Michelangelo, V: The Final Period* (Princeton, 1960), pp. 19–50. Reproduced in Goldscheider, plates 228–37, and Tolnay, plates 1–56 (related material in plates 120–57, 257–90). Salvini's single plate is masterly (vol. ii, plate 9); so are the sixty-one plates provided in *Il Giudizio Universale di Michelangelo*, ed. Redig de Campos (Milan, 1964), which also has a comprehensive introduction.

61 *Croniche di Messer Giovanni Villani cittadino fiorentino* (Venice, 1537), book i, chs i–iii; selections from this work have been translated by R. E. Selfe, ed, P. H. Wicksteed (1896). On Villani, see Nicolai Rubinstein, 'The Beginnings of Political Thought in Florence', *JWCI*, v (1942), 198–227; the standard work by Georg Gervinus, *Historische Schriften: Geschichte der florentinischen Historiographie*, new ed. (Vienna, 1871); and Louis Green, 'Historical Interpretation in Fourteenth-Century Florentine Chronicles', *JHI*, xxviii (1967), 161–78.

62 Herbert Butterfield, *The Statecraft of Machiavelli* (1955); see further below, p. 113, note 9. On Italian humanist historiography, see Eduart Fueter, *Geschichte der neueren Historiographie*, 3rd ed. (Munich and Berlin, 1936), ch. i; Wallace K. Ferguson, *The Renaissance in Historical Thought* (Boston, 1948), ch. i; Beatrice R. Reynolds, 'Latin Historiography: A Survey, 1400–1600', *SRen*, ii (1955), 7–66; Delio Cantimori, 'Rhetoric and Politics in Italian Humanism', *JWCI*, i (1937–8), 83–102; Peter Burke, *The Renaissance Sense of the Past* (1969); Hans Baron, *The Crisis of the Early Italian Renaissance*, rev. ed. (Princeton, 1966), and *From Petrarch to Leonardo Bruni* (Chicago, 1968); Charles S. Singleton, ed., *Art, Science and History in the Renaissance* (Baltimore, 1968); Donald J. Wilcox, *The Development of Florentine Humanist Historiography in the Fifteenth Century* (Cambridge, Mass., 1969); Felix Gilbert, *Machiavelli and Guicciardini* (Princeton, 1965); Nancy S. Struever, *The*

Language of History in the Renaissance (Princeton, 1970); *et al.* The first three studies also discuss subsequent developments; but see the equally fundamental studies by William J. Bouwsma, 'Three Types of Historiography in Post-Renaissance Italy', *H&T*, iv (1965), 303–14; Giorgio Spini, 'The Art of History in the Italian Counter Reformation', in *The Late Italian Renaissance 1525–1630*, ed. Eric Cochrane (1970), ch. iv; Beatrice R. Reynolds, 'Shifting Currents in Historical Criticism', in *Renaissance Essays*, ed. Paul O. Kristeller and Philip P. Wiener (1968), ch. v; Leonard F. Dean, *Tudor Theories of History Writing*, University of Michigan Contributions in Modern Philology, i (1941), pp. 1–24; and George N. Clark, *The Seventeenth Century* (Oxford, 1929), ch. xvi. There is a stimulating survey by Benedetto Croce, *Theory and History of Historiography*, trans. D. Ainslie (1921), part ii, ch. iv.

63   *The Church-History of Britain* (1655), book x, The Epistle Dedicatory. For the adoption of Machiavelli's principle by Marlowe, see Irving Ribner, 'The Idea of History in Marlowe's *Tamburlaine*', in *Elizabethan Drama*, ed. R. J. Kaufmann (1961), pp. 81–94.

64   B. L. Ullman, 'Leonardo Bruni and Humanist Historiography', in his *Studies in the Italian Renaissance* (Rome, 1955), ch. xvi. See also H. Baron, *The Crisis of the Early Italian Renaissance*, rev. ed. (Princeton, 1966), part iii.

65   Myron P. Gilmore, '*Fides et Eruditio:* Erasmus and the Study of History', in *Teachers of History*, ed. H. S. Hughes (Ithaca, N.Y., 1954), pp. 9–27.

66   Vincent Luciani, *Francesco Guicciardini and his European Reputation* (1936), ch. v; revised in the Italian ed., *Francesco Guicciardini e la fortuna dell'opera sua* (Florence, 1949), ch. v. Cf. Thomas Wheeler, 'Francesco Guicciardini and the Clouded Crystal Ball', *Renaissance Papers 1958, 1959, 1960* (Durham, N.C., 1961), pp. 58–65. For further references see the bibliography in Edoardo Bizzarri, *L'italiano Francesco Guicciardini* (Florence, 1942), pp. 363–73.

67   Ch. vii; trans. Beatrice Reynolds, *Method for the Easy Comprehension of History* (1945). I have consulted two replies to Bodin's attack: Dresser (above, note 30), vol. i, pp. 550 ff.; and Diggory Wheare, *The Method and Order of Reading . . . Histories*, trans. Edmund Bohun (1685), part i, sections iii–v. See further J. B. Bury, *The Idea of Progress* (1920), pp. 37 ff.; Henri Sée, 'La philosophie de l'histoire de Jean Bodin', *RH*, clxxv (1935), 497–505; John L. Brown, *The Methodus . . . A Critical Study* (Washington, D.C., 1939); Julian H. Franklin, *Jean Bodin and the Sixteenth-Century Revolution in the Methodology of Law and History* (1963); and Leonard F. Dean, 'Bodin's *Methodus* in England before 1625', *SP*, xxxix (1942), 160–6.

68   Even Herodotus, who had fallen on particularly evil times; see A. D. Momigliano, 'The Place of Herodotus in the History of Historiography', *History*, xliii (1958), 1–13.

69   *Elegantiarum linguae latinae*, ii, Pr., 41; *apud* J. H. Whitfield, *Petrarch and the Renaissance* (Oxford, 1943), p. 126. Fidelity to historical sources affected also epic poetry, but with disastrous results! The victim was Schelandre's incomplete *Stuartide* (two books published, 1611), a celebration of the House of Stuart; see D. W. Maskell, 'The Transformation of History into Epic: The *Stuartide* of Jean de Schelandre', *MLR*, lxvi (1971), 53–65.

70   Paul van Tieghem, 'La littérature latine de la Renaissance', *BHR*, iv (1944),

200. On the importance of style, consult Peter Burke, *The Renaissance Sense of the Past* (1969), ch. v.

71 Gentili, *De jure belli* (Hanau, 1598); Grotius, *De jure belli ac pacis* (Paris, 1625). On the foundation of international law as laid by Grotius *et al.*, see John N. Figgis, *Studies of Political Thought from Gerson to Grotius*, 2nd ed. (Cambridge, 1916), pp. 241 ff.

72 W. S. M. Knight, *The Life and Works of Hugo Grotius* (1925), p. 212; see further F. J. C. Hearnshaw, *The Social and Political Ideas of Some Great Thinkers* (1926), p. 148, and *Some Great Political Idealists of the Christian Era* (1937), p. 100.

73 1st ed., Paris, 1576; trans. Robert Ashley, *Of the Interchangeable Course or Variety of Things in the Whole World* (1594). The work is discussed by J. B. Bury, *The Idea of Progress* (1920), pp. 44 ff.; Kathrine Koller, 'Two Elizabethan Expressions of the Idea of Mutability', *SP*, xxxv (1938), 228–37; and esp. Werner L. Gundersheimer, *The Life and Works of Louis Le Roy* (Geneva, 1966), part iv. See further Herschel Baker, *The Wars of Truth* (1952), pp. 65 ff., and below, p. 117, note 53. The best studies of the background are by Howard R. Patch, *The Goddess Fortuna in Medieval Literature* (Cambridge, Mass., 1927), and Willard Farnham, *The Medieval Heritage of Elizabethan Tragedy* (Berkeley, 1936), *passim*, esp. in chs iii, iv, vii–x.

74 Most explicitly by Machiavelli, who appears to have displaced Providence by the arbitrary goddess Fortune; see Burleigh T. Williams, 'Machiavelli on History and Fortune', *BR*, viii (1959), 225–45.

75 Erwin Panofsky, 'The Early History of Man in Two Cycles of Paintings by Piero di Cosimo', in his *Studies in Iconology* (1939), ch. ii.

76 Thomas Fortescue, *The Foreste* (1571), fo. 23ᵛ. This work contains (in part i, ch. xi) one of the finest summary statements on the Six Ages, translated from Pedro Mexía's *Silua de varia lection* (Valladolid, 1551), part i, ch. xxvi. One of the best English accounts is by William Gouge, *The Progresse of Divine Providence* (1645), pp. 13 ff. On the background see above, p. 25, note 27; also p. 60, note 11.

77 Villani, for instance, adopted an astrological periodisation, while Sabellicus divided his *Enneades* at the sack of Rome by Alaric.

78 For fuller discussions, upon which this paragraph is based, see H. Spangenberg, 'Die Perioden der Weltgeschichte', *HZ*, cxxvii (1923), 1–49; Wallace K. Ferguson, 'Humanist Views of the Renaissance', *AHR*, xlv (1939), 1–28 (reprinted in *The Renaissance in Historical Thought*, above, note 62); and esp. Theodor E. Mommsen, 'Petrarch's Conception of the "Dark Ages" ', in his *Medieval and Renaissance Studies* (Ithaca, N.Y., 1959), ch. vii. See further Myron P. Gilmore, 'The Renaissance Conception of the Lessons of History', in *Facets of the Renaissance*, ed. W. H. Werkmeister (Los Angeles, 1959), pp. 73–86; George Gordon, *Medium Aevum and the Middle Age*, S.P.E. Tract, xix (1925), pp. 1–28; Erwin Panofsky, 'Renaissance and Renascences', *KR*, vi (1944), 201–36; Federico Chabod, 'The Concept of the Renaissance', in *Machiavelli and the Renaissance*, trans. David Moore (1958), ch. iv; William J. Bouwsma, *The Interpretation of Renaissance Humanism* (Washington, D.C., 1959); Denys Hay, *The Italian Renaissance in its Historical Background* (Cam-

bridge, 1961), ch. ii; and the numerous references to the 'Renaissance problem' in Erwin Panofsky, *Renaissance and Renascences in Western Art* (Stockholm, 1960), pp. 5n, 9n. Panofsky's work is the most brilliant recent attempt to uphold the existence of the 'Renaissance'; cf. Roberto Weiss, *The Renaissance Discovery of Classical Antiquity* (Oxford, 1969).

Five

Tradition in Renaissance England

To a superficial observer of *Divine Providence* many things
there are that seem to be nothing else but *Digressions*
from the main End of all. . . . But a wise man that looks
from the Beginning to the End of things, beholds them all
in their due place and method acting that part which the
Supreme Mind and Wisedome that governs all things
hath appointed them, and to carry on one and the
same Eternal designe.

JOHN SMITH[1]

I

Sir David Lindsay's *Dialog betuixt Experience and ane Courteour* (*The
Monarche*),[2] a lengthy poem composed some time in the middle of
the sixteenth century, epitomises the three most important strains
in the Christian view of history. First, it is didactic, and includes
an account of 'ye miserabyll end off certane tyrane princis'. It is
also a metrical version of the typical history of the universe,
beginning with the creation and terminating in 'the moste terrabyll
day of the extreme iugement'. It expounds, lastly, the providential
theory of history,[3] especially the common view that

> God, aye sen the warld began,
> Hes maid of tyrrane Kyngis Instrumentis
> To scurge peple, and to keill mony one man,
> Quhilkis to his law wer Inobedientis
> Quhen thay had done perfurneis his ententis,
> In dantyng wrangus peple schamefullye,
> He sufferit thame to be scurgit creuellye.

As Dante, Janus-like, looks both backward and forward, so
Lindsay not only closes the Middle Ages but leads directly into

the Renaissance. His threefold formulation of the traditional views, far from expiring with him, survived beyond the Renaissance.

The Renaissance view that history is 'a most clere and perfect myrror' wherein one may behold 'the very lyuely Image and expresse figur of his inward mind enstructyng him how to gwyde and order himself in all things',[4] needs no elaboration here; its reiteration makes it a great commonplace of the age.[5] To Christian writers the capital lesson of history was self-apparent. Richard Brathwait, after glancing swiftly across the centuries, became positively ecstatic:[6]

> What ambitious Tyrants proud of their owne strength, and secure of diuine power, are laid flat in the height of their expectancies: so as where they planted the foundation of their hopes, there they were most defeated, to expresse the prouidence, & all-working Maiesty of God, who disposeth of all gouernments, pulling down the tyrannical Empires, and setting wise and discreet Princes in their places.

From here it is only a step to the widely accepted theory that God, as Lindsay had observed, 'Hes maid of tyrrane Kyngis Instrumentis/To scurge peple', while George Petter's summary exposition of God's intervention in human affairs supplies its traditional base:[7]

> in the times of the Old Testament, God punished the wicked Jews by the *Chaldeans* or *Assyrians*, and therefore the King of *Assyria* is called the rod of Gods anger, Esay 10.5. Afterward he punished the *Chaldeans* or *Assyrians*, by the *Persians*; the *Persians*, by the *Grecians*, the *Grecians*, by the *Romans* . . . the *Romans* by other Nations, as by the *Goths* and *Vandalls* . . . . And of later times, how God hath scourged one Nation by another for their sins, and doth at this day, is well known unto all.

The Ottoman Empire was 'at this day', as I have earlier pointed out, foremost among the scourges of God.[8] Yet extension of the theory initiated long ago by Isaiah also stirred argument that God uses all aspects of the created order, as 'by shooting out his three *evill arrowes* (so called in regard of their evill effects) *Plague, Famine, Sword'*.[9] In the summary statement of a versifier of the period,[10]

> When God seuerely scourgeth any land,
> He seconds plagues, with plagues, and woes with woes,
> He taketh his three stringed whip in hand,
> Of derth, of death, of home, of farraigne foes,
> And from these three, all desolation growes.

The darker the clouds of discontent over England, the greater the stress placed on God's evil arrows. But the English, convinced that God supervises select nations for a benevolent end, eventually persuaded themselves that the nation most favoured by God in the later sixteenth century was England. The celebrated Sir Henry Wotton provided one of the many eulogies of Elizabeth I in terms of the providential theory of history:[11]

> I am fully perswaded, that her Grace is preserved and reserved to great fortune to some marvelous purpose; her qualities exceeding other Princes conditions; her fortune being more than ordinary, and her dangers escaped, not prudently, but providently, not by humane policy, but by divine prevention; give me good occasion to presume, that he that disposeth of Kings, and all Kings Actions lengtheneth her days, and hath dedicated her years to some notable accident: For what he hath intended, man cannot prevent: what he purposeth, humane wit cannot change or alter, his resolutions are in Heaven, ours on earth; his eternal, ours changeable; his immutable, ours subject to alteration; We propose, he dispotheth, we intend, he changeth; we desire, he ruleth, yea so ruleth, that he directeth our thoughts, leadeth our counsels, inclineth our dispositions to his will and pleasure.

Similar affirmations of God's supervision of the destiny of England were also ventured in connection with such miraculous events as the abortive invasion of the 'bloudie and cruell' Spaniards, smashed by God's 'owne hand', or the discovery of that 'damnable and diuellish proiect', the Gunpowder Plot, prevented just in time 'by the wisedome of our gratious God'.[12] But examples are endless, in measure equal to man's boundless capacity to claim divine support for any task whatsoever.

Renaissance England had such a preference for explicit formulations of the providential theory of history that indirect statements were avoided or, if made, were amended as soon as possible. Sir Geoffrey Fenton, for example, regarded Guicciardini's *Storia d'Italia* as unsatisfactory because its rather vague Deity appeared to have been displaced by Fortune; in translating it, therefore, he so altered the original as to make it lucidly orthodox.[13] Similarly, the first edition of Holinshed's *Chronicles* (1577) was so revised in the second (1587) that while initially only immersed in providentialism, it was later sunk in it.[14] This insistence on clarity, displayed by all 'sound' historians, is even more explicit in their accounts of the battle at Agincourt. Edward Hall's typical description contains nothing new, for he related what others had said before and were to say again. He remarks on the unwise reliance of the French on their numerical superiority and – obviously in preparation for the subsequent moral lesson – comments on their 'haute courage and proud stomackes'. He contrasts the orations of the Constable of France, who spent his energy ridiculing the English, and of Henry V, who invoked the assistance of God and later 'caused *Te deum* with certaine anthemes to be song geuying laudes and praisynges to God, and not boasting nor braggyng of him selfe nor his humane power'.[15] Still not content, however, Hall proceeded to make the obvious more explicit by glancing all the way back to ancient Israel:[16]

> This battail maie be a mirror and glasse to al Christian princes to beholde and folowe, for kyng Henry nether trusted in the puissance of his people, nor in the fortitude of his champions, nor in the strength of his banded horses, nor yet in his owne pollicy, but he putte in GOD (which is the corner stone and immouable rocke) his whole cõfidence hope & trust. And he which neuer leaueth them destitrute [*sic*] that put their confidence in hym, sent to hym this glorious victory, whiche victory is almoste incredible if we had not redde in the boke of kynges that God likewise had defended and aided them that onely put their trust in him and committed them selfes wholy to his gouernaunce.

Hall's account is only superficially related to Shakespeare's *Henry V*, for as we shall see, the single-minded obsession of the one hardly affected the myriad-minded interpretation of the other. Significantly, persistent analogies with events in ancient Israel are no less absent from Shakespeare than they are omnipresent in lesser writers. Drayton, who resolutely regarded history as a record of divine judgements, pointedly related the defeat of the Spanish Armada to the destruction of the Egyptian army in the Red Sea. In his words,[17]

> What for a conquest strictly they [the Spaniards] did kepe,
> Into the channel presently was pour'd,
> *Castilian* riches scattered on the deepe,
> That *Spaines* long hopes had sodainly devour'd.
> Th' afflicted English rang'd along the Strand
> To waite what would this threatning power betide,
> Now when the Lord with a victorious hand
> In his high justice scourg'd th' *Iberian* pride.

II

The avalanche of universal chronicles testifies even more eloquently to the persistence of the traditional view of history in England. Nor is the metaphor hyperbolic. In addition to innumerable translations of Continental works,[18] England managed to produce a formidable collection of native universal chronicles – 'our own *Moderne Chronicles*', as one writer proudly declared.[19] The first such work of the sixteenth century, *The Cronycle of Fabyan* (1516), did not begin with the creation because, as Robert Fabyan explained, 'in the accomptynge of the yeres of the worldle from yᵉ Creacion of Adam vnto the incarnation of Crist been many and sundry oppynyons'; and so, displaying remarkable critical acumen, Fabyan began with a much more reliable event, the Flood. Next we have *The Chronicle of Iohn Hardyng* (1543), which conveyed another aspect of the tradition into the sixteenth century, since it was a metrical version of the usual universal history. Hardyng, less scrupulous than Fabyan, chose to begin with Adam ('in all vertue/Was none him lyke in no place that men knewe'). Shortly after, John Bale, who concerned himself endlessly with 'origins', took matters even further. In *A Tragedye*

74

or Enterlude manyfestyng the Chefe Promyses of God unto Man (1547?),
he offered a dramatised panorama of the most significant events
from 'before the heavens were create' to John the Baptist.[20] The
influence of the Mystery Plays, now adjusted to the purposes of
newly-emergent Protestantism, is self-evident. But we may not
claim that Bale's 'preoccupation with the past stamps him in the
end as an historian, not an apologist';[21] he himself, one suspects,
would have denied this accusation promptly. His other works
include *The Image of both churches after the moste wonderful and
heauenly Reuelation of Sainct John* (1548?) which is representative
of the increasing Protestant tendencies to interpret history in
accordance with the 'prophecies' of the Johannine Apocalypse.[22]

In the meantime a young man, Thomas Lanquet, was com-
posing *An Epitome of Cronicles* which started from the creation and
reached out, 'through the thicke mistes and darkenes' of the past,
to the Incarnation. Lanquet left his work unfinished, but Bishop
Thomas Cooper completed it for him (1549) and Robert Crowley
continued it to the reign of Elizabeth I (1559). Four years later
Richard Grafton published an abridgement of yet another world
history, expanded later into *A Chronicle at large and meere History
of the Affayres of Englande* (1569), which also commenced with the
account of creation by that 'deuine Prophet and Historiographer'
Moses. But a far more ambitious project was already being
planned as Reginald Wolfe, printer to the Queen, began to
think in terms of 'an vniuersall Cosmographie of the whole world'.
But Wolfe's death reduced his grandiose plans to a mere collection
of *The Chronicles of England, Scotland, and Irelande* (1577), which still
did not fail to begin 'in the beginning whẽ God framed the worlde'.
The editor of this composite work was Raphael Holinshed.

The traditional attitude again received support from the antiquary John Stow, who in *A Summarie of Englyshe Chronicles* (1565),
later renamed *Annales*, started his account with the Flood. It is,
moreover, a sign of the times that Stow's work had by 1631 run
through more than twenty revised editions. Equally interesting
is the attitude of John Speed, for critical-minded though he
showed himself to be when commenting on the futility of attempting to discover 'things so farre cast into the mistie darknesse of
obscuritie and obliuion', he nevertheless signalled his agreement
with Stow by commencing his own narrative with the Flood.[23]
Encouraged by such formidable example, greater and lesser

writers only too naturally compiled numerous similar chronicles. Most started with the creation, among them Lodowick Lloyd's *The Consent of Time* (1590), John More's *A Table from the Beginning of the World* (1593), Roger Cotton's *A Spirituall Song: containing an Historicall Discourse from the Infancie of the World* (1596), William Perkins's *Specimen digesti* (1598), and Anthony Munday's *A Briefe Chronicle . . . from the Creation* (1611). However, no work attained the popularity either of Joshua Sylvester's translation of the poem by Du Bartas, or Sir Walter Ralegh's magniloquent *History of the World*.

Du Bartas's *La Semaine ou création du monde* was first published in 1578 and was followed six years later by its sequel, *La Seconde Semaine ou enfance du monde*. By the first decade of the seventeenth century the work had already been translated, in whole or in part, into Italian, German, Dutch, English, and Latin. Du Bartas, praised with restraint on the Continent,[24] achieved in England phenomenal popularity: Sylvester's translation[25] was a tremendous success, going through countless editions, Du Bartas thereby receiving unmerited recognition as 'a Poet above the ordinary level of the world'.[26] Judged as poetry, his work is found wanting; but judged by its scope and influence, it amounts to a major achievement, for it is easily the most ambitious metrical history of the universe available to Renaissance England at that time. It expounds in strict orthodoxy the providential view of history; and though the narrative is carried only to 586 B.C., history's end is kept firmly in view through the vision of the universal conflagration to be initiated by 'the *Chief-Chief-Iustice*, venging Wrath'.[27]

Ralegh's *History of the World* (1614) is equally orthodox.[28] Fifty years after its publication Thomas Fuller could fault it only because it was left unfinished;[29] but though Ralegh did interrupt his narrative in 168 B.C., his work was as unaffected by its incompleteness as is *The Faerie Queene*. The Preface, later known as 'A Premonition to Princes', sets the tone by asserting God's total control of historical events. The narrative proper begins with an account of the creation and thereafter posits one 'truth' in particular, that within the historical process mankind forms an interdependent entity, a spiritual unity. The remaining books are constructed as a series of interlocked parallel movements performed by man himself yet always orchestrated by God, 'the infinite Spirit of the *Universall,* piercing, moving, and governing all things'.[30] Ralegh's *History* ran through ten editions before the Restoration, which attests its enormous popularity, and repeated quotations from it throughout the seventeenth century attest equally an approbation verging on hagiolatry. The decision of Alexander Ross to abridge and continue it[31] is the most eloquent testimony to its essential orthodoxy. Nor can we dismiss lightly Ross's undertaking because he was excessively preoccupied with any deviation from the straightest and narrowest of paths: he chastised for their 'unorthodoxy' Sir Thomas Browne, Sir Kenelm Digby, Sir Francis Bacon, William Harvey, Thomas Hobbes, and all the followers of Copernicus and Galileo!

Though Ralegh's universal history is the best, it is far from unique in the seventeenth century. In 1659, introducing Denis Pétau's world chronicle to England, 'R.P.' observed that 'Sir *Walter Rawleigh* and others that have highly deserved by their Atchievements in the Theatre of History, have so voluminously inlarged themselves, that the Reader's patience is too discourteously oppressed'.[32] Such thoughtful concern, once expressed, was soon forgotten; and universal histories and annals continued to be written: James Gordon's *Opus chronologicum* (1617), Henry Isaacson's *Saturni ephemerides* (1633), William Vaughan's *The Church Militant* (1640), James Ussher's *Annales* (1650–4), Thomas Allen's *Chain of Scripture Chronology* (1659), William Howell's *Institution of General History* (1661). Moreover, a host of other writers, both before and after Ralegh, although preoccupied with enterprises other than the composition of world chronicles, still exemplify in their works certain aspects of the traditional attitude. Thomas Heywood's best non-dramatic work, the *Troia britanica* (1609), a comprehensive depository of myths cast within the framework of 'an Vniuersall Chronicle from the Creation', is a good example; so is Samuel Purchas's *Purchas his Pilgrimage* (1613), representative of the literature of travel, which he expanded into a universal history out of sheer inability to discard any of the consulted 'seuen hundred Authors, of one or other kind' (the kinds: 'Sacred, Prophane, Learned, Vnlearned, Ancient, Moderne, Good, and Bad').[33] Finally we have Joseph Mede's *Clavis apocalyptica* (1632), typical of the numerous apocalyptic interpretations of history that naturally focus on the Day of Wrath but, mindful of history's linear nature, glance back to the creation as well;[34] John Swan's *Speculum mundi* (1635), an encyclopaedic work of such catholic scope that it includes everything conceivable, and many things inconceivable, from the beginning to the end of history; and even Sir Thomas Urquhart's ambitious outline of historical events in terms of his own family, proudly 'deducing the true pedigree . . . of the Urqvharts since the Creation of the World'![35]

In order to appreciate the multitude of branches sprouting from the single tree, we should glance also at perhaps the most moving prose work of the English Reformation, the martyrology of John Foxe.[36] Neither the author nor the work has fared well in modern times. The uncompromising verdict is that the work is 'the longest pamphlet ever composed by the hand of man', and its author 'the first great journalist in English history'.[37] Admittedly Foxe was a partisan, but he was writing in an age of profound partisanship. However, the purpose of the work is what matters, transcending its frequent lack of literary merit. The capital concern of Foxe was not so much to prove that the Vatican had turned 'truth into heresie' as to celebrate the 'true christian fortitude' which is patience and heroic martyrdom. His labours are for our purposes only too relevant: for in claiming that his work constitutes 'a liuely testimony of Gods mighty working in the life of man', he accepted the providential view of history; in placing his vision under the shadow of the Book of Revelation, he agreed with the distinctly Protestant interpretation of history; in harking back to the apostolic times, he clasped hands with all ecclesiastical historians; in recording the acts and monuments of the heroes of the faith as 'examples of great profite', he allied himself with the tradition of the *exempla*; while in his conception of true fortitude he looked not only back to the impressive tradition that had already translated patience from weakness into strength,[38] but also forward to the exposition of the same ideal at the outset of the ninth book of *Paradise Lost*.

III

The dramatic literature of the English Renaissance fully reflects the contemporary interest in history.[39] Initially grown on the soil of the Mystery Plays, sixteenth-century drama retained both the comprehensive vision of its mediaeval predecessors and their distinctly moral tenor. Increasingly, however, other concerns were so grafted to the pre-existent pattern as to transform it radically. The newly-emergent nationalistic and religious loyalties, in particular, gradually transplanted the destiny of the chosen people from its Biblical context to that of the people of England.[40] Marlowe and Chapman[41] alike hovered between a world destined to vanish all too soon, and a world pressing to be born. Shakespeare also began his dramatic career constrained by the forces of tradition, but ended by transcending their barriers.

Shakespeare's ten history plays include two independent entities: *King John* and *Henry VIII*. The rest are normally grouped into two tetralogies: the 'minor' tetralogy of the three parts of *Henry VI* together with *Richard III*; and the 'major' tetralogy of *Richard II*, the two parts of *Henry IV*, and *Henry V*.[42] Traditional modes of thought persist in all, especially in connection with the curse which Tudor historians had claimed lay heavily on the English crown after the dethronement of Richard II. Shakespeare agreed:

> The blood of the English shall manure the ground,
> And future ages groan for this foul act,
> Peace shall go sleep with Turks and infidels,
> And, in this seat of peace, tempestuous wars
> Shall kin with kin, and kind with kind, confound.
> (*Richard II*, IV, i, 137–41)

Equally traditional is the concept of sovereignty which in *Richard II* is phrased in words borrowed from the tradition-bound account by Holinshed.[43] According to the Bishop of Carlisle, the king is

> the figure of God's majesty,
> His captain, steward, deputy-elect,
> Anointed, crowned.
> (IV, i, 125–7)

The sentiment is endorsed by Richard himself:

> Not all the water in the rough rude sea
> Can wash the balm off from an anointed king;
> The breath of worldly men cannot depose
> The deputy elected by the Lord.
> (III, ii, 54–7)

Despite appearances to the contrary, however, Shakespeare's

history plays are not extensions of the Tudor chronicles.[44] True, he leaned heavily on chroniclers like Hall and Holinshed (above, pp. 73 and 75), and made free use of the age's most sacrosanct commonplaces. Increasingly, however, he subordinated tradition to the demands of his dramatic art. Richard's endorsement of the traditional concept of sovereignty, for instance, appears to be a mere repetition of a commonplace. But it is promptly qualified by Richard's violation of its essence, in so far as he has already resolved 'to farm our royal realm' (I, iii, 45). The irony has transmuted theory into art.

Shakespeare's progress from the 'minor' tetralogy to the 'major' one could tempt us to favour the first less than the second.[45] The 'major' tetralogy displays Shakespeare at the height of his inventive powers, already poised to embark on the tragedies. He writes with greater authority, a keener awareness of what is dramatically appropriate, an increased sense of realism. On the other hand, to claim that Shakespeare developed by advancing along a straight line were itself grossly unrealistic. In between the two tetralogies intervened, for one, that uneven play, *King John*; while the final play in the 'major' tetralogy was the paean that is *Henry V* – 'a propaganda-play on National Unity: heavily orchestrated for the brass'.[46] It was moreover not in the 'major' but in the 'minor' tetralogy that Shakespeare first co-ordinated the divers materials at his disposal, imposing form on formlessness.[47] He also adjusted the Christian view of history to the requirements of his art. The theme of time – omni-present in the history plays but particularly emphatic in the 'major' tetralogy[48] – reveals how unprepared Shakespeare was dramatically to assert the Christian burden of time, much less explicitly to maintain it. Yet echoes of the traditional interpretation linger just the same, notably in the prophecy that Prince Hal will eventually imitate a higher example by forswearing Falstaff 'in the perfectness of time'.[49] Other plays adapt commonplaces in like manner, sometimes to the point of inverting them. In *Antony and Cleopatra* the concept of history's consummation beyond time is transferred to the fortunes of the two lovers within it, as Cleopatra is drawn by 'Immortal longings' to join Antony in death (V, ii, 283) which alone effects their apocalyptic expectations of a 'new heaven, new earth' (I, i, 17). *Macbeth,* on the other hand, dramatises the aspiration to jump beyond 'this bank and shoal of time' (I, vii, 6); but the fruitless attempt 'to beguile the time' (I, v, 64) terminates in a catastrophically negative vision as the meaningless days are seen to advance relentlessly 'To the last syllable of recorded time' (v, v, 21).

The action in Shakespeare's plays unfolds against a background darkened by the presence of supernatural forces. But as they are forces that evade the comprehension of man, they afforded Shakespeare opportunities for dramatic irony which he rarely if ever missed. The follies of man – misguided, self-centred, proud man – are constantly exposed; and interest is focused not on the forces hovering in the background but on the lives of men unfolding against it. Shakespeare knew it were absurd to deny that humanity labours *sub specie aeternitatis*; but he also knew that the claims of the tradition-bound Tudor chroniclers, as of all Christian historians, were not accurate representations of total reality, based as these claims were on 'patterns' apprehended by faith and not necessarily confirmed by experience. As an artist who was interested less in dogmatic affirmations than in their dramatic potentialities, Shakespeare resolutely declined to take upon him the mystery of things as if he were God's spy:

> O God, that one might read the book of fate,
> And see the revolutions of the times
> Make mountains level, and the continent,
> Weary of solid firmness, melt itself
> Into the sea, and other times to see
> The beachy girdle of the ocean
> Too wide for Neptune's hips; how chance's mocks
> And changes fill the cup of alteration
> With divers liquors! O, if this were seen,
> The happiest youth, viewing his progress through,
> What perils past, what crosses to ensue,
> Would shut the book and sit him down and die.
>
> (2 *Henry IV*, III, i, 45–56)

IV

Throughout the seventeenth century the greatest respect was reserved for Ralegh's *History of the World* (1614), Cromwell himself advising his son to 'Recreate yourself with Sir Walter

Raughleye's History: it's a body of history, and will add much more to your understanding than fragments of story.'[50] But the traditional interpretation was no less zealously welcomed by Anglicans. Publicly asserted as a leitmotif in Donne's sermons, it was also privately contemplated by Lancelot Andrewes in his *Preces privatae*, itself a sustained meditation on the progress of the temporal order toward the City of God.[51] The same attitude distinguishes the thought of the Cambridge Platonists who conflated all events into a unified vision of history described by Henry More as 'that large voluminous Period of Providence, which, beginning with the first *Fiat lux* in *Genesis*, ends not till the last *Thunder-clap* intimated in *Revelation*'.[52] English Catholics concurred. Crashaw frequently emphasised the Christocentric nature of world history through his inimitable celebrations of Jesus:[53]

> All-circling point. All centring sphear.
> The world's one, round, Æternal year.

But an even more impressive development during the seventeenth century is the influence which the Christian view of history exerted on the actual structure of several works of literature. George Herbert's dramatic poem, 'The Collar', for instance, compresses within its thirty-six lines the broad circumference of the traditional vision of history. The narrator's anguished predicament is placed within a context far wider than is at first apparent. His initial resolution to escape 'abroad' is deliberately phrased by Herbert in language reminiscent of man's first disobedience ('there is fruit,/And thou has hands'). In effect, therefore, the narrator is unwittingly re-creating the Fall of Man. But at the same time he is boldly misappropriating to himself those terms which collectively remind us of man's redemption by the Christ (my italics):[54]

> Have I no harvest but a *thorn*
> To let me *bloud*, and not *restore*
> What I have lost with *cordiall fruit*?
> Sure there was *wine*
> Before my *sighs* did drie it: there was corn
> Before my *tears* did drown it.
> Is the year only lost to me?
> Have I no bays to *crown* it?

The narrator, subconsciously cognisant of the real context of his blatant aspirations, responds at last to the call not of the first but of the second Adam. His interior monologue ends, as history is to do, with the individual's absorption into the Eternal:

> Me thoughts I heard one calling, *Child!*
> And I reply'd, *My Lord.*

The Christian view of history is no less relevant to the art of Sir Thomas Browne. Ravished as we are by his seductive sentences, we do not always discern the underlying structure of the divers meditations comprising his *Religio Medici* (1642). At times, indeed, we are even tempted to censure him for a lack of 'architectonic imagination'.[55] True, we are now aware that the two parts of *Religio Medici* resemble the common division of theological treatises into Faith and Hope on the one hand, and Charity on the other.[56] Equally true, we have observed of late that the meditations in Part I (Faith and Hope) are woven round themes that advance from the creation to the Last Judgement.[57] Yet Browne did not so much acknowledge the validity of the Christian view of history as employ it to link every sentence of his *Religio Medici*.

Browne's fundamental article of belief is Order, most succinctly affirmed near the end of *The Garden of Cyrus* (1658): 'All things began in order, so shall they end, and so shall they begin again; according to the ordainer of order and mysticall Mathematics of the City of Heaven.'[58] Order according to the conception in *Religio Medici* encompasses in the first instance a vertical unity that pervades the entire creation: 'there is in this Universe a Staire, or manifest Scale of creatures, rising not disorderly, or in confusion, but with a comely method and proportion.'[59] But Order also dictates the unfolding of history as a play which advances in a straight line toward 'that one day, that shall include and comprehend all that went before it, wherein as in the last scene, all the Actors must enter, to compleate and make up the Catastrophe of this great peece'.[60] Man is obliged to see the play sequentially, but God beholds its various scenes simultaneously. As Browne remarks early in *Religio Medici*,[61]

> that terrible terme *Predestination*, which hath troubled so many weake heads to conceive, and the wisest to explaine, is in respect of God no previous determination of our

estates to come, but a definitive blast of his will already fulfilled, and at the instant that he first decreed it; for to his eternitie which is indivisible and altogether, the last Trumpe is already sounded, the reprobates in the flame, and the blessed in *Abrahams* bosome. Saint *Peter* spake modestly when hee said, a thousand yeares to God are but as one day; for, to speake like a Philosopher, those continued instants of time which flow into a thousand yeares, make not to him one moment; what to us is to come, to his Eternitie is present, his whole duration being but one permanent point, without succession, parts, flux, or division.

Browne was utterly fascinated by the concept of the Eternal Present. In several meditations which follow its initial formulation here, he repeatedly indulges in paradoxes which cumulatively assert the concept by upholding the unity of the created order in the omniscient eyes of God. In such instances the tone rises steadily as Browne's serene assurance in his own election yields to a triumphant proclamation of the contemporaneity of all events:[62]

That which is the cause of my election, I hold to be the cause of my salvation, which was the mercy and bene-placit of God, before I was, or the foundation of the world. *Before Abraham was, I am*, is the saying of Christ, yet is it true in some sense if I say it of my selfe, for I was not onely before my selfe, but *Adam*, that is, in the Idea of God, and the decree of that Synod held from all Eternity. And in this sense, I say, the world was before the Creation, and at an end before it had a beginning; and thus was I dead before I was alive; though my grave be *England*, my dying place was Paradise, and *Eve* miscarried of mee before she conceiv'd of *Cain*.

The Christian view of history affected also the seventeenth century's greatest literary achievement, *Paradise Lost*. But Milton displayed his full awareness of the traditional interpretation even earlier, in his 'Nativity Ode', a poem that is in more ways than one a prelude to *Paradise Lost*.

But it is a poem, we have been told, in which the Atonement is 'an abstract and remote performance'.[63] This judgement may apply if, as often happens, Milton's treatment of the birth of Jesus is compared to Crashaw's.[64] But the advantages of such a comparison are questionable, for are there two poets of the seventeenth century more in opposition to each other temperamentally, in their loyalties, and in their approach to poetry, than Milton and Crashaw? Crashaw approaches the Nativity 'vertically', focusing attention on the manger and dwelling upon the directly perpendicular relationship between God and man. Milton, by contrast, concentrates on the 'horizontal' significance of 'the rude manger' as it affected the relationship not between God and man but between God and all mankind, the totality of human beings. The devotional Crashaw concentrated on the one specific moment in history that witnessed the union of God and man. Milton chose to go much further, affirming the birth of Jesus as an event affecting the whole universe. Milton's far-ranging references to the idols and deities of Assyria and Egypt, Greece and Rome, were imperative, for collectively they argue that the Atonement was all-embracing in its effect, that the infant Jesus achieved not merely peace but, in Milton's words, 'a *universal* Peace'. Nor did Milton forget to observe that, although mankind's bliss began upon the birth of the Saviour, its consummation cannot be until after the Second Coming, when the wakeful trump of doom shall thunder through the deep

> With such a horrid clang
> As on mount *Sinai* rang
>   While the red fire, and smouldring clouds out brake:
> The aged Earth agast
> With terrour of that blast,
>   Shall from the surface to the center shake;
> When at the worlds last session,
> The dreadfull Judge in middle Air shall spread his throne.
>
> And then at last our bliss
> Full and perfect is.
>
> (ll. 157–66)

Many critics have commented on the 'Nativity Ode'. One alone has recognised that in it Milton 'celebrates the meaning of the Incarnation not only in history but after history is over, an event both in and not within created nature, a peace both in and not within created time'.[65]

The 'Nativity Ode' was Milton's dress rehearsal for his performance in *Paradise Lost*. In *Paradise Lost* we have the most successful attempt in poetry to fuse the essential aspects of the Christian view of history into a magnificent whole. First, we have the didactic spirit that pervades Michael's revelation of the future to Adam. Second, we have explicit affirmation that temporal events are a record of divine judgements. Above all, we have the universalistic and Christocentric view of history.

The vision of the future in Books XI and XII may be a convention of epic poetry,[66] but it differs fundamentally from other such parallel visions and its purpose is clearly set forth in Michael's words to Adam:

> I am sent
> To shew thee what shall come in future dayes
> To thee and to thy Offspring; good with bad
> Expect to hear, supernal Grace contending
> With sinfulness of Men; thereby to learn
> True patience, and to temper joy with fear
> And pious sorrow, equally enur'd
> By moderation either state to beare,
> Prosperous or adverse: so shalt thou lead
> Safest thy life, and best prepar'd endure
> Thy mortal passage when it comes.
>
> (xi, 356–66)

This statement itself, and the vision in its entirety, attempt to establish what Christian writers had repeatedly maintained, that history is a teacher of the highest order. St John Chrysostom, in a sermon translated in 1542, stated in prose precisely what Milton was to transmute into poetry: 'the holy scripture, as it were done in a large image & picture, hath peinted to the many lyues of the olde fathers, from Adam to the tyme of our maister Christ, that thereby thou mightest see the synnes and faultes of some, and also the rewardes of som other: and by bothe examples thou mightest be instructed'.[67] Milton's Adam is similarly informed that as events unfold before him, he should observe 'what reward/ Awaits the good, the rest what punishment' (xi, 709 f.). The two 'cities' are, accordingly, delineated clearly. In the *civitas terrena* are such persecutors as the Pharaoh and Nimrod. In the *civitas Dei* are the servants of God extending from Enoch and Noah, through Abraham and David and Solomon, to Jesus the Christ of God.[68] With the Incarnation, the vision in *Paradise Lost* reaches its climax. Before the coming of Jesus, events have meaning only in so far as they herald his way 'by types/And shadowes' (XII, 232 f.). After his advent, all events are likewise related to him by reversion to his Incarnation, which is a historical verity.

But I might seem to confuse the poem with the tradition. The consensus, after all, appears to be that Milton had 'no profound belief in the incarnate Christ', that his account of the Incarnation is 'sketched, hastily and prosaically, in the Twelfth Book', and that the mere 'hundred lines' allotted to it even there is 'surely insufficient treatment'.[69] Even so, I am persuaded that the God-man in *Paradise Lost*, far from being relatively unimportant to Milton, gives coherence to the entire epic. *Chronologically* the narrative proper begins with Raphael's account of the exaltation of the Son of God 'on such day/As Heav'ns great Year brings forth' (V, 577 f.), and ends with Michael's prophecy of the God-man's Second Advent to raise 'New Heav'ns, new Earth, Ages of endless date,/Founded in Righteousness and Peace and Love' (XII, 549 f.). Between these two all-important dates in the history of the universe, in all that is past and passing and to come, the Word is presented by Milton as acting both continually and continuously. The War in Heaven, the first event in which he figures, is adequate warning of Milton's attitude. It was held traditionally that Michael opposed and defeated Lucifer,[70] but Milton displaced the angel in favour of the Son of God (VI, 671–866). The role of protagonist, once assigned to him, is maintained in all subsequent events. As Creator he erects the universal edifice (VII, 210 ff.); as Saviour he volunteers to redeem man long before the Fall (III, 236 ff.); as Judge he passes sentence on Adam and Eve (X, 97 ff.); through his Prevenient Grace he is instrumental in their regeneration (XI, 2 ff.); as the incarnate Christ he consummates the salvation for which he had earlier offered himself (III, 236 ff.; XII, 360 ff.); through his Comforter he supports his faithful followers (XII, 485 ff.); and as the Supreme Judge he is to return in order to terminate the history of the world.[71] All this is considerably more, I think, than just a hundred lines. It is the epic itself.

Milton, by frequent use, has emphasised two words in *Paradise Lost*. One is the word 'all';[72] the other, 'seed'. The word 'all' occurs, with greater intensity than on any other occasion, when in Book III the Father speaks after the Son has offered to die for fallen man:

>   *all* Power
> I give thee, reign for ever, and assume
> Thy merits; under thee as Head Supream
> Thrones, Princedoms, Powers, Dominions I reduce:
> *All* knees to thee shall bow, of them that bide
> In Heav'n, or Earth, or under Earth in Hell;
> When thou attended gloriously from Heav'n
> Shalt in the Skie appear, and from thee send
> The summoning Arch-Angels to proclaime
> Thy dread Tribunal: forthwith from *all* Windes
> The living, and forthwith the cited dead
> Of *all* past Ages to the general Doom
> Shall hast'n, such a peal shall rouse thir sleep.
> Then *all* thy Saints assembl'd, thou shalt judge
> Bad men and Angels. . . .
> Then thou thy regal Scepter shalt lay by,
> For regal Scepter then no more shall need,
> God shall be *All* in *All*. But *all* ye Gods,
> Adore him, who to compass *all* this dies,
> Adore the Son, and honour him as mee.
>
>   (III, 317–43)

'All' is used with singular appropriateness in connection with the God-man, since the word indicates that the Christ Jesus should ultimately be spoken of in the total terms befitting the axis of history.[73]

The word 'seed' is also introduced in Book III ('be thyself Man . . . of Virgin seed' [283–4]. But later, in the sentence God passes on Satan after the Fall of Man, the word explodes into history:

> Between Thee and the Woman I will put
> Enmitie, and between thine and her Seed;
> Her Seed shall bruise thy head, thou bruise his heel.
>
>   (X, 179–81)

To prevent any misunderstanding, Milton proceeds to explain that these 'mysterious terms' were

> verifi'd
> When *Jesus* son of *Mary* second *Eve*,
> Saw Satan fall like Lightning down from Heav'n,
> Prince of the Aire; then rising from his Grave
> Spoild Principalities and Powers, triumphd
> In op'n shew, and with ascension bright
> Captivitie led captive through the Aire,
> The Realme it self of *Satan* long usurpt,
> Whom he shall tread at last under our feet.
>
> (x, 182–90)

Hereafter the 'seed' is mentioned constantly. The peace of mind finally regained by Adam and Eve is attributed directly to that 'first gospel'.[74] Adam's recollection of the promise that Eve's 'Seed shall bruise/The Serpents head' (x, 1031 f.) leads eventually to his acknowledgement of its peculiar role in their regeneration:

> peace returnd
> Home to my brest, and to my memorie
> His promise, that thy Seed shall bruise our Foe.
>
> (xi, 153–5)

The archangel Michael had by this time received his charge to reveal to Adam how the covenant would be 'in the Womans seed renewd' (xi, 116). The result is the vision of the future which unfolds largely in terms of the 'seed'[75] and culminates in its identification with the incarnate Christ:

> The Womans seed, obscurely then foretold,
> Now amplier known thy Saviour and thy Lord.
>
> (xii, 543–4)

Nor is this a mere 'incident' in *Paradise Lost*. Milton in the opening lines states his choice of theme:

> Of Mans First Disobedience, and the Fruit
> Of that Forbidd'n Tree, whose mortal tast
> Brought Death into the World, and all our woe,
> With loss of *Eden*, till one greater Man
> Restore us . . .

At the other end of the poem, in Eve's last speech, this 'greater Man' reappears as the 'Seed':

> though all by mee is lost,
> Such favour I unworthie am voutsaft,
> By mee the Promised Seed shall all restore.
>
> (XII, 621-3)

In *Paradise Lost* 'restore' is the final word to be spoken. Thus the end of the poem looks across the ages at the translation of the vision into history.[76]

V

Milton's concern in *Paradise Lost* is with Man, yet his philosophy is not anthropocentric. The action of the poem moves always *sub specie aeternitatis*; the story told is not a sentence in the history of the world, it is a parenthesis in eternity that opens with Raphael's account of the 'great Year' before the creation, and closes with Michael's vision of the end of time. Within and without this span stands the God-man, making *Paradise Lost* Christocentric and securing for Milton an honoured position in the long line that stretches from Eusebius to Augustine, thence to Jerome and Orosius, Isidore and Bede, Otto of Freising and Vincent of Beauvais, and finally to Dante, the authors of the Mystery Plays, and the numerous exponents of the traditional conception during the Renaissance. As Christians, all believed history to be a record of divine judgements and mercies revealed progressively from the creation to the Second Advent, a palpable testimony that 'the same iust God who liueth and gouerneth all thinges for euer' – as Ralegh said in *The History of the World* – does 'giue victorie, courage, and discourage, raise, and throw downe Kinges, Estates, Cities, and Nations'.[77]

Notes

1 *Select Discourses* (1660); in *The Cambridge Platonists*, ed. C. A. Patrides (1969), p. 190.
2 1st ed. *c.* 1554; *The Works of Sir David Lindsay of the Mount*, ed. Douglas Hamer (Edinburgh, 1931), vol. i, pp. 198–386.

3 *The Monarche*, ll. 4147–53.

4 Arthur Golding, *Thabridgment of the Histories of Trogus Pompeius* (1564), The Epistle Dedicatory. Parallel statements occur in the introductory matter to numerous other translations: Alexander Barclay's Sallust (1520?), Sir Anthony Cope's Livy (1544), Peter Ashton's Giovio (1546), Nicholas Smyth's Herodianus (1550?), Golding's Bruni (1563), Meredith Hanmer's Eusebius (1577), Fenton's Guicciardini (1579), Barnaby Rich's Herodotus (1584), Sir Henry Saville's Tacitus (1591), Thomas Bedingfeld's Machiavelli (1595), Richard Grenewey's Tacitus (1591), Sir Clement Edmondes's Caesar (1600), Thomas Lodge's Josephus (1602), Edward Grimeston's Jean de Serres (1607) and Pierre d'Avity (1615), John Bingham's Xenophon (1623), Dacres's Machiavelli (1636, 1640), *et al.*

5 See especially W. H. Woodward, *Studies in Education* (Cambridge, 1906), pp. 42 ff., 135 ff., etc.; D. T. Starnes, 'Purpose in the Writing of History', *MP*, xx (1923), 281–300; Willard Farnham, 'The Progeny of *A Mirror for Magistrates*', *MP*, xxix (1932), 395–410; Lily B. Campbell, 'The Use of Historical Patterns in the Reign of Elizabeth', *HLQ*, i (1937–8), 135–67, and *Tudor Conceptions of History and Tragedy in 'A Mirror for Magistrates'* (Berkeley, 1936); Firth (below, note 28), pp. 42 ff.; W. A. Armstrong, 'The Elizabethan Concept of the Tyrant', *RES*, xxii (1946), 161–81; William Peery, 'Tragic Retribution in the 1599 *Mirror for Magistrates*', *SP*, xlvi (1949), 113–30; and below (note 44): Holzknecht, pp. 296 ff., Tillyard, pp. 54 ff., and Campbell, part i *passim*. The tremendous popularity of history is most ably set forth by Louis B. Wright, 'The Elizabethan Middle-Class Taste for History', *JMH*, iii (1931), 175–97, expanded in his *Middle-Class Culture in Elizabethan England* (Chapel Hill, 1935), ch. ix; cf. H. S. Bennett, *English Books and Readers 1558 to 1603* (Cambridge, 1965), pp. 214 ff.

6 *The Schollers Medley* (1614), p. 112; reprinted verbatim in *A Survey of History* (1638), p. 395.

7 *Commentary upon . . . Mark* (1661), vol. ii, p. 1077. Parallel summary statements will be found in Luther, *Tischreden*, trans. Henry Bell, *Colloquia mensalia* (1652), p. 519, and Richard Eburne, *The Two-folde Tribvte* (1613), vol. i, p. 18. The theory is lucidly expounded by Guillaume du Vair, *De la Constance*, trans. Andrew Court, *A Buckler against Adversitie* (1622), pp. 76 ff.

8 See above, p. 48.

9 William Gouge, *Gods Three Arrowes* (1631), *passim*. The Roman Catholic position was identical; see Leonardus Lessius, *De providentia numinis*, trans. 'A.B.' as *Rawleigh his Ghost* (St Omer, 1631), pp. 80 f.

10 Sir Francis Hubert, *The Deplorable Life and Death of Edward the Second* (1628), p. 73.

11 *The State of Christendom* (1657), p. 87. For similar statements, lengthier but less eloquent, see George Whetstone, *The Englysh Myrror* (1586), pp. 128 ff., 145 ff.; Thomas Jackson, *Davids Pastorall Poem* (1603), pp. 214 ff.; and Christopher Lever, *The Historie of the Defendors* (1627), ch. xxix. The standard 'universalised' approach to the Virgin Queen is admirably expounded by Frances A. Yates, 'Queen Elizabeth as Astraea', *JWCI*, x (1947), 27–82.

12 Oliver Pigge, *Meditations concerning . . . the Saftie of England* (1589), p. 26, and

Samuel Garey, *Great Brittans Little Calendar* (1618), pp. 184, 185, respectively. But God's protection did not extend to poetic accounts of the Plot, witness the typically atrocious verses of John Rohdes, *A Briefe Summe of the Treason* (1606).

13 Rudolf B. Gottfried, *Geoffrey Fenton's 'Historie of Guicciardin'*, Indiana University Publications, Humanities Series, No. 3 (1940).

14 R. Mark Benbow, 'The Providential Theory of Historical Causation in Holinshed's *Chronicles*: 1577 and 1587', *TSLL*, i (1959), 264–76.

15 *The Vnion of the two noble and illustrate famelies of Lancastre and Yorke* (1548), i, 50ᵛ. On the traditional attitude toward the battle, see Charles L. Kingsford, *Henry V: The Typical Mediæval Hero* (1901), ch. x, and the account in an anonymous biography (1513) based on Tito Livio's *Vita Henrici Quinti*, ed. C. L. Kingsford, *The First English Life of Henry the Fifth* (Oxford, 1911), pp. 51 ff., 93. For other accounts similar to Hall's, see *The Cronycle of Fabyan* (1516), ii, 178 ff.; John Stow, *Annales* (1631), pp. 349 ff.; John Speed, *The History of Great Britaine* (1611), pp. 631 ff.; and the anonymous play discussed by Bernard M. Ward, '*The Famous Victories of Henry V: Its* Place in Elizabethan Dramatic Literature', *RES*, iv (1928), 270–94.

16 Ibid., folios 52–52ᵛ.

17 'Moses', iii, 67–74; in *The Works of Michael Drayton*, ed. J. William Hebel (Oxford, 1932), vol. iii, p. 399.

18 For example, Sleidanus (above, p. 49: trans. Stephen Wythers, *A Briefe Chronicle of the Four Principall Empyres* (1563), and Abraham Darcie, *The Key of Historie. Or . . . Abridgment of the Four Chiefe Monarchies* (1627; 4th ed., 1661); Carion (above, p. 61, note 12): trans. Walter Lynne, *The Thre Bokes of Chronicles* (1550); Pétau (p. 62, note 23): trans. Anon., *The History of the World* (1659); Doglioni (p. 62, note 24): *The Recovery of Lost Time, being Part I of The Historians Guide* (1676); Faria y Sousa (p. 62, note 27): trans. John Stevens, *The History of Portugal from the first Ages of the World* (1698); Galvão (p. 63, note 34): trans. Anon., ed. Richard Hakluyt, *The Discoveries of the World from their first Originall* (1601); Bullinger (p. 63, note 35): trans. Miles Coverdale, *The Old Fayth* (1547); Naudé (p. 63, note 36): trans. John Davies of Kidwelly, *The History of Magick . . . from the Creation* (1657).

19 Richard Brathwait, *The English Gentleman*, 3rd ed. (1641), p. 121. On English historical literature from the late fifteenth to the early seventeenth century, see the surveys by James Gairdner in *Early Chroniclers of Europe* (1883), pp. 292 ff.; Charles L. Kingsford, *English Historical Literature in the Fifteenth Century* (Oxford, 1913), ch. x; Sir John Sandys, 'Scholarship', in *Shakespeare's England* (Oxford, 1916), vol. i, pp. 251 ff.; Charles Whibley, 'The Chroniclers and Historians of the Tudor Age', in his *Literary Studies* (1919), pp. 1–59; James W. Thompson, *A History of Historical Writing* (1942), vol. i, chs xxxv–vi; Denys Hay, 'History and Historians in France and England during the 15th Century', *BIHR*, xxxv (1962), 111–27, and Introduction to *The Anglica Historia of Polydore Vergil* (1950), pp. xxiii ff.; William R. Trimble, 'Early Tudor Historiography, 1485–1548', *JHI*, xi (1950), 30–41; Glanmor Williams, 'Some Protestant Views of Early British Church History', *History*, xxxviii (1953), 219–33; Thomas Wheeler, 'The

New Style of the Tudor Chroniclers', *TSL*, vii (1962), 71–7; Douglas Bush, *English Literature in the Earlier Seventeenth Century*, 2nd rev. ed. (Oxford, 1962), pp. 220 ff.; F. Smith Fussner, *Tudor History and the Historians* (1970); May McKisack, *Medieval History in the Tudor Age* (Oxford, 1971); and the more comprehensive studies by Herschel Baker, *The Race of Time: Three Lectures on Renaissance Historiography* (Toronto, 1967); F. J. Levy, *Tudor Historical Thought* (San Marino, Calif., 1967); F. Smith Fussner, *The Historical Revolution: English Historical Writing and Thought 1580–1640* (1962); and J. G. A. Pocock, *The Ancient Constitution and Feudal Law: A Study of English Historical Thought in the 17th Century* (Cambridge, 1957). See also the collection of essays on different aspects of *English Historical Scholarship in the 16th and 17th Centuries*, ed. Levi Fox (1956).

20 Among other works by Bale: *The Actes of English Votaryes* (1546 ff.), a survey 'frõ the worldes begynnynge, to a full complete thousand years sens Christes incarnacyon'; and *Illustrium Maioris Brittaniae scriptorvm, hoc est, Angliæ, Cambriæ, ac Scotiæ summariũ* (1548), which modestly commences as late as the post-inundation period.

21 Honor McCusker, *John Bale* (Bryn Mawr, 1942), p. 127. I myself tend to prefer the discussion of the *Chefe Promyses* by Thora B. Blatt, *The Plays of John Bale* (Copenhagen, 1968), pp. 68–95.

22 The *Image* was evidently printed in Antwerp; see Colin Clair, *The Library*, 5th series, xviii (1963), 284 f. The widespread interest in the Apocalypse (above, p. 50) also affected Spenser. Consult Josephine W. Bennett, *The Evolution of 'The Faerie Queene'* (Chicago, 1942), ch. ix; J. E. Hankins, 'Spenser and the Revelation of St. John', *PMLA*, lx (1945), 364–81; and J. F. Kermode, 'Spenser and the Allegorists', *PBA*, xlviii (1962), 261–79.

23 *The History of Great Britaine* (1611), pp. 161 ff.

24 See the survey by U. T. Holmes, Jr, in *The Works of . . . Du Bartas* (Chapel Hill, 1935), vol. i, pp. 28–66.

25 Though the principal translator of Du Bartas, Sylvester was not the only one. Among others were Sir Philip Sidney, whose partial version of the 'First Week' is no longer extant, and James VI of Scotland, the first to introduce Du Bartas in English (*L'Uranie*, trans. 1584). Sylvester's piecemeal translations, begun in the 1590s, were completed in 1608; see Lily B. Campbell, *Divine Poetry and Drama in Sixteenth-Century England* (Cambridge, 1959), part i, chs ix–xi.

26 William Hodson, *The Divine Cosmographer* (Cambridge, 1640), p. 147. On the influence of Du Bartas, consult Sir Sidney Lee, *The French Renaissance in England* (Oxford, 1910), pp. 333–55; Alfred H. Upham, *The French Influence in English Literature* (1911), ch. iv; and esp. Harry Ashton, *Du Bartas en Angleterre* (Paris, 1908). The enthusiastic work of George C. Taylor, *Milton's Use of Du Bartas* (Cambridge, Mass., 1934), is an overstatement.

27 *Du Bartas his Deuine Weekes and Workes* (1621), p. 9; I have quoted the pertinent passage in its entirety in the *HTR* study cited below (p. 98, note 71), 174–5. For other French poets besides Du Bartas who commenced with the creation, see M. Thibaut de Maisières, *Les Poèmes inspirés du debut de la Genèse a l'époque de la Renaissance* (Louvain, 1931), and R. A. Sayce, *The French Biblical Epic in the Seventeenth Century* (Oxford, 1955), *passim*.

28 Substantial extracts in my edition (1971); I have drawn heavily upon its Introduction for my present account. For other discussions see Sir Charles Firth, *Essays Historical and Literary* (Oxford, 1938), pp. 34–60; C. F. Tucker Brooke, *Essays on Shakespeare and Other Elizabethans* (New Haven, 1948), ch. xiv; Ernest A. Strathmann, '*The History of the World* and Ralegh's Skepticism', *HLQ*, iii (1940), 265–87, and *Sir Walter Ralegh* (1951), pp. 109 ff. and *passim*; and F. Smith Fussner, *The Historical Revolution* (1962), ch. vii. Divergent interpretations are offered by Christopher Hill, *Intellectual Origins of the English Revolution* (Oxford, 1965), ch. iv, and Pierre Lefranc, *Sir Walter Ralegh écrivain* (Paris, 1968), chs x–xi.

29 *The History of the Worthies of England* (1662), 'Devon-shire', p. 262.

30 IV, ii, 3; ed. C. A. Patrides (1971), p. 253. Ralegh's work adheres casually to the concept of the Four Monarchies, which is much more clearly affirmed in the 'exquisite abstract' issued later as *Tvbvs historicvs: An Historical Perspective* (1636).

31 *The Marrow of Historie, or an Epitome of . . . Rawleigh* (1650; 2nd ed., 1662); and *The History of the World: The Second Part* (1652). But Ross still managed to find something to complain about, as in *Som Animadversions and Observations upon Sr Walter Raleighs Historie of the World* (1653). Sir William Sanderson in defending Ralegh declared that Ross's abridgement had ruined the original 'Master-peice', while his animadversions left it unaffected: Ralegh 'yet indures the examination of his Errours' (*The Lives and Reigns of Mary Queen of Scotland, and . . . James* [1656], i, 'Proeme').

32 *The History of the World* (1659), 'To the Reader'.

33 The *Pilgrimage*, while entirely different from *Pvrchas his Pilgrim* (1619), has decisive affinities with the encyclopaedic *Haklvytvs Posthumus or Pvrchas his Pilgrimes* (1625), the longest single work published in English until that time.

34 Trans. Richard More, *The Key of Revelation* (1643).

35 I quote the title page of his Παντοχρονοχανον [*sic*] (1652). Other works still further afield include: Robert Glover's *Nobilitas political vel civilis* (1608), later translated by Thomas Milles, typical of the host of historical defences of 'the bright estate of noblenesse', all commencing with the first nobleman of them all, Adam; Thomas Lydiat's *Emendatio temporvm compendio facta ab initio mundi* (1609), the Latin counterpart to numerous computations of chronology in English, all harking back to Adam; John Speed's *The Genealogies recorded in the Sacred Scriptvres . . . with the Line of ovr Saviour . . . observedfrom Adam* (1611 et seq.), prefixed – 'cvm privilegio' – to the editions of the King James Bible; Edward Cooke's *Bartas Junior. Or, the Worlds Epitome* (1631), part of the legacy bequeathed by an obvious master, in atrocious verses; Peter Heylyn's massive *Cosmographie* (1652), a history *and* a geography of the whole world, introduced with the standard account of the creation; Alexander Ross's Πανσεβεία: *Or, a View of all Religions in the World, from the Creation* (1653), a sub-primitive effort in comparative religion, with a running commentary denouncing past and present deviates from the author's severe orthodoxy; and Thomas Fuller's *The Chvrch-History of Britain; from the Birth of Jesus Christ* (1655), the English counterpart to the Continental compilations of Flacius and Baronius. If these works do not suffice to demonstrate the universalising tendencies of Renaissance

England, we may glance at extremes like George Hakewill's historical study of regicide, *Scvtvm regivm. id est, adversvs omnes regicidas et regicidarvm patronos, ab initio mundi* (1612); also Robert Sibthorpe's *Apostolicke Obedience* (1627), which harks back to the early Church in a desperate attempt to justify, of all things, taxation; and finally the most fascinating work of all, George Owen Harry's *The Genealogy of the High and Mighty Monarch, James* (1605), which traces His Majesty's descent not only from Brut but from Noah, here triumphantly crowned 'the first Monarch of the world'. But even Harry's work was soon superseded by that of William Slatyer, whose appendix to *The History of Great Britanie* (1621) traces the 'stemma Iacobi' beyond even Noah – to Adam!

36 1st ed., Strasbourg, 1554; revised in 1559, 1570 (the last two editions in English). The title *Actes and Monuments* dates from 1563; since 1776 the work has been known as *The Book of Martyrs*. Here I am using the text of *The Ecclesiastical History contaynyng the Actes* (1570).

37 Charles Whibley, *Literary Studies* (1919), p. 45, and Hugh Massingham, 'John Foxe', in *Great Tudors*, ed. Katharine Garvin (1935), p. 379; respectively. But see further the estimate by J. F. Mozley, *John Foxe and his Book* (1940), ch. vi, and especially the study by William Haller, *Foxe's Book of Martyrs and the Elect Nation* (1963).

38 As in the case, particularly, of the *Vitæ Patrum*. These, collected by Heribert Rosweyde, S.J. (Antwerp, 1615), are now accessible in *PL*, lxxiii–iv; there is a partial translation by Helen Waddell, *The Desert Fathers* (1936). But note also the extension of the tradition in France, in d'Aubigné's *Les Tragiques* (above. p. 50).

39 Irving Ribner, 'The Tudor History Play: An Essay in Definition', *PMLA*, lxix (1954), 591–609, and 'Marlowe's *Edward II* and the Tudor History Play', *ELH*, xxii (1955), 243–53. See also Ribner's survey of *The English History Play in the Age of Shakespeare* (Princeton, 1947), and F. P. Wilson's suggestive study of 'The English History Play', in his *Shakespearian and Other Studies*, ed. Helen Gardner (Oxford, 1969), ch. i.

40 The argument is essentially E. Catherine Dunn's, as before (above, p. 46, note 64).

41 See G. R. Hibbard, 'George Chapman: Tragedy and the Providential View of History', *SS*, x (1967), 27–31.

42 The 'major' tetralogy is said to constitute an epic; see Alvin Kernan, 'The Henriad: Shakespeare's Major History Plays', *YR*, lix (1969), 3–32.

43 Cf. above, pp. 73, 75. On Shakespeare's indebtedness to Holinshed, see W. G. Boswell-Stone, ed., *Shakspere's Holinshed: The Chronicle and the Historical Plays Compared* (1896), and Geoffrey Bullough, ed., *Narrative and Dramatic Sources of Shakespeare* (1960–2), vols iii–iv.

44 The case is succinctly argued by Leonard F. Dean, '*Richard II* to *Henry V*: A Closer View', in *Studies in Honor of DeWitt T. Starnes*, ed. T. P. Harrison *et al.* (Austin, 1967), pp. 37–52; but see further R. Poisson, '*Richard II*: Tudor Orthodoxy or Political Heresy?', *Humanities Association Bulletin*, xiv (1963), 5–11, and esp. A. P. Rossiter, 'Ambivalence: The Dialectic of the Histories', in his *Angel with Horns*, ed. G. Storey (1961), ch. iii; M. M. Reese, *The Cease of Majesty: A Study of Shakespeare's History Plays* (1961); S. C. Sen Gupta,

Shakespeare's Historical Plays (1964); cf. Roland M. Frye, *Shakespeare and Christian Doctrine* (Princeton, 1963). But consult also the contrary thesis of E. M. W. Tillyard, *Shakespeare's History Plays* (1946); Lily B. Campbell, *Shakespeare's 'Histories': Mirrors of Elizabethan Policy* (San Marino, Calif., 1947); Irving Ribner, 'Shakespeare's History Plays Revisited', *Bulletin de la Faculté des Lettres de Strasbourg*, xliii (1965), 855–62, and above, note 39. Shakespeare's treatment of history has also been discussed by M. W. MacCallum, *Shakespeare's Roman Plays* (1910), pp. 73–94; F. J. C. Hearnshaw, 'Shakespeare as Historian', *CR*, cxxiv (1923), 728–38; Karl J. Holzknecht, *The Backgrounds of Shakespeare's Plays* (1950), pp. 307 ff.; Karl Brunner, 'Middle-Class Attitudes in Shakespeare's Histories', *SS*, vi (1953), 36–8; Michael Quinn, 'Providence in Shakespeare's Yorkist Plays', *SQ*, x (1959), 45–52; Tom F. Driver, *The Sense of History in Greek and Shakespearean Drama* (1960), esp. part iii; Sigurd Burckhardt, '*King John*: The Ordering of this Present Time', *ELH*, xxxiii (1966), 133–53; Ronald Berman, 'Anarchy and Order in *Richard II* and *King John*', *SS*, xx (1967), 51–9; and Henry A. Kelly, *Divine Providence in the England of Shakespeare's Histories* (Cambridge, Mass., 1970), which I reviewed in *ELN*, ix (1971), 108–10. See also the bibliographical essay by Harold Jenkins, *SS*, vi (1953), 1–15, and below, notes 45–8.

45 Studies of Shakespeare's progress to the 'major' tetralogy include: John F. Danby, *Shakespeare's Doctrine of Nature* (1949), part ii, ch. i; Derek Traversi, *Shakespeare: from 'Richard II' to 'Henry V'* (Stanford, 1957); John Lawlor, *The Tragic Sense in Shakespeare* (1960), ch. i; and Rossiter (previous note).

46 Rossiter (above, note 44), p. 57. See also Zdeněk Stříbrný, '*Henry V* and History', in *Shakespeare in a Changing World*, ed. Arnold Kettle (1964), pp. 84–101.

47 See Philip Brockbank, 'The Frame of Disorder: *Henry VI*', in *Early Shakespeare*, ed. J. R. Brown and B. Harris (1961), ch. iv; also his comprehensive survey, 'Shakespeare: his Histories, English and Roman', in *English Drama to 1710*, ed. Christopher Ricks (1971), pp. 166–99.

48 See e.g. Benjamin T. Spencer in *UTQ*, xiii (1944), 394–9; Harold E. Toliver in *SQ*, xvi (1965), 63–80; Hugh Maclean in *UTQ*, xxxv (1966), 229–45; Paul A. Jorgensen, *Redeeming Shakespeare's Words* (Berkeley, 1962), ch. iv; Robert L. Montgomery, Jr, in *SS*, iv (1968), 73–85; *et al.* Consult also the definitive study by Ricardo J. Quinones, *The Renaissance Discovery of Time* (Cambridge, Mass., 1972).

49 *2 Henry IV*, iv, iv, 74.

50 Letter of 2 April 1650, in *The Writings and Speeches of Oliver Cromwell*, ed. Wilbur C. Abbott (Cambridge, Mass., 1939), vol. ii, p. 236. Scholars were equally enthusiastic. 'Of al modern Writers', wrote Diggory Wheare in 1623, 'Sir *Walter Rawleigh* our Country-man deserves the first place' (*The Method and Order of Reading . . . Histories*, trans. Edmund Bohun [1685], p. 41).

51 Elizabeth McCutcheon, 'Lancelot Andrewes' *Preces Privatae*: A Journey through Time', *SP*, lxv (1968), 223–41.

52 *Divine Dialogues* (1688), vol. ii, p. 287. See also John Smith's statement, quoted above, p. 70.

53 'In the Glorious Epiphanie of our Lord God, a Hymn', ll. 26–7, in *Carmen Deo nostro* (Paris, 1652). See the discussion by A. R. Cirillo, 'Crashaw's "Epiphany Hymn": The Dawn of Christian Time', *SP*, lxvii (1970), 67–88.

54 'The Collar', ll. 7–14. I quote from Herbert's *Works*, ed. F. C. Hutchinson (Oxford, 1941), pp. 153–4. For a different but not unrelated approach, see Stanley Stewart, 'Time and *The Temple*', *SEL*, vi (1966), 97–110.

55 Egon S. Merton, *Science and Imagination in Sir Thomas Browne* (1949), p. 63.

56 Cf. the typical twofold division of Milton's *De doctrina christiana*, and the discussion by Frank L. Huntley, *Sir Thomas Browne* (Ann Arbor, 1962), pp. 107 f.

57 Consult Huntley, ibid., ch. viii.

58 Ed. John Carter (Cambridge, 1958), p. 114.

59 Ed. Jean-Jacques Denonain (Cambridge, 1955), p. 44 (i, 33).

60 Ibid., p. 61 (i, 47). Browne's analogy of history to a play is similar to Ralegh's in *The History of the World*.

61 Ibid., p. 16 (i, 11). The most important precedent to Browne's formulation is Boethius, *De consolatione philosophiæ*, book v, prose iv et seq.

62 Ibid., p. 74 (i, 59).

63 Malcolm M. Ross, 'Milton and the Protestant Aesthetic', *UTQ*, xvii (1947–8), 351.

64 'A Hymn of the Nativity', in *Steps to the Temple* (1646); augmented as 'In the Holy Nativity of our Lord: A Hymn', in *Carmen Deo nostro* (Paris, 1652).

65 Rosemond Tuve, *Images and Themes in Five Poems by Milton* (Cambridge, Mass., 1957), p. 39. But the thesis has in fact been more persuasively argued by Balachandra Rajan, *The Lofty Rhyme* (1970), ch. ii.

66 *Aeneid*, vi, 757 ff.; *Os Lusíadas*, x, 7 ff.; *La Gerusalemme Liberata*, xviii, 92 ff.; *The Faerie Queene*, II, x; etc. Other precedents are noted by Thomas Greene, *The Descent from Heaven* (New Haven, 1963), p. 136.

67 *A Sermon . . . furnysshed with heuenly wisedome*, trans. Thomas Lupset (1542), sig. C5.

68 Cf. Luther's restatement of St Augustine's thesis (quoted above, p. 17): 'we must divide the children of Adam and all mankind into two classes, the first belonging to the kingdom of God, the second to the kingdom of the world. Those who belong to the kingdom of God are all the true believers who are in Christ and under Christ' (*Works*, ed. Jaroslav Pelikan and H. T. Lehman [St Louis, 1959 ff.], vol. xlv, p. 88). But even as I assert Milton's debt to Augustine, I am not convinced that the epic's broad span of 'time and eternity' conforms to the traditional pattern of the Six Ages (as George W. Whiting claims in *Milton and this Pendant World* [Austin, 1958], ch. vi). The account by Rosalie L. Colie in *Paradoxia Epidemica* (Princeton, 1966), ch. v, is much more apposite.

69 Seriatim: E. M. W. Tillyard, *Milton* (1930), p. 279; David Daiches, *Milton* (1957), p. 210 (cf. his similar statement in *The Living Milton*, ed. Frank Kermode [1960], p. 59); Sir Walter Raleigh, *Milton* (1900), p. 164; W. Menzies, 'Milton: The Last Poems', *E&S*, xxiv (1939), 85.

70 B. Rajan, *'Paradise Lost' and the Seventeenth Century Reader* (1947), p. 48; Grant McColley, *'Paradise Lost'*, *HTR*, xxxii (1939), 186–7; Watson Kirkconnel, *The Celestial Cycle* (Toronto, 1952), pp. 114, 309. Though Milton

accepted this tradition in *De doctrina christiana* (*Works*, Columbia ed., vol. xv, p. 106), we should also note the frequent claim that Christ is 'figured and signified to vs vnder the tipe of Michaell' (thus Heinrich Bullinger, *A Hvndred Sermons vpon the Apocalips*, trans. John Daws [1561], p. 356; but also Augustin Marlorat, *Exposition vpon the Revelation*, trans. Arthur Golding [1574], folios 174 f.; Niels Hemmingsen, *The Faith of the Chvrch*, trans. Thomas Rogers [1581], p. 12; John Boys, *An Exposition of al the Principall Scriptures* [1610–15], part iv, p. 98; Thomas Taylor, *Christs Victorie* [1633], pp. 341 f.; John Robinson, *Endoxa* [1658], p. 30; *et al.*).

71 iii, 323 ff.; xi, 900–1; xii, 458 ff., 544 ff. I discussed Milton's eschatological ideas in 'Renaissance and Modern Thought on the Last Things', *HTR*, li (1958), 169–85, and *Milton and the Christian Tradition* (Oxford, 1966), ch. ix. The intriguing possibility of 'The Apocalypse within *Paradise Lost*' is argued by Michael Fixler in *New Essays on 'Paradise Lost'*, ed. Thomas Kranidas (Berkeley, 1969), ch. vii.

72 First observed in another connection by William Empson, *The Structure of Complex Words* (1951), pp. 101–4.

73 'All' is directly related to the traditional concept of 'recapitulation' which I discussed in 'Milton and the Protestant Theory of the Atonement', *PMLA*, lxxiv (1959), 7–13, and *Milton and the Christian Tradition* (Oxford, 1966), ch. v. For another study of our increasing awareness of the Son's central position in the poem, see Hugh MacCallum, ' "Most Perfect Hero": The Role of the Son in Milton's Theodicy', in *'Paradise Lost': A Tercentenary Tribute*, ed. B. Rajan (Toronto, 1969), pp. 79–105.

74 See my article on 'The "Protevangelium" in Renaissance Theology and *Paradise Lost*', *SEL*, iii (1963), 19–30.

75 See esp. xii, 148–50, 233–5, 325–30, 379–80. Critics are becoming increasingly aware that books xi and xii 'fulfill the rhythm of the poem' (Arnold Stein, *Answerable Style* [Minneapolis, 1953], p. 161). See: F. T. Prince, 'On the Last Two Books of *Paradise Lost*', *E&S*, n.s., xi (1958), 38–52 (reprinted in *Milton's Epic Poetry*, ed. C. A. Patrides [Harmondsworth, 1967], pp. 233–48); Joseph H. Summers, *The Muse's Method* (1962), ch. viii; Lawrence A. Sasek, 'The Drama of *Paradise Lost*, Books XI and XII', in *Studies in English Renaissance Literature*, ed. Waldo F. McNeir (Baton Rouge, 1962), pp. 181–96; H. R. MacCallum, 'Milton and Sacred History', in *Essays . . . presented to A. S. P. Woodhouse* (Toronto, 1964), pp. 149–68; Mary Ann Radzinowicz, ' "Man as a Probationer of Immortality": *Paradise Lost* XI–XII', in *Approaches to 'Paradise Lost'*, ed. C. A. Patrides (1968), pp. 31–51; George M. Muldrow, *Milton and the Drama of the Soul* (The Hague, 1970), ch. ii; Balachandra Rajan, *'Paradise Lost*: The Hill of History', in his *The Lofty Rhyme* (1970), ch. vi; and Michael Cavanagh, 'A Meeting of Epic and History: Books XI and XII of *Paradise Lost*', *ELH*, xxxviii (1971), 206–22.

76 *Paradise Regained* was later to deal with the central episode of the Christian epic of history, the fulfilment of time; see Laurie Zwicky, 'Kairos in *Paradise Regained*: The Divine Plan', *ELH*, xxxi (1964), 271–7. But the poem may also be placed within an apocalyptic context, witness the impressive study by Michael Fixler, *Milton and the Kingdoms of God* (1964).

77 *The History of the World* (1614), II, xix, 3; ed. C. A. Patrides (1971), p. 211.

Six

Innovation in Renaissance England

Some haue written of times so anciently past, that no
means are extant, either to *direct* or to *correct* them.
Many of these liuing in Artlesse ages, haue stuffed their
Stories with most senselesse fictions; nothing better then
country womens tales. . . . After this example *Geoffry* of
Munmouth about 400 yeares since, did first (as some
affirme) draw the originall of the *Britans* from *Brutus* the
Troian: forging such races, names, reignes and passages
of affaires, as may more easily be conuinced to be
false, then supplied with any certaine truth.

SIR JOHN HAYWARD[1]

I

Notwithstanding the acceptance of the traditional view in
Elizabethan England, opinion was already merging with the
stream of Italian historiography to become, in the two centuries
following, a mighty torrent. The feverish activities of translators
in England, more than in Italy, help us in our consideration of
shifting viewpoints – not least because one of the translators was
the Queen herself.[2]
It is of course hardly novel to assert that translation during the
Renaissance in England had become an art in itself.[3] Nearly all
translators apologised for having stripped so many works of their
original garments and dressed them with 'a playne English cote'.
However, this signified little, for no translation was a light burden
but, as William Crosse said of his version of Sallust (1629), each
'smelles of the Lampe'. Thus, despite their open disavowal of
'our vulgar toong', the pride all the translators shared in their

concerted endeavours must be seen as contributing to the severance of the last bond uniting Europe, the Latin language.

But the real story is told by the works selected for translation. Though we are at first glance impressed by the quantity of theological and religious books rendered into English, closer scrutiny reveals that they are predominantly by Continental reformers. Only five of the older traditional texts were made available in English because circumstances of the time subjected them to discrimination. Thomas Lodge, for example, translated Josephus in 1602 probably less for doctrinal reasons than because Josephus was recommended by Scaliger and other humanists as a reliable historian.[4] Meredith Hanmer, in rendering the ecclesiastical histories of Eusebius and others (1577), was motivated by the peculiarly Protestant desire to proclaim what should still be done in order to eliminate 'the difference that is in these our dayes betwene the Church and the Apostolicke times'.[5] Similarly, Thomas Stapleton translated Bede's *Historia ecclesiastica* (1565) in order to demonstrate 'the misse information of a fewe for displacing the auncient and right Christian faith'. Stapleton also pointedly observed that Bede is 'a countreman of oures', sounding a patriotic note which Thomas Habington rang again in 1638 when he published his version of the history of Gildas, who 'above a thousand yeeres ago' proved that England was not 'overwhelmed with Barbarisme' but was in fact the fountain-head of 'wisdome'. John Healey's celebrated translation of *De civitate Dei* (1610), a work only too enthusiastically welcomed by Protestants since St Augustine was the guiding light of the Reformation, caps the five traditional works we have mentioned.

These five works excepted, none of the many expositions since Augustine of the Christian view of history was translated into English. The whole array of mediaeval world chronicles remained imprisoned in the original Latin; even philosophers of history like Sulpicius Severus, Orosius, and Salvian were unavailable in English,[6] which suggests that English eyes were no longer fixed squarely on the Christian tradition but on the historians of Greece, Rome, and Renaissance Italy, as we may infer from the impressive number of classical and humanist texts rendered into English.[7] Translations of Machiavelli's *Discorsi* and *Il Principe* supply our best evidence of the changing climate of opinion. Though numerous translations in manuscript survive,[8] only those by Edward

Dacres were published, the *Discourses* in 1636 and the *Prince* in 1640. Dacres wisely approached his perilous task with caution. In his preface to both translations he denounced Machiavelli's theories as 'pernicious', although he also had the courage to suggest that perhaps some good might still derive from the evil ('From the same flower the Bee sucks hony, from whence the Spider hath his poyson'). Machiavelli was of course widely known even without Dacres's 'English cote'. George Webbe, who was no enthusiast for 'this incarnate Deuill', nevertheless reported faithfully his claim to fame:[9]

> Alas he liueth yet, and is liked too much: his writings are too plentifull in Stationers shops, in Gentlemans studies, in Citizens chambers; yea it is to bee feared, that it is now growne habituall amongst vs, which a French writer complained, was crept in amongst his Coumtrimen; *They make Tacitus their Gospell, They studie Lucian more than the old Testament, and Machiauel more than the new.*

Translations of classical and humanist historians yielded another villain besides Machiavelli. He was Hobbes, the translator of Thucydides in 1629. He embarked on a career whose impact on the old order later caused an alarmed Alexander Ross to answer in exasperation with his tellingly entitled *Leviathan drawn out with a hook* (1653).[10]

The great interest taken in classical and humanist historians was stimulated by a belief that the Greeks and the Romans, as well as their heirs in Renaissance Italy, had drawn closest to the 'truth'. Moses had by no means lost his place as the most accurate historian in the world, but his displacement had begun already in the Renaissance. One of the first signs of the gathering storm appeared in Scotland when John Bellenden – possibly by way of penance for his version of Hector Boece's *Scotorum historiae*[11] – translated the first five books of Livy, whom he categorically described as 'prince of historiographouris'. Bellenden's Livy was not published until the early nineteenth century,[12] but his counterpart in England, Philemon Holland, independently reached the same conclusion. In 1600 Holland, though referring to Livy, also accounted for the increasing partiality to classical historians. He said of 'that which most of all commendeth an historie':[13]

> an historie, . . . being *lux veritatis*,[14] ought especially to
> deliver with synceritie the whole truth & nothing but
> the truth, without respect of face or person: to keep only
> to the substance & train of the subiect argumẽt; the due
> & orderly regard of the important circumstances
> thereto belonging, without inserting extravagant &
> impertinent by-matters, much lesse then, fabulous tales.

Holland failed to specify the 'fabulous tales' he had in mind. Yet
any intelligent reader could deduce that he was thinking of such
legends as those of Brut and Arthur. By 1600 both were in a
decline that was soon to be complete. This decline is attributable
to factors that illuminate the historiographical temper of Renaissance England; and since scholars have been more generous
in their treatment of Arthur, I propose to give my attention
mostly to Brut.[15]

II

Geoffrey of Monmouth (*c.* 1100–54) thought it 'curious' that both
Gildas and Bede were silent about the noble eras of Brut and
Arthur. To fill the omission he translated into Latin 'a certain
most ancient book' that is supposed to have come into his posses-
sion, the *Historia regum Britanniae*.[16] The book, which was almost
certainly his own work, met with such wide and lasting favour
that historical writing in England for the next four hundred years
largely constitutes a series of footnotes to Geoffrey's imaginative
'history'.[17] English mediaeval chroniclers inadvertently elevated
the *Historia* to the level of the Book of Genesis, for if ever they did
not begin with the Mosaic account of creation, they were almost
sure to do so with Geoffrey's Brut. The numerous instances
include Henry of Huntington and Walter of Coventry, whose
chronicles are typical of the mediaeval compilations based on
Geoffrey;[18] Robert of Brunne, who attempted a metrical version
of a similar collection in the 'Inglis tonge';[19] and a number of
French versions in prose as well as in verse.[20] Bishop John Lesley's
adaptation of the legend of Brut, written in Scots during the
middle of the sixteenth century, demonstrates the impressive
continuity of tradition:[21]

Gif quha walde knawe the name of Britannie monie referris it vnto Bru*tus* the sone of Silui*us* Posthum*us* King of the Latines, and oye of Æneas, and him to be author baith of the name and natione of Britannie. The maist com*m*oune speiking is this, that xl. ʒeirs eftir the seige of Troy, quhill Brutus with grett sollicitude and kair was seiking a resting place with some troiane Iwalis and reliques, eftir sair trauell quhen mony dangeris he escaped had, at last he landet in Albion. Thaireftir the Ile he named Britannie, and his cu*m*panie britanis. Bot quhat vthiris lait writeris speik of this name p*er*chance mair curious than true, I, handeng me content with the opinione of ancient Antiquitie, regarde nocht.

At the time Lesley wrote these lines Geoffrey's reputation was secure, but Lesley was well aware that some 'lait writeris' had begun to wonder whether such stories were 'mair curious than true'. Ranulf Higden had already decided that King Arthur was largely a mythical figure,[22] while Erasmus bluntly dismissed the entire Arthurian matter as 'stupid'.[23] Brut fared no better. In the words of John Rastell, written as early as 1529, 'this story semyth more meruelouse thã trew & though it hath cõtynued here in Englõd & takyn for a trewth amõg vs Englyshmẽ yet other pepull do therefore laugh vs to skorne & so semyth they may ryght well'.[24] Five years later the Italian humanist Polydore Vergil in his *Anglica historia*[25] reconsidered the stories and repudiated them both as unauthentic. Though English historians drew generously on Vergil, his book was never once praised during the Tudor era. Indeed, it served as a rallying point of patriotic outbursts against Vergil ('that most rascall dogge knave').[26]

A single blow cannot kill a tradition, and so the legend of Brut – 'Felix Brutus'[27] – persisted in the face of mounting criticism. In 1547 Arthur Kelton, contemptuously disregarding Vergil, published *A Chronycle with a Genealogie declaryng that the Brittons and Welshemen are lineally descended from Brute*, tracing the line even further back to Osiris ('the first king of Egipt'). Such claims, already numerous before Elizabeth's accession,[28] became even more plentiful during her reign. Thus in 1565 the antiquary John Stow, despite 'paynfull searche' into primary sources, accepted Brut's existence in agreement with 'the most ancient and best approued Authours';[29] in 1574 John Higgins confidently commenced with Brut his extension of the *Mirror for Magistrates*; in 1577 Holinshed dismissed criticism of the legend firmly ('wee shall not doubte of Brutes hyther comming');[30] in 1589 William Warner added an appendix to his *Albions England* to clarify the rather remote times of Aeneas, 'Patriarke of our *Brutones*'; while a year later, in the most calculated defiance of that rascal Vergil, appeared the first three books of *The Faerie Queene*. Spenser's account[31] is the most persuasive articulation of the myth that 'noble *Britons* sprong from *Troians* bold'. His imaginary forces gathered 'the *Troians* scattered of-spring' under the leadership of Brut, and saw them building a capital to rival both Priam's Troy and Aeneas's Rome:

> It *Troynouant* is hight, that with the waues
> Of wealthy *Thamis* washed is along.
>
> (iii, ix, 45)

But the new critics proved just as resourceful, since they were able to enlist the co-operation of the antiquary William Camden, widely regarded as England's 'rare ornament' 'vniuersally admyred throughout Christendome', 'the glory of our Nation'.[32] Camden was the most diplomatic of all writers on Brut. He refused in his *Britannia* (1586) to start even with such an event as the Flood by pleading ignorance ('whether there were any Islands at all before the Deluge, it is not my purpose here to argue'), and going on to speak of 'those reports of Brutus' as follows:[33]

> For mine owne part, it is not my intent, I assure you, to discredit and confute that story which goes of him, for the upholding whereof (I call *Truth* to record) I have from time to time streined to the heighth, all that little wit of mine. For that were, to strive with the streame and currant of time; and to struggle against an opinion commonly and long since received. How then may I, a man of so meane parts, and small reckoning, be so bold, as to sit in examination of a matter so important, and thereof definitively to determine? Well, I referre the matter full and whole to the Senate of Antiquaries, for to be decided. Let every man, for me, judge as it pleaseth him; and of what opinion soever the Reader shall be of, verily I will not make it a point much material.

Camden's attitude is a reflection of parallel developments on the Continent. The English were by no means unique in claiming descent from the Trojans; nearly all Western Europeans claimed as much,[34] barring only the Portuguese whose capital is appropriately said to have been founded by a much-travelled mariner, the πολύτροπος Odysseus.[35] By the early seventeenth century, however, acceptance of these legends was declining on the Continent as it was in England. The mediaeval chroniclers of France, for instance, had persistently regarded the Trojans as their direct forefathers;[36] but increasingly through the sixteenth century the myth was subjected to sceptical examination, notably by Paolo Emilio, Beatus Rhenanus, Estienne Pasquier, and particularly François Hotman in *Franco-Gallia* (1573).[37] Thereafter the warning issued by Louis de Mayerne-Turquet was heard repeatedly: 'The beginning and Antiquitie of nations farre fetcht, is alwaies fabulous.'[38] Only poets elected to disagree: Ronsard like Spenser reverted to the 'fabulous' past, and stubbornly celebrated in *La Franciade* (1572) the exploits of the father of the French nation, the Trojan Prince Francus.[39] But presently no less an authority than the royal historiographer Jean de Serres recounted the Trojan legend only in order to dismiss it:[40]

> If we were to seeke truth in vanitie, following the common error, to search for the originall of the FRENCH, in the ruins and ashes of TROY or in the fennes of *Meotides*, for in the most auncient Histories of the *Trojans*, there is no mention of FRANCVS or FRANCION, sonnes of *Hector*, who had but one sonne named *Astianax* slayne at three yeares of age in the sacke of Troy. There is also no likelyhood to find the stemme of our FRENCH nation in the fennes of *Meotides*, where they were first called SICAMBRES, hauing built a Citty by imagination named SICAMBRA: And that they issued from thence in great troups. There is no more proofe that they are come from these marishes, then from the desarts of *Affricke*.

Fifty years later restraint was replaced by abuse. 'In a manner', declared Gabriel Naudé, 'all Histories within seven or eight hundred years past are so hydropically swoln with lying legends, that a man would think the Authors of them had made it their main strife, who should advance the greatest number.'[41]

Developments in England were similar. After Camden two mutually exclusive approaches persisted for a time. We have on the one hand the enlightened attitude of such writers as John Speed, who paused long enough to deliver the pun that 'neuer any such *Brute* raigned in the world';[42] and on the other, the defenders of tradition, still insisting that 'We are not *Brittons*, we are *Brutans*',[43] and still scornfully dismissing such 'strangers' as Vergil, who 'deserue not to be laid in ballance to counterprize the authority of so many learned Authors in our countrey'.[44] The traditionalists were, however, gradually whittled down to a minority. The cautious mood of the early seventeenth century is exemplified by Samuel Daniel's attempt to strike the proper balance between reliable sources ('the best approued Monuments domesticall and forraine') and opinions sanctified by time ('we are not . . . so freed, to trafficque, all vppon our owne coniectures, without custome of tradition'); yet even Daniel was compelled to reject the authenticity of Brut completely and of Arthur tentatively.[45] This conclusion was inevitable for anyone aspiring to be 'of no other side, then of Truth', since in aiming at 'antique Originals', as John Clapham pointed out, 'a man may much more easily shoote wide, then hit the marke'.[46] Poets like Drayton and versifiers like John Taylor continued to cling to the past,[47] but among historians hesitant criticism soon grew into open rebellion, dramatically expedited by the collapse of the monarchy and the break with the past. Only two years before, in 1647, Thomas May asserted in his *History of the Parliament of England* that it was no longer 'needful to begin the Story from times of any great distance',[48] and by 1658 Francis Osborn, at the outset of his *Historical Memoires*, felt at liberty to denounce the traditional confinement to '*Patterns* and *old Forms*' and to challenge his contemporaries to '*new* and *forbidden Discoveries*'.[49] By the Restoration in 1660 William Winstanley was uncompromisingly rebuking all past historians for confounding 'naked truth' with 'ridiculous falsehoods'.[50]

III

Winstanley's denunciation of 'ridiculous falsehoods' did not constitute a revolution. As he himself must have known, it was merely the culmination of an evolutionary process to which translators of classical and humanist historians, and the critics of the 'fabulous tales' of Brut and Arthur, had each contributed a share. The rise of secular biographies as opposed to the hagiographies of the past,[51] and the fragmentation of historiography brought about by Bacon's formidable influence,[52] were also developments of importance. The revival of the cyclical view of history on the Continent too played its part, although it appeared in England under the cloak of an idea related to it. 'Mutability' was its most popular name; and the wheel was its most common metaphor, 'the euer-whirling wheele/Of *Change*, the which all mortall things doth sway'.[53] Perhaps its most forceful appearance in dramatic literature is in Marlowe's *Edward II*. Mortimer's regard of himself as one who 'makes Fortune's wheel turn as he please'[54] leads but to a bitter acknowledgement of the contrary truth:

> Base Fortune, now I see, that in thy wheel
> There is a point, to which when men aspire,
> They tumble headlong down . . .
>
> (v, vi, 59–61)

Appearances were saved so long as the gyrations of this wheel were assumed to be under the ultimate control of Providence. But more and more writers would not be so explicit, while certain others thought it was beyond their province to assume the role of a 'diuyne'. Ralph Carr's epistle dedicatory to *The Mahumetane or Turkish Historie* (1600) furnishes us with an interesting example of changing attitudes. Acknowledging the Turks to be 'the terror of the West', Carr dutifully asserted that 'God almightie in his secret iudgements doth hasten their proceedings, to chastice the ingratitude of vs Christians for the small thankefulnesse wee show for so many his gratious benefits liberally (though vnworthely) bestowed on vs'. Suddenly, however, he strikes a new note. 'But my office', he goes on, 'is not of a diuyne, hauing in purpose to make knowẽ onely what they [the Turks] haue euen from the first done, and daylie doe, rather then the reason of the deede.' Then comes the cyclical view of history: 'I am in opinion often a *Platonist*, assigning all mortall affaires necessarelie a periode in theyr perfection, to which hauing attayned, they fall into a retrograde of declining, vntill they be brought to the lowest degree which miseries can alot: nor there long continuing, againe and againe reuiue and arise from foorth the ashes like to the *Arabian*

Phœnix'. Yet the ladder whereon Jacob saw angels ascending and descending still did not topple. It held firm, for a while at least, because of individuals like Milton.

Milton did not only articulate the poetic vision we examined earlier (pp. 84 ff.). He was also a historian who endeavoured valiantly to merge the traditional and the novel. His *History of Britain*, first published in 1670,[55] was the product of the recent developments in contemporary historiography. Milton, being conscious of the admonitions of the humanists, consulted all the sources at his disposal; and he selected his material in such a diligent and constructive manner that he has been judged 'a judicious and conservative scholar'.[56] In his *History* he retained a number of the portents reported by earlier writers, but lest we are inclined to regard them as an obviously 'mediaeval' element in his work, we must remember that rarely did humanists think it wise to forgo popular superstitions. Even the critical Polydore Vergil wove into the fabric of his *Anglica historia* an overwhelming series of portents. Vergil, though not necessarily one of Milton's 'sources', constitutes one of his finest precedents. Milton not only resorted to portents but carried further Vergil's break with the annalistic form of history by writing as he did a continuous narrative. Milton's work is clearly an application of Vergil's conclusion that 'ther is nothinge more obscure, more uncertaine, or unknowne then the affaires of the Brittons from the beginninge'.[57] Milton's early plans to write an Arthurian epic are too well known for us to elaborate here.[58] Less familiar is his idea of starting with Brut:[59]

> I shall sing of the Trojan prows
> Cleaving the seas beneath the cliffs of Kent,
> And the old Kingdom that was Imogen's,
> And Arvirach, was son of Cymbeline,
> And Bren and Belin, ancient British captains,
> And the Breton coast brought under Britain's law.

Milton finally discarded both Brut and Arthur not because of any 'disillusionment' with his countrymen but because so much doubt had accumulated about 'the affaires of the Brittons from the beginninge'. As he observed in the opening sentence of his *History of Britain*, 'The beginning of Nations, those excepted of whom sacred Books have spok'n, is to this day unknown.' Here is why his *History* commences with the Roman invasion.

Milton was, however, more than a humanist, he was a *Christian* humanist endeavouring always to reconcile the novelties of the present with the august traditions of the past. He paid heed to contemporary notions without losing sight of the opinions of earlier Christian historians. Encyclopaedic as his knowledge was, he had read the contributions of every major writer up to his time, among them Isaiah, St Paul, Eusebius, Augustine, Isidore, and Bede.[60] Among historians of the Renaissance he had read particularly the 'eminent' and 'ever-renowned' Sir Walter Ralegh, one of whose works he edited.[61] So inspired, he states explicitly at the very outset of his *History* that his singular purpose was 'to relate well and orderly things worth the noting, so as may best instruct and benefit them that read'.[62] Such a purpose involved not only an extension of the traditional *exempla* but a reiteration of the providential view of history. Milton, like his great predecessors, believed that human events constitute a record of God's constant intervention in the affairs of the world. Whoever the conquerors of Britain were, whether the Romans or the Danes, they were alike agents of divine justice. Thus Milton stands heir to the Hebrew prophets, the early Christians, and the mediaeval historians.

But where Milton achieved one kind of unity, his friend Marvell achieved another.

IV

Marvell in 'An Horatian Ode upon Cromwell's Return from Ireland'[63] brilliantly utilised the mutually exclusive attitudes of historians past and present, to create a poem whose greatness resides in its elusive ambiguities. Cromwell's progress through history initially described in terms fraught with apocalyptic import:

> like the three-fork'd Lightning, first
> Breaking the Clouds where it was nurst,
> Did thorough his own Side
> His fiery way divide. . . .
> Then burning through the Air he went,
> And Pallaces and Temples rent.
> (ll. 13–16, 21–2)

Were Cromwell's cyclonic activities divinely-sanctioned? Are we to regard the *three*-forked lightning, no less than 'the Clouds where it was nurst', as an allusion to the supernatural? If so, the warning that follows seems entirely appropriate:

> 'Tis Madness to resist or blame
> The force of angry Heavens flame.
>
> (ll. 25–6)

But what if we were to regard the lightning as a merely natural phenomenon? Cromwell's self-urged 'active Star' would then be transformed into a blasphemous presumption and a blight on the created order. The warning itself, moreover, would be abruptly qualified with shattering irony:

> 'Tis Madness to resist or blame
> The force of angry Heavens flame:
> And, if we would speak true,
> Much to the Man is due. . . .
>
> (ll. 61–4)

Charles I, like Cromwell, is also placed at the outset within a supernatural context: the context of the Stuart claim concerning the divine right of kings. But as this 'right' is not invoked even at the moment of execution, the decapitation of the martyred monarch assumes the dimensions of a satanic outrage:

> Nor call'd the *Gods* with vulgar spight
> To vindicate his helpless Right,
> But bow'd his comely Head,
> Down as upon a Bed.
>
> (ll. 25–8)

But Charles is at the same time presented as an 'actor':

> thence the *Royal Actor* born
> The *Tragick Scaffold* [did] adorn:
> While round the armed Bands
> Did clap their bloody hands.
> *He* nothing common did or mean
> Upon that memorable Scene:
> But with his keener Eye
> The Axes edge did try.
>
> (ll. 53–60)

The ironic implications are inescapable. The performance of
Charles may have been the finest of his entire reign; but it was
also his last. More important still, the royal performance was not
initiated by Charles: the stage was set, and the tragedy was
directed, by Cromwell. True, the calculated defiance of the
monarch's 'keener Eye' trying the axe's edge is an obvious attempt
to elicit the reader's admiration. But it may also be a recollection
of the execution of Sir Walter Ralegh, himself victim of the injustice of Charles's father. Ralegh's final moments were widely
reported:[64]

> putting off his doublet, and gowne, he desired the
> headsman to shew him the Axe, which not being suddenly
> granted unto him, he said I prithee, let me see it, dost
> thou thinke that I am afraid of it, so being given unto
> him, he felt along upon the edge of it, and smiling, spake
> unto M. Sheriffe saying, this is a sharpe medecine, but it
> is a physician that will cure all diseases.

'The ghost of Ralegh', a modern historian remarks, 'pursued the
House of Stuart to the scaffold.'[65] Did Marvell concur?

The 'Horatian Ode' as a study of the clash of mighty opposites
might have sanctioned the providential theory of history. But
Marvell was aware that the theory was simultaneously espoused
by republicans in connection with Cromwell, and by royalists
in connection with Charles. Truth – the truth of reality – transcended either partisan claim; and therefore the poem's final lines
appear to celebrate Cromwell even as they proclaim the alarming
ambiguities of the historical process:

> But thou the Wars and Fortunes Son
> March indefatigably on;
> And for the last effect
> Still keep thy Sword erect:
> Besides the force it has to fright
> The Spirits of the shady Night,
> The same *Arts* that did *gain*
> A *Pow'r* must it maintain.

The sombre sound of 'indefatigably', the sinister implications of
'last effect', the allusion of the erect sword to the crusader's zeal
no less than to the tyrant's weapon, merge with the intentional

ambiguity of the last two lines to affirm that the humanist search for truth – 'without respect of face or person'[66] – leads invariably to reality, even to painful, brutal reality.

Notes

1 'To the Reader', in Sir Roger Williams, *The Actions of the Lowe Countries* (1618). The statement is quoted in part by F. P. Wilson, *Elizabethan and Jacobean* (Oxford, 1945), p. 25.

2 But unlike her successor, she published none of her labours. See *Queen Elizabeth's Englishings*, ed. Caroline Pemberton, EETS: OS, cxiii (1899).

3 The classic study is by F. O. Matthiessen, *Translation: An Elizabethan Art* (Cambridge, Mass., 1931). See further O. L. Hatcher, 'Aims and Methods of Elizabethan Translators', *Englische Studien*, xliv (1912), 174–92; Flora R. Amos, *Early Theories of Translation* (1920), ch. iii; Carey H. Conley, *The First English Translators of the Classics* (New Haven, 1927); Charles Whibley, *Literary Studies* (1919), pp. 60–111; Louis B. Wright, 'Translations for the Elizabethan Middle Class', *The Library*, 4th series, xiii (1932–3), 312–31; Henry B. Lathrop, *Translations from the Classics into English from Caxton to Chapman*, University of Wisconsin Studies in Language and Literature, xxxv (Madison, 1933); cf. H. S. Bennett, *English Books and Readers 1558 to 1603* (Cambridge, 1965), ch. iv.

4 Wrote Scaliger: 'Sed de Iosepho nos hoc audacter dicimus, non solum in rebus Iudaicis, sed etiam in externis tutius illi credi, quam omnibus Græcis, & Latinis. Itaque desinat mirari doctus vir, cur tot eruditi, & nos quoque, qui non in illis eruditis, sed huius scriptoris lectione peregrini non sumus, tantum illi deferamus, cuius fides & eruditio in omnibus elucet' (*Opvs de emendatione temporvm*, 2nd rev. ed. [Leyden, 1598], Prolegomena, sigs γ2^v–γ3). But the famous passage on Jesus (above, p. 40, note 4) was already beginning to be regarded as an interpolation. On the ensuing controversy, see Gustav A. Müller, *Christus bei Josephus* (Innsbruck, 1890); Leon Bernstein, *Flavius Josephus* (1938), ch. xi; and esp. Friedrich H. Schoedel, *Flavivs Iosephvs de Iesv testatvs* (Leipzig, 1840). In general, Renaissance England did not question what Donald Lupton called Josephus's 'famous Testimony of our Lord' (*The Glory of their Times* [1640], p. 13); Lodge himself accepted the 'testimony' without comment.

5 Catholics were no less imaginative: an anonymous translation of *The Ecclesiasticall History of Theodoret* ([St Omer], 1612) was made in order to prove that the early Christians were 'quite contrary to the reformed faith of the Protestants'.

6 Unlike their Continental brethren, English Renaissance publishers failed to issue even the Latin texts of Sulpicius and Orosius. Salvian was published only once (Oxford, 1629); later, he was also the first to be translated into English (1700).

7 Convenient lists are available in Conley and Lathrop (above, note 3); but

see esp. Henrietta R. Palmer, *List of English Editions and Translations of Greek and Latin Classics printed before 1641* (1911). A comparative list of translations into English, French, German, Italian and Spanish (to 1600) is provided by R. R. Bolgar, *The Classical Heritage and its Beneficiaries* (Cambridge, 1954), App. II.

8 Napoleone Orsini, *Studii sul Rinascimento italiano in Inghilterra* (Florence, 1937), ch. i, and 'Elizabethan Manuscript Translations of Machiavelli's *Prince*', *JWCI*, i (1937–8), 166–9; one of these versions has been edited by Hardin Craig (Chapel Hill, 1944).

9 *The Pathway to Honovr* (1612), pp. 26–7. Numerous references to studies of the Machiavelli legend during the Renaissance are given by Irving Ribner, 'The Significance of Gentilet's *Contre-Machiavel*', *MLQ*, x (1949), 153–7; but see esp. Mario Praz, *The Flaming Heart* (1958), pp. 90–145, and George L. Mosse, *The Holy Pretence* (Oxford, 1957). There is an extensive bibliography in Chabod (above, p. 68, note 78), pp. 201–47.

10 As was to be expected, Hobbes's translation of Thucydides was preparatory to the formulation of his political philosophy; see Richard Schlatter, 'Thomas Hobbes and Thucydides', *JHI*, vi (1945), 350–62. Hobbes's view of history is discussed by Leo Strauss, *The Political Philosophy of Hobbes*, trans. E. M. Sinclair (Oxford, 1936), ch. vi; the only substantial study of seventeenth-century reactions to Hobbes is by Samuel I. Mintz, *The Hunting of Leviathan* (Cambridge, 1962).

11 Boece's work was first published in 1527; Bellenden's Scots version (c. 1537) was translated into English by William Harrison for Holinshed's *Chronicles* (1577), ii. The work ('a palpably false history') is discussed by J. B. Black, 'Boece's *Scotorum Historiae*', in *Quatercentenary of the Death of Hector Boece* (Aberdeen, 1937), pp. 30–53; R. W. Chambers and Walter W. Seton, 'Bellenden's Translation of the History of Hector Boece', *SHR*, xvii (1919), 5–15; and Kendrick (below, note 15), pp. 65 ff.

12 *The First Five Books of the Roman History* (Edinburgh, 1822); later re-edited for the Scottish Text Society by A. W. Craig (Edinburgh, 1901–3), 2 vols.

13 *The Romane Historie written by T. Livivs* (1600), 'To the Reader'. Holland made a similar observation concerning Suetonius: 'hee seemeth to affect nothing so much as uncorrupt & plaine trueth, (the principall vertue of an Historiographer)' (*The Historie of Twelve Cæsars* [1606], 'To the Reader').

14 Part of Cicero's celebrated 'definition' of history in *De oratore*, ii, 9 ('historia vero testis temporum, lux veritatis, vita memoriæ, magistra vitæ, nuntia vetustatis'). Misreadings of this 'definition' over the ages could provide an interesting study of the changing historiographical assumptions. It is quoted at the outset of Vincent of Beauvais's *Speculum historiale* (above, p. 42, note 25) as readily as on the engraved title page of Ralegh's *History of the World* (reproduced in my edition [1971] with the explanatory verses by Ben Jonson).

15 The material available on Arthur can only be approached through bibliographies, notably John J. Parry, *A Bibliography of Arthurian Critical Literature* (1931 ff.), and the *Bulletin bibliographique de la Société Internationale Arthurienne* (Paris, 1949 ff.). But the following studies are pertinent to our purposes: Edwin Greenlaw, *Studies in Spenser's Historical Allegory* (Cambridge, Mass.,

1932), ch. i; Charles B. Millican, *Spenser and the Table Round* (Cambridge, Mass., 1932); E. K. Chambers, *Arthur of Britain* (1927), ch. iv; Roberta F. Brinkley, *Arthurian Legend in the Seventeenth Century* (Baltimore, 1932); Ernest Jones, *Geoffrey of Monmouth 1640–1800*, UCE, v (1944), pp. 357–77; and T. D. Kendrick, *British Antiquity* (1950). John Leland's great defence of Arthur is also readily accessible: *Assertio inclytissimi Arturii* (1544), trans. Richard Robinson (1582), ed. William A. Mead, EETS: OS, clxv (1925). By contrast, the only study exclusively concerned with Brut is the delightful essay by George Gordon, 'The Trojans in Britain', *E&S*, ix (1924), 9–30, (revised in his *Discipline of Letters* [Oxford, 1946], pp. 35–58); but Kendrick has also collected much valuable information (op. cit., chs iii, vi, vii *passim*), and S. K. Heninger, Jr, has written on 'The Tudor Myth of Troy-novant', *SAQ*, lxi (1962), 378–87. For two more specialised studies, see A. E. Parsons, 'The Trojan Legend in England: Some Instances of its Application to the Politics of the Times', *MLR*, xxiv (1929), 253–64, 394–408, and Sydney Anglo, 'The *British History* in Early Tudor Propaganda', *BJRL*, xliv (1961), 17–48. The ground covered by Parsons is less satisfactorily surveyed by E. M. W. Tillyard, *Some Mythical Elements in English Literature* (1961), ch. iii (2).

16 Ed. Acton Griscom (1929); trans. Sebastian Evans (1904). The best study of the work and its influence is by J. S. P. Tatlock, *The Legendary History of Britain* (Berkeley, 1950). But see also Robert W. Hanning, *The Vision of History in Early Britain* (1966), ch. v.

17 Notwithstanding the severe attacks on Geoffrey by his contemporaries William of Newburgh and Giraldus Cambrensis (James Gairdner, *England* [1883], pp. 167 f.). See further Laura Keeler, *Geoffrey of Monmouth and the Late Latin Chroniclers, 1300–1500*, UCE, xvii (1946).

18 Henry of Huntington, *Historia anglorum*, ed. Thomas Arnold, RB (1879); Walter of Coventry, *Historical Collections*, ed. William Stubbs, RB (1872–3), 2 vols.

19 *The Story of England*, ed. Frederick J. Furnivall, RB (1887), 2 vols. Typical of the numerous other abbreviated versions is *An Anonymous Short Metrical Chronicle*, ed. Ewald Zettl, EETS: OS, cxvi (1935).

20 Among the accounts in prose: the anonymous *Le livere de reis de Brittanie* and *Le livere de reis de Engletere*, ed. and trans. John Glover, RB (1865); John of Wavrin, *Recueil des croniques et auchiennes istories de la Grand Bretaigne*, ed. and trans. William Hardy, RB (1864–91), 8 vols; and *Brut d'Engleterre*, the translation of which has been edited by F. W. D. Brie, *The Brut*, EETS: OS, cxxxi (1906) and cxxxvi (1908). The metrical versions include *The Chronicle of Pierre de Langtoft*, ed. Thomas Wright, RB (1866–8), 2 vols. For a rare visual representation of Brut's arrival in Britain, see the Flemish tapestry (*c.* 1475) now at the Cathedral in Saragossa, reproduced by Heinrich Göbel, *Wandteppiche, I: Die Nederlande* (Leipzig, 1923–34), part ii, plate 225.

21 *The Historie of Scotland*, trans. James Dalrymple, ed. E. G. Cody (Edinburgh, 1888), vol. i, p. 5. Dalrymple's version (1596) was made from Lesley's *De origine, moribus, et rebus gentis scotorum* (Rome, 1579). For another Scots account of Brut, see Andrew of Wyntoun (above, p. 44, note 52), vol. ii, pp. 126–7.

22 John E. Housman, 'Higden, Trevisa, Caxton, and the Beginnings of Arthurian Criticism', *RES*, xxiii (1947), 209–17.

23 Gilmore (above, p. 67, note 65), p. 15.

24 *The Pastyme of People* (1529), 'Prologus'. Among 'other pepull' besides Continental writers who later attacked Brut was George Buchanan, who branded the legend 'the most notorious and impudent Falshood' (*Rerum scoticarum historia* [Edinburgh, 1582; trans., 1690], p. 41). But all Scots writers did not react the same way (as Gordon suggests [above, note 15], 21–2). Besides Lesley, the story of Brut was regarded as authentic by Boece (*The Hystory and Croniklis of Scotland*, trans. John Bellenden [Edinburgh, 1537?], sig. B1) and by John Major (*Historia Maioris Britanniæ* [1521], trans. Archibald Constable, Publications of the Scottish History Society [Edinburgh, 1892], x, p. 3).

25 Basle, 1534; revised in 1546, 1555. A translation made in the later sixteenth century has been edited by Sir Henry Ellis, *Polydore Vergil's English History* (1844–6), 2 vols; books xxvi–vii, covering the period from 1485 to 1537, ed. and trans. Denys Hay (1950). The best study is by Denys Hay, *Polydore Vergil: Renaissance Historian and Man of Letters* (Oxford, 1952).

26 For a more reasoned defence of Brut, see Sir John Price, *Historiae brytannicae defensio* (1573), pp. 40 ff.

27 *Sir Gawain and the Green Knight*, l, 13.

28 For example, the anonymous *A Breuiat Chronicle, contaynyng all the Kynges, from Brute to this day* (1551) reached, within a decade, a ninth revised edition. Inevitably, there were Latin versions as well: 'E.S.', *De rebus gestis Britanniæ commentarioli tres* (1570?).

29 *A Summarie of Englyshe Chronicles* (1565), pp. 9 ff.

30 *The First Volume of the Chronicles* (1577), p. 9.

31 Given in III, ix, 38 ff. See further: C. A. Harper, *The Sources of the British Chronicle History of Spenser's Faerie Queene* (Philadelphia, 1910), partially reprinted with other pertinent material in *The Works of Edmund Spenser*, variorum ed. (Baltimore, 1933), pp. 449–55; and particularly Isabel E. Rathborne, *The Meaning of Spenser's Fairyland* (1937), esp. ch. ii *passim*. Cf. also above, note 15.

32 Thomas Nashe, *The Terrors of the Night* (1594), sig. F3ᵛ, and Henry Peacham, *The Compleat Gentleman* (1622), p. 51, respectively.

33 *Britain*, trans. Philemon Holland (1637), p. 6. See the estimates by Sir Maurice Powicke, 'William Camden', *E&S*, n.s., i (1948), 67–84; Stuart Piggott, 'William Camden and the *Britannia*', *PBA*, xxxvii (1951), 199–217; F. J. Levy, 'The Making of Camden's *Britannia*', *BHR*, xxvi (1964), 70–97; F. Smith Fussner, *The Historical Revolution* (1962), ch. ix; Kendrick (above, note 15), ch. viii; and more generally: H. R. Trevor-Roper's lecture, *Queen Elizabeth's First Historian: William Camden and the Beginning of English Civil History* (1971).

34 See Denys Hay, *Europe: The Emergence of an Idea* (Edinburgh, 1957), pp. 48 f., 108 f. As Professor Hay rightly points out, the idea of a common Trojan origin contributed – 'in its odd fashion' – to the unity of European society (p. 109).

35 Lisbon means, literally, 'the port of Ulysses'. The legend of its foundation is

recounted by Camões, *Os Lusíadas*, VIII, v, 1–4. On the other hand, the seemingly endless hordes of Trojan refugees somehow managed to reach Portugal as well. A peninsula south-east of Lisbon is called, to this day, Tróia.

36 The belief stretched to the late fifteenth century, both in popular compilations like Nicole Gilles's *Annales* and more sophisticated works like Robert Gaguin's *Compendium de origine et gestis francorum* (Paris, 1495); both cited by Huppert (next note). See also the first page of the *Croniques de France* (1477) – the first book in French to be printed in Paris – reproduced in *The Age of the Renaissance*, ed. Denys Hay (1967), p. 169.

37 On the rise and fall of the Trojan legend in France, see the classic study by A. Joly, *Benoit de Sainte-More et le Roman de Troie* (Paris, 1870–1), ch. viii, as well as Maria Klippel, *Die Darstellung der Fränkischen Trojanersage* (Marburg, 1936), and George Huppert, 'The Trojan Franks and their Critics', *SRen*, xii (1965), 227–41.

38 *Histoire generale d'Espagna* (1586); trans. Edward Grimeston, *The Generall Historie of Spain* (1612), p. 1.

39 *La Franciade* was to have been six times as long as it is; but Ronsard's hero never even reached the promised shores of France. *Les qvatre premiers livres de la Franciade* (Paris, 1572) was stillborn.

40 *Inventaire general de l'histoire de France*, 1st complete ed. (Paris, 1600); trans. Edward Grimeston, *A General Inventorie of the Historie of France* (1607), sig. A4.

41 *Apologie* (Paris, 1625); trans. John Davies of Kidwelly, *The History of Magick* (1657), p. 10.

42 *The History of Great Britaine* (1611), p. 164. But lest we think of Speed as unduly 'modern', we should remember that he accepted the legend of Joseph of Arimathea's sojourn in Britain as authentic.

43 Richard Harvey, *Philadelphvs, or a Defence of Brutes, and the Brutans History* (1593), p. 2.

44 Edmund Howes, 'An Historical Preface' to his continuation of Stow's *Annales* (1631). Francis Godolphin made much the same point, though he also acknowledged that '*Polydore Virgill* in the opinion of most excelleth' (*Annales of England*, trans. Morgan Godwin [1630], 'The Avthovrs Preface'). But the prejudice against Vergil persisted; as late as 1663 he was still viewed by some as a 'man not much to be trusted for his relation of English affairs' (Edward Leigh, *Fœlix consortium* [1663], p. 354).

45 *The First Part of the Historie of England* (1612), p. 2. See further May McKisack, 'Samuel Daniel as Historian', *RES*, xxiii (1947), 226–43, and Rudolf B. Gottfried, 'Samuel Daniel's Method of Writing History', *SRen*, iii (1956), 157–74. Cf. Seronsy, below, note 53.

46 *The Historie of Great Britannie* (1606), p. 2, which accordingly begins with the Roman invasion.

47 Song 1 of Drayton's *Poly-Olbion* (1612; completed 1622) contains a lengthy account of Brut, with a prose commentary in his defence (cf. also above, p. 74). John Taylor the Water Poet produced *A Memorial of all the English Monarchs . . . from Brute* (1662).

48 *The History of the Parliament of England* (1647) begins, accordingly, with the

reign of Elizabeth; and after a brief survey of the conditions under her successor, it dwells capitally on the rise of parliamentary power under Charles I.

49 *Historical Memoires* (1658), 'The Epistle'.

50 *England's Worthies* (1660), p. 8. Winstanley is specifically referring to Arthurian legends; he did not even condescend to mention Brut. Fifteen years later Sir Winston Churchill in *Divi Britannici* (1675), pp. 51–2, was significantly indifferent about the legend of Brut ('I leave it to the free Censure of each Reader').

51 Donald A. Stauffer, *English Biography before 1700* (Cambridge, Mass., 1930); F. P. Wilson, *Seventeenth Century Prose* (Berkeley, 1960), ch. iii.

52 *Of the Proficience and Advancement of Learning* (1605), book ii; *The Historie of the Raigne of King Henry the Seuenth* (1622). See the estimates by F. J. C. Hearnshaw, 'Bacon as Historian', *CR*, cxxiii (1923), 606–14; Wilhelm Busch, *England under the Tudors*, trans. A. M. Todd (1895), vol. i, pp. 416–23; Leonard F. Dean, 'Sir Francis Bacon's Theory of Civil History-Writing', *ELH*, viii (1941), 161–83; Vincent Luciani, 'Bacon and Guicciardini', *PMLA*, xlii (1947), 96–113; Thomas Wheeler, 'The Purpose of Bacon's *History of Henry the Seventh*', *SP*, liv (1957), 1–13, and 'Bacon's Henry VII as a Machiavellian Prince', *Renaissance Papers 1957* (Durham, N.C., 1957), pp. 111–17; and Fussner (above, note 33), ch. x.

53 *The Faerie Queene*, VII, i, 1–2; see further Samuel C. Chew, *The Pilgrimage of Life* (New Haven, 1962), ch. iii. On the 'cyclical' view of history during the Renaissance, see – in addition to the studies cited above (p. 68, note 73) – Samuel C. Chew, 'Time and Fortune', *ELH*, vi (1939), 83–113; Ernest L. Tuveson, *Millennium and Utopia* (Berkeley, 1949), pp. 56–75; Raymond Chapman, 'The Wheel of Fortune in Shakespeare's Historical Plays', *RES*, n.s., i (1950), 1–7, and 'Fortune and Mutability in Elizabethan Literature', *CJ*, v (1952), 374–82; Hiram Haydn, *The Counter-Renaissance* (1950), pp. 428 ff.; Herschel Baker, *The Wars of Truth* (1952), pp. 65 ff.; Cecil C. Seronsy, 'The Doctrine of Cyclical Recurrence and Some Related Ideas in the Works of Samuel Daniel', *SP*, liv (1957), 387–407; Joseph A. Mazzeo, *Renaissance and Revolution* (1965), ch. ii; and Herbert Weisinger, 'Ideas of History during the Renaissance', in *Renaissance Essays*, ed. Paul O. Kristeller and Philip P. Wiener (1968), ch. iii.

54 *Edward II*, v, ii, 55. Cf. *Tamburlaine 1*: 'I hold the Fates bound fast in iron chains,/And with my hand turn Fortune's wheel about' (I, ii, 174–5).

55 Ed. French Fogle, in *Complete Prose Works* (New Haven, 1971), vol. v, part i. Lloyd S. Berry suggests (in *RES*, n.s., xi [1960], 150–6) that Milton's *History* was probably written *c.* 1632–8.

56 Harry Glicksman, *The Sources of Milton's 'History of Britain'*, University of Wisconsin Studies in Language and Literature, xi (1921), p. 140. In addition to Glicksman's study, see especially Sir Charles Firth, 'Milton as an Historian', *PBA*, iii (1908–9), 227–57 (reprinted in his *Essays Historical and Literary* [Oxford, 1938], pp. 61–102); but also J. Milton French, 'Milton as a Historian', *PMLA*, l (1935), 469–79; Ernest Sirluck, 'Milton's Critical Use of Historical Sources: An Illustration', *MP*, l (1953), 226–31; Constance Nicholas, *Introduction and Notes to Milton's 'History of Britain'*, Illinois Studies

in Language and Literature, xliv (1957); Harris F. Fletcher, *The Intellectual Development of John Milton* (Urbana, 1961), vol. ii, pp. 323–36; French R. Fogle, 'Milton as Historian', in *Milton and Clarendon*, by Fogle and H. R. Trevor-Roper (Los Angeles, 1965), pp. 1–20; Merritt Y. Hughes, 'Milton's Treatment of Reformation History in *The Tenure of Kings and Magistrates*', in his *Ten Perspectives on Milton* (New Haven, 1965), ch. ix; Michael Landon, 'John Milton's *History of Britain*: its Place in English Historiography', *UMSE*, vi (1965), 59–76; and Irene Samuel, 'Milton and the Ancients on the Writing of History', *Milton Studies*, ii (1970), 131–48. On Milton's other historical work, the *Brief History of Moscovia*, see in particular Robert R. Cawley, *Milton's Literary Craftsmanship* (Princeton, 1941), and John B. Gleason, 'The Nature of Milton's *Moscovia*', *SP*, lxi (1964), 640–9.

57 *English History*, ed. Sir Henry Ellis from a late sixteenth-century anonymous translation (1844), vol, i, p. 33.

58 The best account of Milton's gradual revision of his plans is by Roberta F. Brinkley, *Arthurian Legend in the Seventeenth Century* (Baltimore, 1932), pp. 126–41.

59 *Epitaphium Damonis*, ll. 162–5; from Helen Wadell's free but admirable translation, reprinted in *Milton's 'Lycidas': The Tradition and the Poem*, ed. C. A. Patrides (1961), p. 24.

60 But also an incredible array of other historians; see the discussion by William R. Parker, *Milton* (Oxford, 1968), pp. 145 ff., and the favourite historians enumerated by Ruth Mohl, *John Milton and his Commonplace Book* (1969). Cf. Constance Nicholas, 'The Editions of the Early Church Historians used by Milton', *JEGP*, li (1952), 160–2.

61 *The Cabinet-Council* (1658), which is not in fact by Ralegh (cf. E. A. Strathmann, *TLS*, 1956, p. 228). Significantly, the work bears Machiavelli's imprint all too clearly; see Nadja Kempner, *Raleghs staatstheoretische Schriften* (Leipzig, 1928), pp. 32 ff., 62 ff.

62 In Fogle's edition (above, note 55), p. 4.

63 In *Poems and Letters*, ed. H. M. Margoliouth, 2nd ed. (Oxford, 1952), vol. i, pp. 87–90. Throughout the italics are Marvell's.

64 Sir Thomas Overbury, *The Arraignment and Conviction of Sr Walter Rawleigh* (1648), p. 34.

65 G. M. Trevelyan, *History of England*, 3rd ed. (1945), p. 388.

66 Philemon Holland, quoted above, p. 102.

Seven

Restatements in the New World

... a body of divinity in an entire new method, being
thrown into the form of a history; considering the
affair of Christian theology, as the whole of it, in each
part, stands in reference to the great work of redemption
by Jesus Christ; which I suppose to be of all others the
grand design of God, and the *summum* and *ultimum* of
all the divine operations and decrees; particularly considering all parts of the grand scheme in their historical
order.

JONATHAN EDWARDS
on his *History of the Work of Redemption*[1]

I

Spain's conquest of the New World was achieved on the physical
level by brute force, and on the metaphysical level by millennial
expectations. Columbus himself was evidently affected by an
apocalyptic interpretation of history not entirely unconnected
with Joachimist 'prophecies'.[2] In time, however, the initial
optimism was arrested as the Spanish Empire eventually declined
and fell. But the great expectations survived to be inherited by
another group of optimists, the sojourners in New England in
1620.[3]

The events in New England from 1620 to 1647 are recounted
in William Bradford's *Of Plimmoth Plantation*.[4] The work is not
necessarily history; much less is it literature. But as an application
of the providential theory of history to developments in New
England, it heralds the extension of the traditional view across
the Atlantic and anticipates two somewhat more substantial
productions, Cotton Mather's *Magnalia Christi Americana* and

Jonathan Edwards's *A History of the Work of Redemption*. The centre of gravity is not always the same, witness Edward Taylor's metrical history of Christianity which is largely a paraphrase of the *Magdeburg Centuries*.[5] Generally speaking, however, the historians of New England remained heavily indebted to the cumulative voices of their European predecessors, notably St Augustine, who appears yet again 'like Teneriff or Atlas unremoved'.

New England under the guidance of Providence was transformed by the later seventeenth century into the Holy Commonwealth, the temporal zenith of an eternal design.[6] The development is celebrated in Cotton Mather's *Magnalia Christi Americana* (1702), an ambitious performance cast in the form of an epic and written in an anachronistic baroque style. Its vast circumference gathers echoes of the *Aeneid* as well as of *Paradise Lost*, not least in terms of the 'heroic' theme announced in the opening lines with appropriate magniloquence:[7]

> I write the WONDERS of the CHRISTIAN RELIGION, flying from the depravations of Europe, to the American Strand; and, assisted by the Holy Author of that Religion, I do with all conscience of Truth, required therein by Him, who is Truth itself, report the wonderful displays of His infinite Power, Wisdom, Goodness, and Faithfulness, wherewith His Divine Providence hath irradiated an Indian Wilderness.

Unlike *Paradise Lost*, the *Magnalia* asserts that the lost Eden has been regained within history, replanted by God in the Garden of America. Like *Paradise Lost*, on the other hand, Mather's prose epic not only endorses the providential theory of history: it is also eschatologically oriented, in that Mather envisages the newly elect of God advancing steadily beyond mighty victories over demonic forces toward the consummation of history at the Last Judgement. The work has been hailed as 'perhaps the supreme achievement of American Puritan literature'. It has also been called 'a showcase of pedantry and elephantine wit'.[8]

Jonathan Edwards's *A History of the Work of Redemption* was initially delivered as a series of sermons in 1739, just as the Great Awakening was approaching the apex of its emotional frenzy. Edwards himself described his labour as 'a body of divinity in an

entire new method', and at least one modern scholar has since
agreed that it is indeed 'entirely novel'.⁹ But it is not. The general
pattern 'from the fall of man to the end of the world'¹⁰ is thoroughly
traditional. The details also draw on earlier claims, whether in
connection with the division of universal history into three
periods, or the affirmation that the promise of the Seed – the 'first
gospel' – was 'like the first glimmerings of the light of the Sun in
the east when the day first dawns'.¹¹ The emphasis, however, is
often rather different. The *History* is much more distinctly Christocentric than was common in the standard surveys of history's
progress under God. Millenarian expectations – 'chiliasm in its
starkest form'¹² – are also unusually emphatic, however insistently
Edwards may have upheld the Last Judgement. Yet when all is
said the pattern remains firmly cemented to traditional modes of
thought. For Edwards, as for his predecessors, history reveals a
providential design that 'was begun soon after the fall, and is
carried on through all the ages of the world, and finished at the
end of the world'.¹³

II

Edwards's *History* was first published in London in 1774. An English
reviewer promptly dismissed it with contempt: 'It is merely an
attempt to revive the old mystical divinity that distracted the last
age with pious conundrums: and which, having, long ago, emi-
grated to America, we have no reason to wish should ever be im-
ported back again'.¹⁴ The *History* was evidently published an age
too late. But the reviewer's implied claim that the enlightened
thinkers of the eighteenth century had already dismantled the
traditional theory is a claim which is not supported by facts. As we
shall note in the next chapter, the Christian view of history was
not so much dismantled as rebuilt anew. In colonial America,
on the other hand, the original structure remained clearly recog-
nisable, and provided the foundation of the Republic created in
1776.

The idealistic founders of the United States borrowed two
fundamental aspects of the Christian view of history. The first was
the idea of progress ever-present in the traditional vision of history.
Stripped of its Christocentric burden, however, it was merged
with the widespread millennial expectations so enthusiastically

articulated by Edwards, to produce the distinctly American concept of 'manifest destiny'. The teleological optimism of the new Republic's Constitution, and especially its Bill of Rights, appeals in the end to the persistent belief that salvation is to be attained within history under the aegis of the United States. As reflected in actual events, 'manifest destiny' supplied the metaphysical justification for America's expansion westwards during the nineteenth century. On the domestic scene, moreover, it contributed to the missionary zeal with which the Republic engaged in its Civil War; while later, on the international front, it informed America's enthusiastic participation in the Great War.[15]

But American expectations were gradually reshaped on the anvil of reality. Immediately following the two World Wars in particular, adverse developments hammered the idea of progressive perfection into airy thinness.[16] The immediate literary response appears to have been pessimistic in the extreme, but the lingering American dream never ceased to exert its potent influence. In twentieth-century literature the path leads from the bleak landscape of *The Waste Land* to the orchestrated tones of the *Four Quartets*.[17]

Notes

1 Letter to the Trustees of the College at Princeton, 19 October 1757; in *The Works of President Edwards* (1844–7), vol. i, p. 50.
2 Consult John L. Phelan, *The Millennial Kingdom of the Franciscans in the New World*, 2nd rev. ed. (Berkeley, 1970).
3 See David E. Smith's bibliographical survey, 'Millenarian Scholarship in America', *AQ*, xvii (1965), 535–49. Other available studies are surveyed by Richard S. Dunn, 'Seventeenth-Century English Historians of America', in *Seventeenth-Century America*, ed. J. M. Smith (Chapel Hill, 1959), pp. 195–225; B. D. Bargar, 'Seventeenth Century America: An Historiographic View', in *Historical Essays 1600–1750 presented to David Ogg* (1963), pp. 131–56; and Gay (next note), pp. 119–57. The following may be particularly recommended: Perry Miller, *The New England Mind: The Seventeenth Century* (Cambridge, Mass., 1939), ch. xvi; *idem*, with Thomas H. Johnson, *The Puritans* (1938), ch. i; Kenneth B. Murdock, *Literature and Theology in Colonial New England* (Cambridge, Mass., 1949), ch. iii, and 'Clio in the Wilderness: History and Biography in Puritan New England', *CH*, xxiv (1955), 221–38; Edward K. Trefz, 'The Puritans' View of History', *Boston Public Library Quarterly*, ix (1957), 115–36; Larzer Ziff, *The Career of John*

Restatements in the New World

Cotton (Princeton, 1962), esp. ch. viii; and the studies by Gay (next note) and Buchanan (note 15).

4 See Peter Gay, *A Loss of Mastery: Puritan Historians in Colonial America* (Berkeley, 1966), ch. ii, which also provides full bibliographical details.

5 See Donald E. Standford, 'Edward Taylor's Metrical History of Christianity', *AL*, xxxiii (1961), 279–95. Taylor's verses were never published; which is just as well. On the *Magdeburg Centuries*, see above, p. 52.

6 See Sacvan Bercovitch, 'New England Epic: Cotton Mather's *Magnalia Christi Americana*', *ELH*, xxxiii (1966), 337–50, and Peter Gay, *A Loss of Mastery* (Berkeley, 1966), ch. iii; my own account is fully indebted to the former. On the rise of the Holy Commonwealth, consult Herbert W. Schneider, *The Puritan Mind* (1930), ch. i.

7 Quoted by Bercovitch (ibid.) from the edition by Thomas Robbins (Hartford, Conn., 1853), 2 vols.

8 Bercovitch and Gay (above, note 4), respectively. See further Austin Warren, 'Dr. Cotton Mather's *Magnalia*', in his *Connections* (Ann Arbor, 1970), pp. 24–44.

9 See the quotation opening this chapter, above, p. 119. The scholar alluded to is Perry Miller; see his *Jonathan Edwards* (1949; repr. 1959), p. 307.

10 *A History of the Work of Redemption*, 1st American ed. (1786), p. 28. The text is also available in *Works* (1844–7), vol. i, pp. 293–516. See the estimates by Miller (as in the previous note), pp. 307–30; Gay (note 4), ch. iv; and Edward H. Davidson, *Jonathan Edwards: The Narrative of a Puritan Mind* (Cambridge, Mass., 1968), ch. iv.

11 Ibid., p. 45. On the 'first gospel', see above, p. 89.

12 Miller (note 9). The point is also stressed by C. C. Goen, 'Jonathan Edwards: A New Departure in Eschatology', *CH*, xxviii (1959), 25–40.

13 *Works* (1844–7), vol. i, p. 304.

14 *The Monthly Review*, lii (Jan.–June 1775), 117–20, quoted by Gay (Note 4), p. 117.

15 The preceding remarks are based on the arguments of John G. Buchanan, 'Puritan Philosophy from Restoration to Revolution', *Essex Institute Historical Collections*, civ (1968), 329–48; Frederick Merk, *Manifest Destiny and Mission in American History* (1963); and Timothy L. Smith, *Revivalism and Social Reform: American Protestantism on the Eve of the Civil War* (1957, repr. 1965). On the background to American millennial thought, see above, p. 27, note 57, and also Ernest L. Tuveson, *Redeemer Nation: The Idea of America's Millennial Role* (Chicago, 1968). The changing patterns in American historiography since the 1830s are examined by David W. Noble, *Historians against History* (Minneapolis, 1965).

16 See the surveys on 'The Idea of Progress' by Guy A. Cardwell, Louis J. Budd, John T. Flanagan, and Everett Carter, in *Georgia Review*, xi (1957), 271–97.

17 See below, pp. 134–5. Philip E. Williams, in 'The Biblical View of History: Hawthorne, Mark Twain, Faulkner, and Eliot', *Dissertation Abstracts*, xxv (1965), 4159–60, discusses 'the dialectic of time and eternity from a perspective on history' in *The Scarlet Letter*, *Huckleberry Finn*, *Absalom, Absalom!*, and the *Four Quartets*.

Eight

The Aftermath

all things dying each other's life,
living each other's death.

W. B. YEATS[1]

I

The Christian view of history declined in Europe much earlier than it did in America. Milton's espousal of the traditional outlook marks, indeed, the termination of an era in the history of European thought. Some poets persisted, stubbornly; but inspiration invariably failed them, witness Charles Perrault's *Adam* (1692–7), which is a sweeping but less than persuasive universal history from the creation to the Last Judgement,[2] or Sir Richard Blackmore's *Creation* (1712) and *Redemption* (1722), which are essentially polemical treatises accidentally cast in verse form. Blackmore was rightly dismissed by Pope as a versifier 'Who sings so loudly, and who sings so long'.[3]

It was far otherwise in prose, however. The Christian view of history was reiterated, however tangentially, in Bunyan's *Pilgrim's Progress* (1678), even as it was elegantly argued in France by Bishop Jacques Bossuet (1627–1704), whose *Discours sur l'histoire universelle* was published in Paris in 1681 and translated into English five years later. Bossuet's starting-point is once again the act of creation as described by Moses, 'the most ancient of Historians, the most sublime of Philosophers, and the wisest of Legislators'; and once again the providential theory of history is expounded with the assurance of a latter-day disciple of St Augustine, with whose thought Bossuet was 'thoroughly saturated'.[4] Accordingly, in Bossuet's demonstration of the way that 'the Empires of the world have ministred to Religion', we seem to be listening once again to the voice of St Augustine – and beyond him, to the voices of the great prophets, particularly Isaiah:[5]

Empires have for the most part a necessary Connexion to the History of the People of God. God was served by the *Assyrians* and the *Babylonians* to chastise that People; by the *Persians*, to re-establish them; by *Alexander* and his his first Successors, to protect them; by *Antiochus* the Illustrious and his Successors, to exercise them; by the *Romans*, to maintain their Liberty against the Kings of *Syria*, who made it their whole Business to destroy them. The *Jews* continued unto *Jesus Christ* under the Power of those very *Romans*. When they had ungratefully Crucified him, those same *Romans* lent their hands, without ever thinking that they did so, to the divine Vengeance, and rooted out that ungrateful People.

The changes that were to become evident during the eighteenth century were foreshadowed by 1677 in Dryden's 'opera', *The State of Innocence and Fall of Man*. It was an attempt to rewrite *Paradise Lost* with the permission, Dryden has told us, of Milton. The 'opera' is not Christocentric for the simple reason that Dryden denied the God-man any active role in the affairs of mankind. The sentence on Adam and Eve is passed not by the Son of God, but by a mere angel, Raphael. The same angel reveals the future to Adam in a 'vision', but it is a vision drastically limited – according to the stage directions – to 'deaths of several sorts', with 'a battle at land, and a Naval fight'.[6] Milton's survey of the course of events from the first Adam to the second is missing; and so is the incarnate Christ. The angel does promise that the race of man will 'revive', though precisely how this is to happen, he confesses, is 'Far more than I can show, or you can see'. Yet Adam, undeterred, at once cries out,

> O goodness infinite! whose Heav'nly will
> Can so much good produce, from so much ill!

Eve, whom Dryden gallantly permitted to see the 'vision', promptly adds:[7]

> Ravish'd with Joy, I can but half repent,
> The sin which Heav'n makes happy in th' event.

The 'paradox of the Fortunate Fall', so naturally introduced in *Paradise Lost*, is not necessarily relevant to *The State of Innocence and Fall of Man*.

If Dryden and the Augustan poets failed to imitate Milton's comprehensive vision of history in *Paradise Lost*, they could at least endeavour to fulfil Milton's earlier ambition to write a national epic centred on Brut or Arthur or both. Dryden himself had hoped to compose an Arthuriad, which like Milton's was 'intended chiefly for the Honour of my Native Country'.[8] Pope's parallel expectations involved an epic called *Brutus*. Both projects were stillborn. But Dr Johnson was not displeased: '[Pope] laid aside his Epick Poem, perhaps without much loss to mankind; for his hero was Brutus the Trojan, who, according to a ridiculous fiction, established a colony in Britain'.[9] It was to prove Brut's last appearance in English literature. But the durable Arthur lingered on, resuscitated in time by the poet laureate of Victorian England.

II

Thematically, the single most important development after the later seventeenth century was the advent of the idea of progress in its recognisably modern form.[10] Always implicit within the Christian view of history, the idea of progress was now secularised as the ever-present millennial expectations were transferred to a temporal setting under the promise of the brighter future held out by science. The three ages of the Joachimist interpretation of history, for example, reappeared in several thoroughly secular contexts: during the eighteenth century, in Comte's theory of evolutionary progress in three stages; during the nineteenth, in Marx's theory of the progressive redemption of the proletariat; and during the twentieth, in the Nazi concept of the Third Reich.[11] The metaphysical claims of the Christian view once denied, interpretations varied widely, and reactions came in a flood. Naïve versifiers were content to hail the redeemer of the new order:[12]

> *Newton* the unparallel'd, whose Name
> No Time will wear out of the Book of Fame,
> Cælestial Science has promoted more,
> Than all the Sages that have shone before.

Other writers lived only for the world before them, eschewing like Fielding both the past and the future in favour of the immediate present.[13] Profound philosophers like Vico, on the other hand, lapsed into scepticism whose import very few appreciated, and even fewer were prepared to endorse.[14] Pope did endeavour to adapt the Christian view of time in his *Pastorals*, but his youthful exuberance yielded in the end to the sombre apocalyptic vision of *The Dunciad*.[15] Only occasionally did anyone persist in the Christian vision of the unity of the divers families on earth. Christopher Smart's *Jubilate Agno* led the way:[16]

> For the Danes are of the children of Zabulon.
> For the Venetians are the children of Mark and Romans. . . .
> For the Mogul's people are the children of Phut.
> For the Old Greeks and the Italians are one people, which are blessed in the gift of Musick by reason of the song of Hannah and the care of Samuel with regard to divine melody.

But Smart was thought to have been insane.

Thematic considerations went hand in hand with questions concerning the style appropriate to the new historiography. Conscious of the inadequacies of English writers in the earlier eighteenth century, Bolingbroke complained in a letter to Pope that 'our Historys are Gazettes ill digested, & worse writ. The case is far otherwise in France and in Italy. Eloquence has been extreamly cultivated in both Countrys.'[17] The remark would have been phrased differently had Bolingbroke lived to evaluate the full range of the achievement of Voltaire and, in England, of Gibbon.

Voltaire is the foremost representative of the new temper in European thought: 'ce n'est pas un homme, c'est un siècle', as Victor Hugo said. Voltaire refused to differentiate between history and literature. 'The art of writing history well is very rare', he observed. 'It requires a grave, pure, varied, agreeable style.'[18] But he also pleaded for an emphasis on recent history, which he himself demonstrated in *The Age of Louis XIV* (1752): 'Above all, inculcate in the young a greater liking for the history of recent times, which is essential for us to know, than for ancient history, which only serves to satisfy our curiosity. Let them reflect that modern history has the advantage of being more certain, from the very fact that it is modern.'[19] More important still, Voltaire circumvented God. His celebrated *Essai sur les mœurs et l'esprit des nations* (1756), nominally a continuation of Bossuet's

Discours, actually denied the validity of the providential theory of history. But much the same temper was manifest in his 'Poème sur le désastre de Lisbonne'. The earthquake that devastated 'wicked' Lisbon on 1 November 1755 was widely interpreted as a visitation of Divine Justice. Voltaire's caustic response was to wonder why Paris was spared:

Lisbonne est abîmée, et l'on danse à Paris.[20]

But the poem is not only an attack on traditional modes of thought. It is also a censure of the naïve optimism of Leibniz and Pope, and as such anticipates *Candide* (1759).

Voltaire's view of organised religion as the major obstacle to enlightenment was fully shared by Gibbon. In *The Decline and Fall of the Roman Empire* (1776–88), consequently, Gibbon looked on the triumph of Christianity as a catastrophe, and on the rise of the Byzantine Church as the advent of sheer barbarism.[21] But his magisterial work remains the high-water mark of Augustan historiography, no less impressive in its staggering range and sustained interpretation of the past than in its justly admired style. It compares favourably with *Paradise Lost*; but where Milton consolidated the heritage of his predecessors, Gibbon stood facing the future.

III

The liberation of historiography from the chains of tradition affected also the response of William Blake (1757–1827). He looked on the history of experience as the history of the destruction of innocence:

I saw it was filled with graves,
And tomb-stones where flowers should be;
And Priests in black gowns were walking their rounds,
And binding with briars my joys & desires.

Each of history's Seven Ages should have led to birth but is circumscribed by death, 'a state of dismal woe'.[22] Man – 'slothful vegetating Man' – is 'cavern'd', a prisoner of his self-imposed restrictions and stony lethargy. But the visionary Bard 'Who Present, Past, & Future, sees', bursts through the darkness of systematised existence to proclaim the imminent apocalypse:[23]

The groans of Enitharmon shake the skies, the lab'ring Earth,
Till from her heart rending his way, a terrible child sprang forth
In thunder, smoke & sullen flames, & howlings & fury & blood ...

Blake, like the Hebrew prophets, promised redemption even as he
threatened annihilation. But the promise was not in the least
bound to tradition. It posits the transcendence of good and evil,
not because the one is to triumph over the other at some datable
post-historic Day of Wrath, but because they are alike part of the
unity of creation in which 'every thing that lives is Holy'. Blake's
aspiration to raise men 'into a perception of the infinite' was
achieved by the abolition of all contrary states and by the marriage
of Heaven and Hell:[24]

> The pride of the peacock is the glory of God.
> The lust of the goat is the bounty of God.
> The wrath of the lion is the wisdom of God.
> The nakedness of woman is the work of God.

Blake regarded the Christian view of history as another of the
'mind-forg'd manacles', a mere 'System' which further bound,
restricted, limited the caverned men who invented it. He therefore
transcended its confines by internalising the whole traditional
sequence of events from the creation to the flames of Doomsday –
now but 'flames of mental fire'. Later, in his major prophecies,
Blake often appears to have replaced one scheme by another
('I must Create a System or be enslav'd by another Man's').
But the initial impulse was ecstatically to celebrate the joyous
unity of the living world 'where every particle of dust breathes
forth its joy'.[25]

The transformation of the Christian view of history is also
clearly reflected in the epic of the Romantic movement, *The
Prelude*. Milton's epic had ended with Adam and Eve exiled from
Eden into history:

> The World was all before them, where to choose
> Thir place of rest, and Providence thir guide:
> They hand in hand with wandring steps and slow,
> Through *Eden* took thir solitarie way.

Wordsworth's epic consciously begins by echoing Milton:

The earth was all before me. With a heart
Joyous, nor scared at its own liberty,
I look about; and should the chosen guide
Be nothing better than a wandering cloud,
I cannot miss my way.

(I, 14–18; from the 1850 version)

But echoes of Milton are not limited to the outset of *The Prelude*.
Like the author of *Paradise Lost* who had hoped to 'leave something
so written to aftertimes, as they should not willingly let it die',[26]
Wordsworth ventured the 'daring thought'

that I might leave
Some monument behind me which pure hearts
Should reverence.

(VI, 55–7)

The monument was to have been *The Recluse*, 'a philosophical
poem, containing views of Man, Nature, and Society'.[27] Only
parts of it were completed: a massive introduction, *The Prelude*;
the opening sections published as 'Home in Grasmere'; and an
intermediate part, *The Excursion*. The argument, though vastly
different from Milton's, was to be no less 'heroic' (III, 184). The
setting would likewise be the universe but resolutely anthropocentric:

In the midst stood Man,
Outwardly, inwardly contemplated,
As, of all visible natures, crown, though born
Of dust, and kindred to the worm; a Being,
Both in perception and discernment, first
In every capability of rapture,
Through the divine effect of power and love;
As, more than anything we know, instinct
With godhead, and, by reason and by will,
Acknowledging dependency sublime.

(VIII, 485–94)

There were to be other fundamental differences. As the structure
of *The Prelude* testifies, the central position allotted to the concept
of time[28] involves in particular the displacement of the Christian
myth of paradise, its loss, and its eventual restoration, by the

myth of the paradise of childhood, its loss, and its eventual restoration. The intention of Wordsworth, said Coleridge in a
significant phrase, was to reveal 'a redemptive process in opera-
tion'.[29] The pattern, then, was to be a nominal 'mimesis' of the
Christian view of history. But the Christ was firmly excluded from
the redemptive process, even as history from the creation to the
Last Judgement was internalised in the mind of Man –

> My haunt, and the main region of my song.[30]

In Milton's epic as in Wordsworth's, however, all events are
alike propelled toward a *telos*. Milton conceived it as the time when
time itself is to stand fixed; Wordsworth, as conflating

> past, present, and to come,
> Age after age, till Time shall be no more;
> (XIV, 110–11)

but especially as a dimension of experience within history when time
is transcended in the apocalyptic serenity of a summer's night
that, breezeless and majestically silent, impels the mind to comprehend the mystery of things (XIV, 11 ff.).

The obsessive attachment of the Romantics to nature necessarily
obliged them to relate their 'philosophy' of life to nature's cycles.
The Prelude is one obvious example; Shelley's 'Ode to the West
Wind' is another. The autumnal leaves – 'Yellow, and black, and
pale, and hectic red,/Pestilence-stricken multitudes' – are conceived by Shelley as victims of the wind that at springtime also
emerges as nature's redeemer. The poem's symbolism recurs else-
where, its precedents once named by Shelley himself[31] as two in
particular: the Homeric lines quoted earlier (p. 1), and the
sombre reflections of that sceptic, Ecclesiastes (p. 6). Still another
precedent, Virgil's celebration of the circling centuries (above,
p. 1), looms behind Shelley's lyrical drama *Hellas*, occasioned
by the Greek Revolution of 1821. The last choric song (*Hellas*,
ll. 1060–5) heralds the abandonment of the Christian conception
of history in favour of the cyclical view:

> The world's great age begins anew,
> The golden years return,
> The earth doth like a snake renew
> Her winter weeds outworn:

> Heaven smiles, and faiths and empires gleam,
> Like wrecks of a dissolving dream.

The anthropocentric universe of *The Prelude* was extended in the egocentric universe of Byron's *Don Juan*. But as quantity displaced quality, Byron's attitude to history. like the design of his great poem, was kept a personal secret.

IV

It is perhaps tempting to see in Wordsworth's concern with time in *The Prelude* an anticipation of a Victorian obsession. But while Wordsworth reflects a common human experience, however personal the terms of its articulation, the Victorians vastly expanded its range in response to the displacement of Newton's perfect but static universe by the concept of evolution that culminated in Darwin.[32] As a geologist remarked in 1858,[33]

> The leading idea which is present in all our researches, and which accompanies every fresh observation, the sound which to the ear of the student of Nature seems continually echoed from every part of her works, is –
> Time! – Time! – Time!

To the extent that the theory of evolution appeared to reinforce the idea of progress, the Victorians were optimistic. But it was an optimism greatly qualified by the concurrent fear engendered by the possibility of decadence.[34] Beliefs so mutually exclusive were bound to produce diametrically opposed reactions. We know how valiantly Tennyson had to struggle in *In Memoriam* to quell his mounting despair; but we also know how utterly Arnold was engulfed by the shroud of his despondency. Increasingly, too, lesser writers turned inwards upon themselves to explore (in Pater's phrase) 'the narrow chamber of the individual mind'.[35] In this sense at least, the nineteenth century terminates in claustrophobia.

Warnings abounded. Hopkins's sonnet 'God's Grandeur' may also be read as an apocalyptic warning of the imminence of the Last Judgement. The initial vision of the world 'bleared, smeared with toil', propels the narrator to a cry of indignation: 'Why do men then now not reck his rod?' But the inevitable threat of annihilation recedes before the assurance of God's eternal love:

And though the last lights off the black West went
Oh, morning, at the brown brink eastward, springs –
Because the Holy Ghost over the bent
World broods with warm breast and with ah! bright wings.

The world after the final conflagration, charred ('brown') and
twisted ('bent') by the apocalyptic fires, continues to be sustained
by the Holy Ghost just as he once brooded over the newly-created
world. Creation continues apace, and darkness yields to light
once more.

But the heirs of the Victorian era, like Hopkins himself in
the 'dark sonnets', were unable to resist the widespread despair.
The Victorian obsession with time, in particular, assumed in
twentieth-century philosophy the dimensions of a major problem.
Literature responded in dramatically diverse ways, first with
Conrad and the late Henry James, and subsequently with
Proust, Virginia Woolf, and Faulkner, among others.[36] In several instances the spectacle of human existence merely *sub specie
temporis* resulted in the interpretation of time as 'a medium
neutral, indifferent, and hostile to man's works and values, a source
of suffering and anxiety, and a reason for despair'.[37] As variously
asserted by T. S. Eliot in 'Gerontion'[38] and Beckett in *Waiting for
Godot*,[39] the conflict is between man's inability to comprehend the
meaning of time and his persistent desire to penetrate its palpable
yet elusive presence. Hence the shattering agony of 'the thoughts
of a dry brain in a dry season' experienced by Eliot's protagonist,
for whom time future like time present is 'sluggish, pale and
monochrome', as Beckett said in speaking of Proust.[40] In fiction,
especially in science fiction, the effort to understand time has
ended in the phantasmagoria of 'an infinite series of times, in a
dizzily growing, ever spreading network of diverging, converging
and parallel times'.[41] In the bitter complaint of Joyce's Dedalus,
'History is a nightmare from which I am trying to awake'.[42]

Yeats also tried. *A Vision*, first published in 1925 and modified
in 1937, is a reduction of select aspects of the Greek conception of
time and history to a personal and highly fanciful theory.[43] Yeats's
time-scheme is governed by the Platonic Great Year; and history,
determined in some curious manner by the Phases of the Moon,
is conceived as a series of 'primary' conical spirals which on
reaching their apex begin a downward movement intercepted by

another rising ('antithetical') spiral. Each spiral, moreover, is divided into several wheels or 'gyres', and each gyre further sub-divided into 'some two thousand odd years'[44] that always terminate in chaos:

> Turning and turning in the widening gyre
> The falcon cannot hear the falconer;
> Things fall apart; the centre cannot hold;
> Mere anarchy is loosed upon the world.
> ('The Second Coming', ll. 1–4)

Yeats rightly held that his gyres had been anticipated by Plato, 'described in the *Timaeus*'.[45] In one form or another, at any rate, Yeats revived the Graeco-Roman theory of temporality as a cyclic movement; he endorsed in particular Virgil's celebration of the circling centuries (above, p. 1): 'the latest age of the Cumaean song is at hand; the cycles in their vast array begin anew; Virgin Astraea returns, the reign of Saturn comes.'[46] But the Christian view of history which Yeats so totally ostracised from his *Vision* was asserted with powerful conviction by T. S. Eliot.[47]

Eliot's Gerontion, as we have seen, wanders in a waste land where history and time have lost their meaning. For Eliot himself, however, the search went on to discover the roots lost beneath the forgetful snow, the water that could spring from desert rocks – the 'sense of the timeless and of the temporal together'.[48] The pattern which he finally observed in history is the traditional view of the linear nature of historical events extending on either side of the Incarnation, itself a predetermined moment 'transecting, bisecting the world of time, a moment in time but not like a moment in time' (above, p. 8). Eliot's words echo Donne's description of the Incarnation as '*timelesse time*, time that is all *time*, time that is no *time*, from all eternity'.[49]

The quest for the pattern led Eliot from 'Gerontion' to the slowly-evolving *Four Quartets*.[50] The waste land persists throughout:

> the world moves
> In appetency, on its metalled ways
> Of time past and time future.
> ('Burnt Norton', ll. 124–6)

There are at best hints half guessed, hints half understood. But:

It seems, as one becomes older,
That the past has another pattern, and ceases to be a
    mere sequence –
Or even development: the latter a partial fallacy
Encouraged by superficial notions of evolution,
Which becomes, in the popular mind, a means of disowning
    the past.

                    ('The Dry Salvages', ll. 85–9)

Past, present, and future are on the contrary related through the single event that invests the entire sequence with significance:

The hint half guessed, the hint half understood, is
    Incarnation.
Here the impossible union
Of spheres of existence is actual,
Here the past and future
Are conquered, and reconciled.

                    (Ibid., ll. 215–19)

However familiar the claim, the process of its discovery for oneself remains always unique. As Eliot argues in the final movement of *Four Quartets*,

We shall not cease from exploration
And the end of all our exploring
Will be to arrive where we started
And know the place for the first time.

Four Quartets demonstrates that the fabric of the Christian view of history has not dissolved utterly, nor its pageant faded. Adapted by other poets and several novelists,[51] it is also current among theologians.[52] Dare one assume that the tide of eternity beats once more upon the high shore of this world? Or have the two 'cities' moved so far apart that redemption is itself beyond redemption? We hover between the persuasion of D. H. Lawrence that

The perfect rose is only a running flame, emerging and flowing off, and never in any sense at rest, static, finished . . .

and the conviction of T. S. Eliot that

    . . . the fire and the rose are one.[53]

Notes

Notes

Notes

1 *A Vision*, 2nd ed. (1937; corrected ed., 1962), p. 271.
2 See R. A. Sayce, *The French Biblical Epic in the Seventeenth Century* (Oxford, 1955), pp. 142 f.
3 *The Dunciad Variorum*, ii, 256.
4 W. J. Sparrow Simpson, *A Study of Bossuet* (1937), p. 4. See further Georges Hardy, *Le 'Civitate Dei' source principale du 'Discours sur l'histoire universelle'* (Paris, 1913).
5 *A Discourse on the History of the World*, trans. Anon. (1686), pp. 437–8. For estimates of Bossuet's achievement, consult Patrick J. Barry, 'Bossuet's *Discourse on Universal History*', in *The Catholic Philosophy of History*, ed. Peter Guilday (1936), pp. 149–86; Karl Löwith, *Meaning in History* (Chicago, 1949), ch. vii; and R. de la Broise, *Bossuet et la Bible* (Paris, 1891), ch. vii.
6 *Dramatic Works* (1932), vol. iii, p. 460.
7 Ibid., p. 461. For studies of Dryden's 'opera', see Bruce King, *Dryden's Major Plays* (Edinburgh, 1966), ch. vi, and Bernard Harris, ' "That soft seducer, love" ': Dryden's *The State of Innocence and Fall of Man*', in *Approaches to 'Paradise Lost'*, ed. C. A. Patrides (1968), pp. 119–36.
8 *The Satires of Decimus Junius Juvenalis* (1693), The Dedication, p. xiii.
9 'The Life of Pope', in *Samuel Johnson*, ed. B. H. Bronson (1958), p. 366.
10 See Carl L. Becker, *The Heavenly City of the Eighteenth-Century Philosophers* (New Haven, 1932); Lois Whitney, *Primitivism and the Idea of Progress in English Popular Literature of the Eighteenth Century* (Baltimore, 1934); Ernest L. Tuveson, *Millennium and Utopia* (Berkeley, 1949); and John Plamenatz, *Man and Society* (1963), vol. ii, ch. vii. More general developments may be approached by way of anthologies: *Philosophy of History*, ed. Alan and Barbara Donagan (1965); *The Philosophy of History in our Time*, ed. Hans Meyerhoff (1959); *Approaches to History*, ed. H. P. R. Finberg (1962); and esp. *The Varieties of History: From Voltaire to the Present*, ed. Fritz Stern, 2nd ed. (1970); *Philosophy in the Mid-Century*, ed. Raymond Klibansky (Florence, 1958), vol. iii, pp. 158–88; and *Theories of History*, ed. Patrick Gardiner (Glencoe, Ill., 1959). The last two collections have exhaustive bibliographies; but see also the survey of eighteenth- and nineteenth-century European historiography by James W. Thompson, *A History of Historical Writing* (1942), vol. ii.
11 Norman Cohn, *The Pursuit of the Millennium* (1957, repr. 1962), pp. 100 f., 308 ff. See also above, p. 41, note 23.
12 John Theophilus Desaguliers, *The Newtonian System of the World, the Best Model of Government* (1728), p. 21.
13 Philip Stevick, 'Fielding and the Meaning of History', *PMLA*, lxxix (1964), 561–8.
14 Vico's *New Science* (1725; revised 1730 and 1744) was 'discovered' only earlier this century. Consult Benedetto Croce, *The Philosophy of Giambattista Vico*, trans. R. G. Collingwood (1913), esp. chs xiii–xiv, but also A. Robert

Caponigri, *Time and Idea: The Theory of History in Giambattista Vico* (1953), and the essays in *Giambattista Vico*, ed. G. Tagliacozzo and H. V. White (Baltimore, 1969). There is a translation of *New Science* by T. G. Bergin and M. H. Fisch (Ithaca, N.Y., 1948).

15 On Pope's adaptation of the Christian view in his *Pastorals*, including the end of history described in his *Messiah*, see Martin C. Battestin, 'The Transforming Power: Nature and Art in Pope's Pastorals', *Eighteenth Century Studies*, ii (1969), 183–204. Like Pope's vision in *The Dunciad*, Hogarth's terminates in the apocalyptic pessimism of his final print, the *Tailpiece, or the Bathos* (1764).

16 *Jubilate Agno*, ed. W. H. Bond (1954), p. 103 (B2, ll. 453–8).

17 18 February 1723/4; quoted by Herbert Davis, 'The Augustan Conception of History', in *Reason and the Imagination*, ed. J. A. Mazzeo (1962), p. 227.

18 From his article 'Histoire', in Diderot's *Encyclopédie*; quoted by Thompson (as before, note 10), p. 67. See further Sir James F. Stephen, 'Voltaire as a Theologian, Moralist, and Metaphysician', in his *Horæ Sabbaticæ*, 2nd series (1892), pp. 211–28; John B. Black, *The Art of History* (1926), pp. 29–75; Friedrich Meinecke, *Die Entstehung des Historismus* (Munich and Berlin, 1936), vol. i, pp. 78–124; Werner Kaegi, 'Voltaire und der Zerfall des christlichen Geschichtsbildes', *Corona*, viii (1938), 76–101; H. Linn Edsall, 'The Idea of History and Progress in Fontenelle and Voltaire', *YRS*, xviii (1941), 163–84; Emery Neff, *The Poetry of History* (1947), ch. i; Wilhelm Weischedel, 'Voltaire', in *Grosse Geschichtsdenker*, ed. Rudolf Stadelmann (Tübingen and Stuttgart, 1949), pp. 149–72; Richard M. Saunders, 'Voltaire's View of the Meaning of History', *UTQ*, xxii (1952), 44–54; G. P. Gooch, 'Voltaire as Historian', in his *Catherine the Great and Other Studies* (1954), ch. iii; Ferdinand Schevill, *Six Historians* (Chicago, 1956), pp. 93–123; Jerome Rosenthal, 'Voltaire's Philosophy of History', *JHI*, xvi (1955), 151–78; and the full account by J. H. Brumfitt, *Voltaire: Historian* (1958), with further references.

19 'On History: Advice to a Journalist', trans. Jacques Barzun, in *The Varieties of History*, ed. Fritz Stern, 2nd ed. (1970), p. 36.

20 See Theodore Bestermann, 'Voltaire and the Lisbon Earthquake: or, The Death of Optimism', in his *Voltaire Essays* (1962), ch. iii, and T. D. Kendrick, *The Lisbon Earthquake* (1956), ch. vii. The latter also details the reaction of traditionalists (chs iv–v).

21 See the accounts by E. M. W. Tillyard, *The English Epic and its Background* (1954), pp. 510–27; Arnaldo Momigliano, 'Gibbon's Contribution to Historical Method', in his *Studies in Historiography* (1966), ch. ii; Ian White, 'The Subject of Gibbon's History', *CQ*, iii (1968), 299–309; and Lynn White, Jr, ed., *The Transformation of the Roman World* (Berkeley, 1966). One of the essays in the latter collection – by Speros Vryonis, Jr, 'Hellas Resurgent', in ch. iii – is a study of Gibbon's prejudices against the Eastern Church.

22 *Songs of Experience*: 'The Garden of Love', and *The First Book of Urizen*, respectively (in *Complete Writings*, ed. Geoffrey Keynes [1966], pp. 215 and 228–9).

23 Seriatim: *Milton*; *Europe*; *Songs of Experience*: 'Introduction'; and *The Four Zoas*: Night v (ibid., pp. 513, 237, 210, and 306).

24 *A Song of Liberty* and *The Marriage of Heaven and Hell*, respectively (ibid., pp. 100, 154, and 151).

25 Seriatim: *Songs of Experience*: 'London'; *The Four Zoas*: Night IX; *Jerusalem*: plate 10; and *Europe* (ibid., pp. 216, 358, 629, and 237). Morton D. Paley, in *Energy and Imagination* (Oxford, 1970), ch. v, reads Blake's thought in terms of the interplay of cyclical and linear time.

26 *The Reason of Church-Government* (1642); in *Complete Works*, gen. ed. Don M. Wolfe (New Haven, 1953), vol. i, p. 810.

27 Preface to *The Excursion* (1814). On the Romantic pursuit of the epic, see Thomas A. Vogler, *Preludes to Vision* (Berkeley, 1971).

28 Most ably discussed by Herbert Lindenberger, *On Wordsworth's 'Prelude'* (Princeton, 1963), chs v–vi, 'Time-Consciousness'.

29 Quoted ibid., p. 184.

30 *The Recluse*, part i, book i ('Home in Grasmere'), l. 794. On the secularisation of theological ideas among the Romantics, see esp. M. H. Abrams, *Natural Supernaturalism* (1971).

31 Note to *Queen Mab* (v, 1–6), in *Complete Poetical Works*, ed. George E. Woodberry (Boston, 1894), vol. i, pp. 346–7. See further I. J. Kaplan, 'The Symbolism of the Wind and the Leaves in Shelley's "Ode to the West Wind"', *PMLA*, li (1936), 1069–79.

32 Theodosius Dobzhansky, 'Evolutionism and Man's Hope', *SR*, lxviii (1960), 274–88. The changing pattern of ideas is more fully studied by Francis C. Haber, *The Age of the World: Moses to Darwin* (Baltimore, 1959).

33 G. P. Scrope, *The Geology and Extinct Volcanoes of Central France* (1858), p. 208; quoted by Haber (previous note), p. 291.

34 The subject is suggestively outlined by Jerome H. Buckley, *The Triumph of Time: A Study of the Victorian Concepts of Time, History, Progress and Decadence* (Cambridge, Mass., 1966).

35 See John Dixon Hunt, *The Pre-Raphaelite Imagination 1848–1900* (1968), ch. iii. On Pater see further William Shuter, 'History as Palingenesis in Pater and Hegel', *PMLA*, lxxxvi (1971), 411–21. On Victorian historiography generally, consult G. P. Gooch, *History and Historians in the Nineteenth Century*, 2nd ed. (1952); Herbert Butterfield, *Man on his Past* (Cambridge, 1955); and Richard A. E. Brooks, 'The Development of the Historical Mind', in *The Reinterpretation of Victorian Literature*, ed. Joseph E. Baker (Princeton, 1950), pp. 130–52, and *Backgrounds to Victorian Literature*, ed. Richard A. Levine (San Francisco, 1967), pp. 181–202. On Arnold, see R. A. Forsyth, ' "The Buried Life": The Contrasting Views of Arnold and Clough in the Context of Dr. Arnold's Historiography', *ELH*, xxxv (1968), 218–53, and Charles R. Moyer, 'The Idea of History in Thomas and Matthew Arnold', *MP*, lxvii (1969), 160–7; on Carlyle: René Wellek, 'Carlyle and the Philosophy of History', in his *Confrontations* (Princeton, 1965), ch. ii; and on Newman: Josef L. Altholz, 'Newman and History', *Victorian Studies*, vii (1964), 285–94.

36 See Frederick R. Karl, *A Reader's Guide to Joseph Conrad* (1960), ch. iii; R. W. Stallman, *The Houses that James Built* (East Lansing, 1961), pp. 34–51; Harry Slochower, 'Marcel Proust: Revolt against the Tyranny of Time', *SR*, li (1943), 370–81; Albert Cook, 'Proust: The Invisible Stilts of Time',

Modern Fiction Studies, iv (1958), 118–26; José Ortega y Gasset, 'Time, Distance, and Form in Proust', trans. Irving Singer, *HR*, xi (1958), 504–13; Margaret Mein, *Proust's Challenge to Time* (Manchester, 1962); Roger Shattuck, *Proust's Binoculars* (1963); John Graham, 'Time in the Novels of Virginia Woolf', *UTQ*, xviii (1949), 186–201; Jean Guiguet, *Virginia Woolf and her Works*, trans. J. Stewart (1965), pp. 382–98; Olga W. Vickery, 'Faulkner and the Contours of Time', *Georgia Review*, lx (1952), 192–201; Jean-Paul Sartre, 'On *The Sound and the Fury*: Time in the Work of Faulkner', in his *Literary and Philosophical Essays*, trans. A. Michelson (1955), pp. 79–87; Perrin Lowrey, 'Concepts of Time in *The Sound and the Fury*', in *English Institute Essays*, ed. A. S. Downer (1954), pp. 57–82; *et al.* More general studies include Wyndham Lewis's polemical account, *Time and Western Man* (1927); A. A. Mendilow, *Time and the Novel* (1952); Hans Meyerhoff, *Time in Literature* (Berkeley, 1955); Georges Poulet, *Studies in Human Time*, trans. Elliott Coleman (Baltimore, 1956); William T. Noon, 'Modern Literature and the Sense of Time', *Thought*, xxxiii (1958), 571–603; S. E. Toulmin and G. J. Goodfield, *The Discovery of Time* (1965); Margaret Church, *Time and Reality: Studies in Contemporary Fiction* (Chapel Hill, 1963); J. T. Fraser, ed., *The Voices of Time . . . as expressed by the Sciences and by the Humanities* (1966), *passim*; *et al.* The modern obsession with time should be compared to older attitudes, e.g. Shakespeare's (above, p. 96, note 48), Racine's (cf. Odette de Mourgues, *Racine* [Cambridge, 1967], ch. ii, 'The Multivalency of Time and Space'), etc.

37 Hans Meyerhoff, *Time in Literature* (Berkeley, 1955), esp. ch. iii, 'Time and the Modern World'.

38 I would personally endorse the reading by Grover Smith, 'The Word in the Whirlwind: "Gerontion"', in his *T. S. Eliot's Poetry and Plays* (Chicago, 1956), ch. iv, rather than that by Harvey Gross, '"Gerontion" and the Meaning of History', *PMLA*, lxxiii (1958), 299–304.

39 See Richard Schechner, 'There's Lots of Time in *Godot*', in *Casebook on 'Waiting for Godot'*, ed. Ruby Cohn (1967), pp. 175–87, and Günther Anders, 'Being Without Time', in *Samuel Beckett: A Collection of Critical Essays*, ed. Martin Esslin (Englewood Cliffs, N.J., 1965), pp. 140–51.

40 *Proust* (1931), p. 4.

41 Jorge Luis Borges, 'The Garden of Forking Paths', in the collection of short stories *The Traps of Time*, ed. Michael Moorcock (1968; Penguin ed., 1970), p. 156.

42 *Ulysses* (1960), p. 42.

43 Discussed by Norman Jeffares, *W. B. Yeats: Man and Poet*, 2nd ed. (1962), pp. 192 ff.; Helen H. Vendler, *Yeats's 'Vision' and the Later Plays* (Cambridge, Mass., 1963); and esp. Thomas R. Whitaker, *Swan and Shadow: Yeats's Dialogue with History* (Chapel Hill, 1964), and T. R. Henn, *The Lonely Tower*, 2nd ed. (1965), ch. xii, '*A Vision* and the Interpretation of History'.

44 *A Vision*, 2nd ed. (1937; corrected ed., 1962), p. 202.

45 Ibid., p. 68. Cf. *Timaeus*, 22 ff.

46 Ibid., pp. 243–4.

47 See Morris Weitz, 'T. S. Eliot: Time as a Mode of Salvation', *SR*, lx (1952), 48–64 (reprinted in Bergonzi, below, pp. 138–52); George Williamson,

'*Four Quartets* and History', in his *A Reader's Guide to T. S. Eliot* (1953), ch. viii; Staffan Bergsten, *Time and Eternity* (Stockholm, 1960); David H. Hirsch, 'T. S. Eliot and the Vexation of Time', *Southern Review*, n.s., iii (1967), 608–24; William F. Lynch, 'Dissociation in Time', in *T. S. Eliot: 'Four Quartets'*, ed. B. Bergonzi (1969), pp. 247–53; John F. Lynen, 'Selfhood and the Reality of Time: T. S. Eliot', in his *The Design of the Present* (New Haven, 1969), ch. vi.

48 'Tradition and the Individual Talent' (1919), in *Selected Essays* (1932), p. 4.

49 *Sermons*, ed. E. M. Simpson and G. R. Potter (Berkeley, 1953–62), vol. ii, p. 139.

50 Written 1935–42, published 1943. All quotations are from the 1959 edition.

51 William T. Noon, in his survey of 'Modern Literature and the Sense of Time' (above, note 36), detects the 'survival of the Christian sensibility' in our day; and Frank Kermode, in *The Sense of an Ending: Studies in the Theory of Fiction* (1967), interestingly relates aspects of the Christian view of history to the strategies of selected novelists and poets. The recipient of *The Waste Land*, 'il miglior fabbro' Pound, also appears to have adapted the traditional view to his purposes: see Daniel D. Pearlman, *The Barb of Time: On the Unity of Ezra Pound's 'Cantos'* (1969).

52. The numerous spokesmen for the Christian view of history include Berdyaev, Bultmann, Cullmann, Daniélou, D'Arcy, Dawson and Niebuhr (see above, p. 10, note 8). See also Paul Henry, S. J., 'The Christian Philosophy of History', *TS*, xiii (1952), 419–32.

53 Lawrence, *Phoenix*, ed. E. D. McDonald (1936), p. 219; Eliot, in the last line of *Four Quartets*.

Index of Names

The asterisk designates individuals *other than* modern commentators. Biblical personalities, as well as translators, are included eclectically, depending on their importance. Editors are not included.

Grendler, Paul F., 62
Gross, Harvey, 139
*Grotius, Hugo, 58, 68
Grundmann, Herbert, 40, 41
Guardini, Romano, 46
Gudzy, N. K., 43
*Guicciardini, Francesco, 57, 67, 91
Guiguet, Jean, 139
Gundersheimer, Werner L., 68
*Gutenberg, Johann, 47
Güterbeck, Hans-Gustav, 9
*Guthberleth, Hendrik, 62
Guthrie, W. K. C., 9

Haber, Francis C., 138
*Habington, Thomas, 100
*Hakewill, George, 95
*Hakluyt, Richard, 94
*Hall, Edward, 73–4, 80, 92
Haller, William, 95
*Hamartolos, Georgios Monachos, 35, 43
Hankins, J. E., 93
*Hanmer, Meredith, 100
Hanning, Robert W., 27, 44, 114
Hanson, R. P. C., 22
Hardy, Georges, 136
*Hardy, Thomas, 4
Hardy, Thomas D., 44
*Hardyng, John, 74
Harper, C. A., 115
Harris, Bernard, 136
*Harry, George Owen, 95
*Harvey, Richard, 116
*Harvey, William, 77
Hashagen, Justus, 41
Haskins, Charles H., 40, 42
Hatcher, O. L., 112
Hausheer, Herman, 25
Hawkins, Robert M., 11
*Hawthorne, Nathaniel, 123
Hay, Denys, 69, 92, 115
Haydn, Hiram, 117
*Hayward, Sir John, 99
Headley, John M., 59
*Healey, John, 100
Heard, Gerald, 11
Hearnshaw, F. J. C., 24, 68, 96, 117

Hebert, A. G., 11
*Helwig, Christoph, 51
*Hemmingsen, Niels, 98
Heninger, S. K., Jr, 114
Henn, T. R., 139
Henning-Pflanz, Hans, 59
*Henry V, 73, 92
*Henry of Huntington, 102, 114
Henry, Paul, 140
*Herbert, George, 12, 82–3, 97
*Hermann of Reichenau, 29, 40
*Herodianus, 91
*Herodotus, 67, 91
Hertzberg, Hugo, 25, 27
*Hesychios Milesios, 35, 43
*Heylyn, Peter, 94
*Heywood, Thomas, 77
Hibbard, G. R., 95
*Higden, Ranulf, 37, 44, 103, 115
*Higgins, John, 104
Hill, Christopher, 94
Hipler, Franz, 25
*Hippolytus, St, 14, 15, 23
Hirsch, David H., 140
Hirsch, Ferdinand, 42
Hirsch, Wolfgang, 65
*Hobbes, Thomas, 77, 101, 113
*Hodson, William, 93
Hoffmann, Ernst, 25
Hofmeister, Adolf, 41
*Hogarth, William, 137
*Holinshed, Raphael, 73, 75, 79, 80, 92, 95, 104, 113
*Holland, Philemon, 101, 113, 118
Holmes, U. T., Jr, 93
Holzknecht, Karl J., 91, 96
Hóman, Bálint, 43
*Homer, 1, 131
*Homologetes, *see* Theophanes, St
*Honorius of Autun, 29, 40
Hope, V., 64
*Hopkins, Gerard Manley, 132–3
Hoppe, Heinrich, 24
*Horn, Albert Otto, 63
*Horn, Georg, 63
*Hotman, François, 105
*Howell, William, 77
*Howes, Edmund, 116

*Hubert, Sir Francis, 91
Hughes, Merritt Y., 118
*Hugo of Flaviny, 29, 40
*Hugo of Fleury, 29, 40
*Hugo, Victor, 127
Hunt, John Dixon, 138
Huntley, Frank L., 97
Huppert, George, 116
Hussey, Joan M., 43
*Hydatius of Chaves, 19, 25

*Illyricus, *see* Flacius, I.
*Ioannes, *see* Malalas, Zonaras
*Isaacson, Henry, 52-3, 77
*Isaiah, 4, 5, 6, 18, 48, 71, 109, 124
*Isidore of Seville, St, 21-2, 27, 28, 41, 58, 90, 109

*Jackson, Thomas, 91
*Jacopo della Quercia, 65
*James I, 93
*James VI of Scotland, *see* previous entry
*James, Henry, 133
Jastrow, Morris, Jr, 11
Jeffares, Norman, 139
Jenkins, Harold, 96
Jensen, Jens Christian, 65
*Jerome, St, 14, 15, 16, 18-19, 20, 25, 28, 29, 62, 90
*Joachim of Fiore, 30-1, 41, 61
Joachimsen, Paul, 59, 60
*Joannes of Gerona, 19, 25
*Joannes I, Tzimisces, 35
*John, St, the Divine, 12
*John Chrysostom, St, 86
*John of Nikiu, 43
*John of Oxnead, 36
*John of Salisbury, 33
*John of Wavrin, 114
Johnson, James W., 23
*Johnson, Dr Samuel, 126
Johnson, Thomas H., 122
Joly, Aristide, 116
Jones, Charles W., 25, 26, 27
Jones, Ernest, 114
Jones, Rufus M., 60
*Jonson, Ben, 113

Jorgensen, Paul A., 96
*Josephus, Flavius, 15, 23, 28, 91, 100, 112
*Joyce, James, 133
*Julius Africanus, 14, 15, 23, 34
*Justin Martyr, St, 13, 14

Kaegi, Werner, 41, 137
*Kallwitz, Seth, 63
Kantrowitz, Joanne S., 12
Kaplan, I. J., 138
Karl, Frederick R., 138
Keeler, Laura, 114
Keller, M. Jerome, 24
Kelly, Henry A., 96
*Kelton, Arthur, 103
Kempner, Nadja, 118
Kendrick, Sir Thomas, 113, 114, 115, 137
Kermode, Frank, 93, 140
Kernan, Alvin, 95
Kestenberg-Gladstein, Ruth, 41
Keyes, G. L., 24
King, Bruce, 136
Kingsford, Charles L., 92
Kirkconnel, Watson, 97
Klausner, Joseph, 11
Klippel, Maria, 116
Knappe, Karl-Adolf, 66
Knight, W. S. M., 68
Knowles, David, 45
Koller, Kathrine, 68
Kolve, V. A., 45, 46
Krautheimer, Richard, 65
*Kremer, Gerhard, 62
Krouse, F. Michael, 12
Krumbacher, Karl, 42
Krusch, Bruno, 26
Kümmel, Werner, G., 12

*Labbé, Philippe, 62
La Boise, R. de, 136
Labriolle, Pierre de, 26
Lafond, Paul, 65
Laistner, M. L. W., 26
*Lambert of Hersfeld, 29, 40
Lampe, G. W. H., 11
Landon, Michael, 118

Laneau, Auguste, 25
*Lanquet, Thomas, 75
Lathrop, Henry B., 112
Lawlor, John, 96
*Lawrence, D. H., 135
Lear, Floyd S., 40
Lee, Sir Sidney, 93
Lefranc, Pierre, 94
*Le Grand, Antoine, 62
*Leibniz, Gottfried Wilhelm, 128
Leigh, David J., 46
*Leigh, Edward, 26, 116
*Leland, John, 114
*Leo Diaconus, 36
*Le Roy, Louis, 58
*Lesley, John, 102–3, 114
*Lessius, Leonardus, 91
*Lever, Christopher, 91
Levison, Wilhelm, 25, 27
Levy, F. J., 93, 115
Lewalter, Ernst, 24
Lewis, Wyndham, 139
Lightfoot, J. B., 23
Lilje, Hans, 59
Lindenberger, Herbert, 138
*Lindsay, Sir David, 70–1, 90
Littell, Franklin H., 64
*Livy, 2, 9, 15, 58, 91, 101
*Lloyd, Lodowick, 11, 76
*Lodge, Thomas, 100, 112
Löwith, Karl, 10, 24, 136
Lohia, Rammanohar, 9
Lovejoy, Arthur O., 9, 64
Lowrey, Perrin, 139
*Lucas of Tuy, 29, 41
*Lucian, 101
Luciani, Vincent, 67, 117
*Lucido, Giovanni, 62
*Lucinge, René de, 60
*Lupton, Donald, 112
*Luther, 48, 59–60, 61, 91, 97
*Lydgate, John, 45
*Lydiat, Thomas, 94
Lynch, William F., 140
Lynen, John F., 140

*Mabuse, *see* Gossaert
MacCallum, Hugh R., 98

MacCallum, M. W., 96
McColley, Grant, 97
McCusker, Honor, 93
McCutcheon, Elizabeth, 96
*Machiavelli, Niccolò, 57, 67, 68, 91, 100–1, 113
MacKinnon, Elfie, 45
McKisack, May, 93, 116
Maclean, Hugh, 96
Macnab, Ludovico D., 40
Madsen, William G., 12
*Maimonides, Moses, 33
*Maitani, Lorenzo, 65
*Major, John, 115
*Malalas, Ioannes, 35, 43
*Maldonado, Alonso, 62
*Manasses, Constantinos, 35, 43
Manitius, Maximilianus, 27, 40
Manson, W., 10
*Mantegna, Andrea, 64
*Marcellinus Comes, 19, 25
*Marcus Aurelius, 1, 9
*Marianus Scotus, 29, 40
Markus, R. A., 11, 24
*Marlorat, Augustin, 98
*Marlowe, Christopher, 67, 79, 95, 107, 117
Marsh, John, 10
Marshall, F. H., 42
*Marshall, William, 64
*Marsilius of Padua, 33
*Marvell, Andrew, 109–12
*Marx, Karl, 126
*Masaccio, 64
Mascall, E. L., 10
Maskell, D. W., 67
Massingham, Hugh, 95
*'Master of Sentences', *see* Peter Lombard
*Mather, Cotton, 119, 120, 123
*'Matthew of Westminster', 37, 44
Matthiessen, F. O., 112
*May, Thomas, 106
*Mayerne, Turquet, Louis de, 105
*Mead, *see* next entry
*Mede, Joseph, 77
Mein, Margaret, 139
Meinecke, Friedrich, 137

Rubinstein, Nicaolai, 66
*Rudolf of Ems, 30, 41
*Rufinus of Aquileia, 16, 21, 24
Runciman, Sir Steven, 43
Ruotolo, Giuseppe, 24
Rupp, E. Gordon, 10
Russell, J. L., 25
Russo, Francesco, 41
Rust, Eric C., 10
Ryan, E. A., 64

*Sabellicus, Marcantonio Coccio, 51, 68
*Salian, Jacques, 62
*Sallust, 91, 99
*Salvian of Marseilles, 20, 26, 100, 112
Salvini, Roberto, 66
Samuel, Irene, 118
*Sanderson, Sir William, 94
Sandys, Sir John, 92
Sanford, Eva M., 40
*Sansovino, Francesco, 62
Sartre, Jean-Paul, 139
Saunders, Richard M., 137
Sayce, R. A., 93, 136
*Scaliger, Joseph Juste, 20, 51, 112
Schechner, Richard, 139
*Schedel, Hartmann, 47, 59
*Schelandre, Jean de, 67
Schevill, Ferdinand, 24, 137
Schlatter, Richard, 113
Schmidlin, Joseph, 41
Schneider, Herbert W., 123
Schoedel, Friedrich H., 112
Schoene, Alfred, 23
Schoeps, H. J., 11
Scholz, Heinrich, 24
*Schotanus, Christiaan, 62
Schott, Rolf, 66
Schwoebel, Robert, 60
*Scoglius, Orazio, 62
Scott, E. F., 11
*Scrope, G. P., 138
Sée, Henri, 67
Séjourné, Paul, 27
*Seneca, 1
Sen Gupta, S. C., 95

Seronsy, Cecil C., 116, 117
*Serres, Jean de, 91, 105
Seyrich, Georg, 24
*Shakespeare, 74, 79–81, 95–6, 139
Shattuck, Roger, 139
*Shelley, Percy Bysshe, 131–2, 138
Shinn, Roger L., 10, 25, 60
Shotwell, James T., 10, 23, 25
Shuter, William, 138
*Sibthorpe, Robert, 95
*Sicard of Cremona, 29, 40
*Sidetes, Philippos, 34
*Sidney, Sir Philip, 93
*Sigebert of Gembloux, 28–9, 40
Simard, Georges, 24
*Simeon, *see* Metaphrastes
Simon, G., 60
Simpson, W. J. Sparrow, 136
Singleton, Charles S., 46
Sirluck, Ernest, 117
*Slatyer, William, 95
*Sleidanus, Johann Philippson, 49, 92
Slochower, Harry, 138
*Smart, Christopher, 127
Smith, David E., 122
Smith, Grover, 139
*Smith, John, the Cambridge Platonist, 70, 96
Smith, Timothy L., 123
*Socrates 'Scholasticus', 16, 21
Söderblom, Nathan, 10
*Sozomen, 16, 21
Spangenberg, H., 68
Spanheim, Friederich, 63
Speed, John, 75, 92, 94, 106, 116
Speiser, E. A., 10
Spencer, Benjamin T., 96
Spenser, Edmund, 47, 76, 93, 97, 104, 105, 107, 115, 117
Spini, Giorgio, 67
*Spondee, Henri de, 52, 62
Stallman, R. W., 138
Standford, Donald E., 123
*Stapleton, Thomas, 100
Starnes, DeWitt T., 91
Stauffer, Donald A., 117
Stauffer, Ethelbert, 64
Stein, Arnold, 98

Stephen, Sir James F., 137
*Sterry, Peter, 47
Stevenson, J., 23
Stevick, Philip, 136
Stewart, Stanley, 97
*Stoughton, John, 11
*Stow, John, 75, 92, 103–4
Strathmann, Ernest A., 94, 118
Strauss, Leo, 113
Stříbrný, Zdeněk, 96
Struever, Nancy S., 66
*Suetonius, 113
*Suleiman the Magnificent, 48–9
*Sulpicius Severus, 20, 26, 62, 100, 112
Summers, Joseph H., 98
Swain, Joseph W., 61
*Swan, John, 77
*Sylvester, Joshua, 76, 93
*Symeon, *see* Metaphrastes
*Synkellos, Georgios, 35, 43
*Székely, István, 63

*Tacitus, 58, 91
*Tasso, Torquato, 97
Tatlock, J. S. P., 114
Taylor, Archer, 63
*Taylor, Edward, 120, 123
Taylor, George C., 93
*Taylor, John, the water poet, 106, 114
*Taylor, Thomas, 98
Temple, William, 10
*Tennyson, Alfred Lord, 126, 132
*Tertullian, 14, 25
*Theodoret of Cyrrhus, 16, 21, 112
*Theodoros Prodromos, 43
*Theophanes Homologetes, St, 35
*Theophilus of Antioch, St, 14, 15, 22–3
Thibaut de Maisières, Maury, 93
*Thomas Aquinas, St, 33, 43
*Thomas of Malmesbury, 37, 44
Thompson, James W., 92, 136, 137
*Thornton, John, of Coventry, 53
*Thucydides, 2, 101, 113
Thyssen, Johannes, 25, 40
Tieghem, Paul van, 68

Tillyard, E. M. W., 91, 96, 97, 114, 137
*Tintoretto, 64
*Titian, 64
Toliver, Harold E., 96
Tolnay, Charles de, 65, 66
Tondelli, Leone, 41
*Tornamira, Francisco Vincente de, 63
*Tornielli, Agostino, 62
*Torsellino, Orazio, 62
*Totila, 57
Toulmin, S. E., 139
Tout, T. F., 40
Toynbee, Arnold, 9
Toynbee, Paget, 46
Trapp, J. B., 64, 65
Traversi, Derek, 96
Trefz, Edward K., 122
Trevelyan, G. M., 118
Trevor-Roper, H. R., 115, 118
Trimble, William R., 92
Troeltsch, Ernst, 25
*Trogus, Gnaeus Pompeius, 15
Trostler, Josef, 43
Turner, C. H., 23
Tuve, Rosemond, 12, 97
Tuveson, Ernest L., 27, 42, 61, 117, 123, 136
*Twain, Mark, 123
*Tyconius, 25
*Tyndale, William, 60

Ullman, Berthold L., 41, 61, 67
Upham, Alfred H., 93
*Urquhart, Sir Thomas, 78
*Ussher, James, 77

*Valla, Lorenzo, 58
*van der Goes, Hugo, *see* Goes
*van der Weyden, Rogier, *see* Weyden
*van Eyck, *see* Eyck
*Vasari, Giorgio, 65
Vasiliev, A. A., 41, 42, 43
Vaughan, Dorothy M., 60
Vaughan, Richard, 45
*Vaughan, Thomas, 64
*Vaughan, William, 77

Index of Subjects

Aeneas, 104
ages, six, *see* six ages
Agincourt, battle at, 73, 92
allegory, 14, 33, 42, 48
American view of history, 119–23
Anabaptists on martyrdom, 52, 64
anagogical sense, 33, 42
Apocalypse, St John's, 12; *see also* millennial expectations
apocalyptic views of history, *see* eschatology; millennial expectations; Revelation
apocatastasis, 14
Arianism, 13
Arthur, King, 102, 103, 106, 107, 108, 113–14, 117, 126
Astraea, 91, 134
atonement, 85; Protestant theory of, 98
Augustan views of history, 125–8, 137
Augustinian view of history, 16–19, 24–5, 30, 34, 39, 46, 48, 100, 124
Aztec view of history, 3

Bible, interpretation of, *see* four senses
Brut, legend of, 37, 95, 102–6, 108, 114–17, 126
Bulgarian historiography, 43
Byzantine view of history, 34–6, 42–4

Cambrai altarpiece, 54, plate 4
Cambridge Platonists, 82
chain of being, 52, 64, plate 1
Chester cycle of plays, 38
chiliasm, *see* millennial expectations
Christ: history's centre, 7–8; seed of

woman, 88–90; testimony of, by Josephus, 40, 112
Christian chronology, 8, 20–1, 59, 134
Christian view of history, 6–9, 10, and *passim*
Christianity predates creation, 14; cf. 51
chronology, 8, 12, 14, 15, 18–19, 20–1, 23, 26, 32, 51, 56; *see also* Christian chronology
cities, two, *see* two cities
Communist view of history, 126
conflagration, universal, *see* eschatology
Constantinople: centre of universe, 35; fall of, 34
continuous narration, 53, 55, 64
Corpus Christi, the play called, 38–9
covenant, 4–5
'Coventry' cycle of plays, 38
creation: year of, 63; predated by Christianity, 14; *see also* universal histories
cyclical view of history, 1–3, 6, 13–14, 30, 58, 68, 107, 117, 131, 133–4

Daniel, Book of, interpretations, 49–50, 60–1
Dark Ages, 68
Day of the Lord, *see* eschatology

Eastern view of history, *see* Byzantine view of history
Ecclesiastes, history according to, 6, 131
eighth age, 22, 27; *see also* six ages

154

DATE DUE